CORDOBA
A HISTORY OF THE CITY
AND HER PEOPLE
THROUGHOUT THE AGES

by

ANTONIO JAÉN MORENTE

Translated by
Magdalena Gorrell Jaén Guimaraens
Cristina Gorrell Jaén von Zeppelin
Angela Gorrell Jaén McKay

CORDOBA. A HISTORY OF THE CITY AND HER PEOPLE THROUGHOUT THE AGES

©Magdalena Gorrell Jaén Guimaraens, Cristina Gorrell Jaén von Zeppelin, Angela Gorrell Jaén McKay
© Sam Guimaraens, 2016 cover photograph

This book is written to provide information and motivation to readers. Its purpose is not to render any type of psychological, legal, or professional advice of any kind. The content is the sole opinion and expression of the author/translator, and not necessarily that of the publisher.

Paperback: 978-1-964035-29-1
eBook: 978-1-964035-28-4
Library of Congress Control Number: 2024914433

SWEETSPIRE LITERATURE
— MANAGEMENT —

*I dedicate this fourth edition of my book to
my wife, María Cristina Goicoechea
because she and Cordoba share a special place in my heart*

Antonio Jaén Morente
San José, Costa Rica

View of the Mesquita-Cathedral
Photograph Sam Guimaraens 2017

TABLE OF CONTENTS

DETAILED CHAPTER INDEX

CORDOBA
A HISTORY OF THE CITY OF CORDOBA
AND HER PEOPLE THROUGHOUT THE AGES
INTRODUCTION

As a tribute to their grandfather in recognition of his lifetime researching and studying Cordoba, his granddaughters undertook to translate and publish Antonio Jaén Morente's *História de Córdoba* with a view to sharing this remarkable, detailed History with everyone, especially visitors to Cordoba and interested readers who are more at ease with the English language.

First published in 1921, this history book is unlike any you have ever read, a true textbook, annotated by Antonio Jaén Morente himself, expresses his intense love of Cordoba, the city of his birth. In translating the text, care was taken to preserve the author's unique style when addressing his students, as he sketches the background of a given topic in the past tense, only to switch back and forth to the present tense when discussing, commenting on, or underscoring the subject in question.

The last official edition of his work, posthumously printed in 1971, seven years after his death in 1964, has been reprinted several times since then and continues to lead sales of Histories of Cordoba nationwide.

Antonio Jaén Morente addressing students in Guatemala[i]

Antonio Jaén Morente in front of the Puerta de Almodóver
In the background on the right, the large house in which he was born
Calle Judios 1, Córdoba[ii]

ANTONIO JAÉN MORENTE
BRIEF BIOGRAPHY

Antonio Rafael Blas Nicolás de Jesus Jaén Morente de Austria was born in Cordoba 3 February 1879. He died in exile 8 June 1964, in San José, Costa Rica.

Held to be one of the great Spanish intellectuals – historian, university professor, lawyer, author of more than 50 books, diplomat, Member of Parliament and dedicated Republican politician, special attention is drawn to the heartfelt prologues to Antonio Jaén Morente's posthumous last edition, by two eminent intellectuals of his time and close friends of his: Rafael Castejón[iii] and Ramon Otero Pedrayo[iv]

Graduated with Honour from his secondary school in Cordoba, he then obtained a graduate degree in Teaching and went on to teach Geography and History in Segovia, Seville and Cordoba at the Cordoba Provincial Institute and the University of Seville.

After marrying Carmen Domingo Sanchís in Cordoba 31 July 1903, Antonio Jaén Morente moved to Madrid where he obtained a Ph.D. in Philosophy and Letters (History) from the Universidad Complutense. His 1908 doctoral thesis on the historical value of the San Jerónimo of Valparaiso monastery in Cordoba, that had been lost and remained unpublished until it was found and transcribed by his granddaughters and great-nephew, was published by the Cordoba Municipal Archives in June 2022.

In 1918 he obtained an LL.D Degree from Santiago de Compostela University. The records of the Cordoba College of Law show that he was registered as a lawyer with offices on the Gran Capitán Boulevard and in his home on Calle Juan de Mena. Settling in Cordoba, in 1920, he was appointed Professor of History at the Cordoba Institute, and it was here than he began his political activities as an active founding member of the Spanish Republican Party, the *Izquierda Republicana*.

During his lifetime, Antonio Jaén Morente was appointed or elected to the following positions, among others:

- Elected to the Spanish Cortes as Member of Parliament for the province of Cordoba 1931-1933
- Civil Governor pro-tem of Cordoba Province 1931
- Civil Governor of Malaga Province 1931
- Spanish Ambassador to Peru in 1933
- Member of Parliament for Cordoba 1933-1936
- Minister of Spain to the Philippines and Far East and Consul General in Manilla from 1937-1939
- Exiled to Ecuador then to Costa Rica 1939-1964, guest Professor at several universities in Ecuador and throughout South America.
- Menéndez Pidal Chair of History at the Costa Rican Institute of Hispanic Culture 1959-1964

FORWARD
by
Rafael Castejón Martínez de Arizala, 1971

The history of the city of Cordoba, whose brilliance encouraged so many illustrious sons (Ambrosio de Morales, Ruano, Morales y Padilla, Casas-Deza, Ramirez de Arrellano and so many others, not forgetting the magnificent men of the Arab era), who in Antonio Jaén Morente, found a spokesperson whose short, flashing summaries, delight whoever reads him.

The first edition of the *History of Cordoba* which he published in 1921 gave the Cordobans their first modern and complete up-to-date historic summary of the city, its deeds and its sons, for which he was honoured by the Municipality. With his second edition, published in 1935, he extended the prologue and retouched some chapters, although he removed the few, excellent illustrations that had embellished the previous edition.

Until he died in San José de Costa Rica 8 June 1964, Antonio Jaén Morente continued to foster his desire to re-edit his book, preparing the necessary changes, including the Prologue by the illustrious Galician professor Ramón Otero Pedrayo, his colleague and friend. Sadly, it was only after his death in 1964 that this was achieved, thanks to the insistence of his widow, Cristina Goicoechea, the editorial decision of the Librería Luque and the popular support of all the students who in this notable book found a manual to glorious Cordoban pride.

It was Antonio Jaén Morente's wish that this should be regarded as the fourth edition of his book as he considered that his many other publications, conferences, courses, lectures on Cordoba, that he participated in and wrote about while in exile in all the countries he visited, were the equivalent of a third edition. We respected his wish.

Lastly, I wish to say that when I was entrusted by the Librería Luque to revise the posthumous edition, I had many doubts because this History is written in a very personal style and any change to any one of his paragraphs would have erased its original flavour. I limited myself to correcting some dates and to adding a short note here and there, in a chapter such as the one on the pre-history which quite logically has been the most updated over time.

Moreover, as fortune entrusted me with this delicate task in my quality as Director of the *Academia* of Cordoba which he praised so highly, it is up to me to thank his memory for that praise in the hopes that each compliment shall, like yet another flower, perfume the place where he rests forever, he who unquestionably loved Cordoba with an enhanced accent of erudite and noble passion.

PROLOGUE
by
Ramon Otero Pedrayo, 1971[v]

My heart is beating so strongly as I attempt to compose these lines that I can barely hold my pen. These are pulses from the soul – broad, hushed, and soothing tidal waves of memory that flow with increasing speed over the tired beach of our present days. They rise from extremely far and very deep and take shape in the most intimate levels of our being. The sails on the masts of our lives and our travels swell with the generous wind of presences from the past.

This wind carries the vibrant accents and the lengthy and passionate echoes of our early days as young scholars in the classes of the old and noble University on the Calle Ancha de San Bernardo in Madrid, of the nights in the Ateneo library, of fiery and serious discussions, of student gatherings and the pure, radiant silences of our student days – all driven, permeated and led by an immortal sense of friendship. This has always been the glory and the reward of our days, the priceless privilege of many years and countless journeys. Among the first and decisive friendly accents, Antonio Jaén Morente's affectionate Cordoban accent, almost always tinged with a subtle mantle of grief, lives and sustains us.

So it was in 1905, in 1906, in 1907. As each Autumn drew to a close, every anticipation of Spring lay in a sometimes bitter and redeeming fruit, a flower, a book. This was the magnificent era of the young and great masters. Admired, debated, denied, they did not experience the barrenness of indifference. Unamuno, Azorín, Orega, Valle Inclán, Baroja. Names bathed in a particular light and distant mystery by those of us who remember them when they were young.

The shadows were cooling around the great figures of the 19th century. A profound revolution between bitterness and enthusiasm was taking shape in the world of the University and of the indolent reader. The threshold of the history of Spain was crossed with another decisiveness, with love and sworn vows, with impassioned criticism, as new roads towards the future were impatiently awaited with each tremor of the approaching dawn. Academia searched for the key to the past among the intimate reality of Art, in the heart of the home of Ethnography, and in the twinkling lights across the evening landscape.

Dogmatic arrogance, the reflection of distant constellations in cold galleries of mirrors of admiration, was forsaken.During those years, Antonio Jaén Morente, with his gentle student air, prepared with his characteristic combination of enthusiasm and disdain, his application for a university teaching position that bore an ancient and evocative title: Theory of Literature and the Arts. He spent many hours in the Ateneo Library, studying the wisdom contained in pages illuminated by Sainte-Beuve's irony, Taine's captivating methodology and the diamond alignment of Goethe's thought. A formidable and passionate reader, Jaén skipped from Hegel to Ruskin, lingering a while as a romantic traveler in afternoons filled with golden Andalusian radiance. Time and again he returned to illustrations of the old Spanish cities. He loved them with the fiery dedication of the pilgrim, the artist of the senses. He knew how to pluck the unedited or forgotten chords of Toledo, of Segovia, of old Madrid, of Santiago de Compostela and during his pulsing silences I accompanied him to these four cities. Not to Cordoba.

As the first light of day shone upon the golden Archangel which crowns the towers of Cordoba I did not reap the benefit of his Cordoban lesson in a Tartessian night crossed by the shadows of all the cultures and every manly disappointment.

Indeed, it was with a smooth and sparkling discourse that he shared his memories and the living presence of his city, such as the music of the fountains and breezes and birdsong from a forest dedicated to the highest muses and to the concept and achievement of illustrious destinies.

Antonio Jaén Morente would have been an admirable professor of Aesthetics and an even better teacher of History of Art. A distilled knowledge pervaded his fine and precise Cordoban feelings. In those days, Jaén was good friends with the only young and at the time modern, Professor of Philosophy and Letters, Andrés Ovejero Bustamante. He guided and enthused young people. A marvelous speaker, when he improvised, he gave lessons in the Toledo Miradero, the Prado Museum, or in the early morning by the fountain in Segovia. When Iglesias and Matías, the librarians, clapped their hands to close the reading rooms at 1 pm, Ovejero and Jaén left to wander the streets of old Madrid.

Good fortune took him along other, no less honorable, paths. After a heated and intense competitive public examination due to the quality of the other contenders, many of whom were friends of ours, he won a professorship in Geography and History at the Instituto in Segovia. I attended those competitions. Another excellent professor, Rafael Ballester, and our compatriot Primitivo R. Sanjurjo, excellent poet and geographer with a fine sense of brevity, also competed against Antonio Jaén Morente who employed the same intense and vigorous eloquence at the lectern. Years later and already a University Professor in Cordoba, Jaén competed for other university professorships, one of which he won: Professor of History at the University of Seville. In other competitions presided by Antonio Sánchez Moguel, old fakir of professorships and also an Andalusian, there were sporadic picturesque situations which Jaén described in his unique style, occasionally resulting in indelible literary etchings.

I tarry with pleasure a while on these reminiscences. They rekindle my memories of the unwavering friendship that neither distance nor circumstances between us could destroy. Both of us were committed Instituto teachers. We both loved, with a devotion that was rarely understood, the young people, not much more than children, who attended our classes. Although both of us, like our teacher and friend, won a university professorship in an open and hard-fought combat, Jaén and I gave of our best and the essence of our lives to the Instituto. As to our knowledge – Antonio Jaén Morente's was both assured, imponderable, and subtle – we imparted the example of deportment, the lesson of enthusiasm and the respect for high ideals, to our students.

Young people will not forget the Instituto lessons when they flow from a clear, clean source, worthy of reflecting the purity of adolescent brows and the clarity of their souls. They may forget them in the violent and boring course of time. They will always resurface, even more so at moments of indecision and despair. With the last of Antonio Jaén Morente's students, and I have met some, dies the authentic and living memory of an exemplary lesson.

Such was Jaén's love for his city and its Instituto that he returned to it as if to a loved one, to his classroom like a vocational calling, renouncing the University lectern and its greater prominence and wider horizons. There was another professorial situation that united us. Antonio Jaén Morente, as a judge in the jury of our competitive examinations, voted first place for me and openly celebrated our relationship. I knew and appreciated his brilliant textbooks, conceived and written with a form of gentle affection, so pleasing to the spirit of our young students. Also, both of us, professors of the same subject and directors of Institutos in our respective hometowns, represented these in Parliament in difficult times, albeit as members of political parties that were not separated by any fundamental ideology.

After Cordoba, without a doubt my friend's greatest love was for the ancient city of Segovia. He dedicated unforgettable pages to the accented, serious, and restrained expressionism of the city's noble architecture. He knew how to blend veiled elements in the landscapes with emerging works of art.

Perhaps understanding that Segovia possessed something similar to the doctrine of a Castilian Cordobaism, Jaén became particularly heated when speaking of the damaged stones of Segovia. Those were the days of the discovery of the intimate and veiled Spain. Whenever I reread Pío Baroja's *Camino de perfecció*n I am overwhelmed by memories of Antonio Jaén Morente.

His outlook, his willingness to dialogue and his expertise as an intellectual dreamer, only interrupted when duty called him to fight, were inseparable from the Ateneo and some Madrid cafés. Jaén was one of those people whose love of Madrid keep them returning. They were awaited and received with affection. They are happy when they arrive and even happier when they leave. For Jaén, Andalusia began on the Atocha railway station platforms.

His friendliness, his words always ready to express emotion, were his weapons in a hard and uneven political fight, tools and focus of his boundless energy. In his decisiveness and the manner with which he reacted to victory and later, to defeat, there was something of the courteous and redeeming elegance of the romantic speakers. I remember once, one of a thousand such occasions, after some Cordoban elections in which Antonio Jaén Morente was running for a seat against Sánchez Guerra. A group of friends, including Manuel García Miranda and Julio Prieto Villabrille, surrounded Jaén in the portrait gallery at the Ateneo, asking him for his impressions and for news. Though weary, our friend slowly and proudly said: "Yes, I lost, but I got one vote! One vote! One worth a consensus: Guerra's vote."

He was always passionately devoted to the glories of Spain. In the same way that the Baetis River flows to Seville and there from the Alameda de Hércules to assume its status as Capital of the Indies, Antonio Jaén Morente dedicated much well-applied study to the history of America in Seville. He had splendid occasions to display his knowledge. His political career took him to two lands sublimely impressed by the fertile Spanish spirit, to Peru and to Morocco. In both he is remembered as a noble friend through the footprint of his plan and the echo of his words. His sense of duty - whose stoic observance extolled and honored his countryman by blood and choice, Seneca - led him to travel to many lands and to sail distant seas. I can imagine the pain and pleasure of his exile as he nurtured and refined the memory of the Homeland in his soul. The light of the Homeland – the pilgrims' reward - became more beautiful and purer as it was reflected in so many mirrored landscapes.

He never wavered from the dictates of his timetable as a scholar, and he produced from near and afar and with affection and knowledge, notable studies regarding Hispanic art and thought.

He unveiled magnificent and exhaustive subjects; their beauty untouched by the august melancholy of the golden twilight of Viceroyal Art. He was accompanied and guided by the spirit of the land that inspired him. Spanish-speaking America is variously imbued by the light and immortal essence of Andalusia. In Ecuador, as in Central America, Antonio Jaén Morente's vocation as a University Professor in which he excelled, lessened the weight and hopelessness of his desire to return home.

As he created a new home, America unveiled in him a gold with a finer and less variable standard than that which was smelt in the serene fires of Indian mines, and the sonorous silver of his affection. He could never forget his first home, with its charming failings of youth and initial combats, nor his excellent daughter who was soon to collaborate with her father. The ancients, when they founded a colony, first brought their house gods and the sacred fire with them. So did Antonio Jaén Morente. Flames from the embers of his fire ensured the continuity of his convictions. Here, in the trajectory of an exemplary Spaniard, Spain and America symbolically achieved their common destiny.

See Cordoba and die, wrote Antonio Jaén Morente in the twilight of his life. He returned to Spain. He was his wife's affectionate, emotive guide. I welcomed them and conversed at length with both in Madrid and in the haven of the inspired towers of Santiago de Compostela. Not for the first time. I had accompanied Antonio Jaén Morente on a previous occasion for a cycle of conferences in our homeland. I had the pleasure of taking him to the high baroque monastery of San Rosendo de Celanova. As another illustrious Andalusian, Américo Castro, would do some years later, Antonio Jaen entered the cloister already laden with the heavy shadows of the orchard of sleepless cypresses with considerable emotion.

Like a subtle sun through clouds and woodlands, a poignant affection illuminates the wording, the letters from Antonio Jaén Morente's wife, Cristina. A sensitive culture, a respect for works of art. She reflected, slowly and gently, without rhetoric, his love for the Spain of old. A noble feeling that perseveres and grows with her response to the pain she feels when she is called to assume the noble role of celebrant at the altar of a beloved memory.

Antonio Jaén Morente's immediate, personal presence shall not die as long as it is nurtured by his daughter and his wife, and I dare say, as long as we, his friends, live. It is to this friendship that I owe the honor of writing the prologue to a book whose simple and profound pages were fuel for the love, knowledge and hopes of its author. A well-known and acclaimed book. In this posthumous edition, it appears enveloped with a new dignity of yearning, consolation, and love.

For a cherished book, a new edition is like a new and honest Spring. It contributes to a Horatian *Non omnis moriar*, the sentence that fortifies true humanists' sullen faces and lightens their soul before death. And so, Antonio Jaén Morente. For his studies, for his Cordobanism. In this year of events overseen by the mark of Seneca's stoic elegance, thanks to the resolve of its cultural institutions and of Señor Luque the editor (a genuine Cordoban, as Jaén declared with a spontaneous emphasis in his letters to me), Cordoba responds to the unanimous desire to re-edit this beautiful book of history and passion – even more strongly so as it is eagerly awaited – whose qualities the modest reader will appreciate right from the first page.

One more thing – and this is important: the Prologue. This is a serious matter in all respects and even more so because it is about the city that since its origins and through five cultures, was able to adjust to the mantle of conceptual and expressive elegance, with a skill never excelled in the Latin world. Something fundamental saves us. Antonio Jaén Morente repeatedly expressed, in writing and in speech, his desire that a few pages by me, his old friend and companion, should precede this new edition of his best-loved book. So be it. With thanks and strong emotions, inasmuch as I am able, I must obey this sacred mandate. A mandate fashioned by friendship, strengthened by exile, sealed with his death.

We loved Cordoba from the moment we read that marvelous passage in Caesar's *Comments on Civil War* as students, and through the works of its great poets, from Lucan, young genius of immortal ruins, to the Duke of Rivas, with sustained enthusiasm, tragic passion, pure romance. With comments and marginal notes, we acknowledged Averroes and Maimonides and measured our youthful hours according to Juan de Mena's zodiac. Everything gave way for us before the memory of a distant Cordoban night – the main street in old Cordoba bearing the name of a discreet, ironical, and educated Galician, the Count of Gondomar. Pink and rose-colored shadows. Tall and concealed presences. At the break of day, the voices of the milkmaids rising early, calling out their unique rhyme: "The King can do a lot, but God can do much more than the King!"

Night always carries morning in its breast. To await it in places consecrated by genius, love and death is the reward, not always deserved, of the traveler. For us, on that unforgettable occasion, the Cordoban night was undoubtedly courteous and generous as the white rose of morning flowered for us in the magic enclosure of the Mesquita, as in a marvelous forest of corals and minerals. Like flowers, we responded to the light of the crystallized colors and the praying of the Introit to the mass never before appeared so beautiful.

Thus, with renewed affection for the memory of my friend, I dedicate my tribute to Cordoba, his Homeland, placing it like an urn of warm ashes of emotion and memory on the altar of Góngora's sonnet:

> *¡Oh excelso muro, oh torres coronadas*
> *de honor, de majestad, de gallardía!*
> ¡Oh gran río, gran rey de Andalucía
> *de arenas nobles, ya que no doradas!*
> ¡Oh fértil llano, oh sierras levantadas
> *que privilegia el cielo y dora el día!*
>
> ¡Oh siempre gloriosa patria mía,
> *tanto por plumas como por espadas!*
> ¡Sí entre aquellas ruinas y despojos
> *que enriquece Genil y Dauro baña*
> *tu memoria no fue alimento mío*
> *nunca merezcan mis ausentes ojos*
> *ver tu muro, tus torres y tu río,*
> *tu llano y sierra, oh patria, oh flor de España!*

Real Academia de Ciencias, Bellas Letras y Nobles Artes de Córdoba[vi]

DEDICATION TO THE
REAL ACADEMIA DE CIENCIAS, BELLAS LETRAS Y NOBLES ARTES DE CÓRDOBA[vii]
by
ANTONIO JAÉN MORENTE

The ideas and emotions that inspired the first edition of this book so many years ago, may have evolved but they have never wavered. Then, as today, the intent had more merit than the end result.

1921 was the first time that a book intending to describe the guidelines of the historical evolution of Cordoba was published, albeit in the form of a succinct synopsis. This remains the case. With more love. Over time, intense and detailed work on the History of Cordoba has been achieved and almost all the fertile furrows have been ploughed by locals, natives to the city or ones who were spiritually adopted.

The generation that animated the last third of the 19th century awaited the organizing sign from Madrid. Today's generation waits and recognizes the work that was done and the creative talent of he who has it.

There is more…

I am pleased to state that there are not many places in Spain with as select a group of individuals as the Cordoban group, a group which knows its city and loves the gallantry of its past. How many are they? You can count them in the Cordoban Academia. They are all there. Probably not one more nor one less. If someone is missing, he shall be included.

The *Semana Califal* and the *Semana de Góngora* they promoted as if each was a spiritual crusade, are pure stirrings of our historical selves.

Then there is Maimonides, another great figure, followed by Romanticism, and almost at the same time, Lope de Vega. There is a magnificent flow of cultural activity. The *Boletín de la Academia* (BRAC), first published in 1922, is a serious local work without equal.

It is well known that Cordoba, who kindly labels these men *wise men* (I also contributed to launching this soubriquet), does not realize how much the city owes this group and the Academia, which in all its existence never shone as brilliantly as it did between 1920 and 1930.

To them …

To them, I send this book. I, who for official reasons frequently had to go out of town and was therefore unable to participate as an academic.

To everyone, without exception.

Cordoba, once again agitated, resentful, passionate, and violent in the midst of a civil battle for souls, resorting without measure to subtle cunning – an emblematic image that I reject – in praise of both white and red beliefs, whilst a path painfully opens before it. Occasionally, Judas is not alone in strolling with muffled steps through the orchard of this spiritual night.

It is because of who you are, an entirety regardless of our individual human failures, magnificent guardians of this hidden and fragrant orchard, the resting place of the sacred soul of Cordoba. The affable and unbiased arrow speaks…

PREAMBLE
TO THE 4TH EDITION
by
ANTONIO JAÉN MORENTE

Light

Dear reader, if only my soul were filled with light to guide you through Cordoba. Long ago, Horace began one of his poems *Micat inter omnes estella Julia...* I do not know why I adopted this as my personal motto for my city. It may be because Cordoba has outshined all Spanish cities, past and present

Its cardinal points

Cordoba takes the lead in the teeming crossroads of the Peninsula, melting pot of races. Its history is a tapestry woven with the blood of a thousand nations, each of which left the finest of its lineage in Cordoba. With Seneca, the Iberian, which is to say the racial, mixes with the Roman gentleman; he dons the turban with the Abderramanes; he ennobles himself with Maimonides and very soon, with Osio, he drapes the cross around his chest. This is why there are four cardinal points in Cordoba's shining constellation: SENECA, OSIO, AVERROES and MAIMONIDES.

Although you will hear others mentioned as the matrix is extremely fertile, in the end you will only see the great furrow these four ploughed.

Four swords

They are like four swords that cross to form a vault of steel. Listen to them speak...

One day, Seneca, the sublime one, said: *Speak badly of yourself,* adding *Live with men as if God were watching you, speak with God as if men were listening to you,* and a thousand more works and a thousand beads of philosophic gold that made huge inroads in the philosophy that nurtured the Cordobans.

Then Osio, the implacable arrived and, one day, presided over the Universal Council where he is dogmatized *in eternum.* Do you want greater glory? The entire world, when it recites the Apostles' Creed, prays with the words of this Cordoban. Cordoba is universal.

This was not enough. The 12th century brings us Maimonides, the great Moses, of whom the study of the people's proverbs declared that from Moses to Moses there has been no other Moses. His is the most profound talent of the Hebrew race.

Later, Averroes completes the cardinal points. Do you know of his glory? Averroism is found in the history of philosophy, but it is more than that. It is at the peak of the Arab influence in all European thought as, to his great credit, he fights intolerance and defends the freedom of thought.

In order to understand Cordoba in its deepest hues, you must remember that is in these initial furrows that the fertile seed was sown and it is here that you shall find a people who magnified the ideal routes for those thoughts and constellated the World with their works.

Low points? Yes, the depth of the pit is enormous. Today, Cordoba appears to be enjoying a rebirth. A difficult rebirth. Like Spain, Cordoba has a historic tormentor: the weight of its crown.

What Cordoba was

The name of Cordoba has been heard since the first days of history. Is it Iberian? One cannot point to its origin with any certainty, nor search for a loftiness based on a haughty genealogy of origins, because today nobody believes that the nobility of a people resides in its antiquity. Is it from the land of the Turduli? One of the most civilized provinces in southern Hispania, all the peoples travelled across it and blended into the racial melting pot that was the Peninsula.

The stamp of Rome

Rome establishes Cordoba as the centre of Baetica, a privileged district; the Arabs declare it Queen of their empire.

There were two great civilizations in Spain: the Roman and the Arab. Cordoba was the centre for both, and it is there that one sees the prolific blending of their ideas and thoughts.

This is why the list of Cordoban writers and scholars is so long and so illustrious: Romans, Muslims, Jews and Christians, the entire ethnic flora.

There were days and years when the districts that were subject to the Roman Empire even fought Rome for leadership of the world empire as well as for the cultural leadership. Cordoba stands out in this quarrel, which is why the following is said:

Tú solo España con honor bien nuevo
Distes al Lacio por tributo Augustos

because the first non-Roman emperors of Rome were Spanish. The Cordoban gathering had once shone. It taught in Rome and wrote wonderful verses, spoke in its forum and taught in its universities. This first sally of Cordoba outside of Cordoba has never been equalled. Seneca is the synthesis of this period.

The importance of the Arabs

The Arabs and their name will forever be linked with ours as the more than 500 years of Arab dominion renders Cordoba, properly speaking, one of their cities. There has been much discussion regarding what the Arabs did for Cordoba and whether their civilization was original or whether it emerged through contact with the elements of the ancient Hispano-Roman culture. In order to correctly judge this, one cannot forget the earlier culture which they found here and which the Mozarab group (San Eulogio, Alvaro) continued, mutually affecting and influencing each other. Though Cordoba's great days are Arabic, from leader of the Arab empire it becomes a modest kingdom, and later a Christian city.

Nonetheless, as long as the kingdom of Granada perseveres and the Arabs threaten it, Cordoba remains full of life, is frequently visited by kings and serves as a bulwark for the battle that is yet to come.

Afterwards...

Later, once unity was achieved and life in Spain revolved around the Court on the one hand, Spain simultaneously expanded its activities to the four corners of the world. Cordoba goes into decline, as do almost all cities in Spain, a decline that increases from the 15th to the 20h century.

Cordobans have linked their names to all the great Hispanic enterprises. As Blanco Belmonte states, there is no wonderful world event that does not include the name of a Cordoban.

Place names – The tug of home

As Spain doubled its map by taking the name of all its cities to America, Cordoba does the same with its name. There is a Cordoba in Argentina, founded by Luis de Cabrera in 1573; a Mexican Cordoba, founded with Guadalcázar by a Fernández de Córdoba in 1617; two Cordobas in the Philippines (one in Cebu and other in Panay); two smaller ones in Mexico and another in Peru; Cordoba Lagoon (Valparaiso) and Cordoba Peninsula (Strait of Magellan); a river by that name in Colombia and two more small towns. It is as if we had showered the entire world with constellations bearing the name of our city.

The meaning of glory changes

The glory of a civilization, however, does not only rest in resonant and warlike deeds, but also to the extent by which it has used the art of peace to contribute to the well-being and the progress of the world.

The plough, the book, the paintbrush, the pen are all of use to a nation and in that sense, Cordoba has done a great deal as its assets have made a formidable contribution to Hispanic culture. How can one describe such a history in a brief article?

Cordoban art

It exists with supreme grandeur. Although the artistic prestige of Cordoba has always been exemplified and justly so, in the unique work of the Mesquita, all the peoples who have travelled through here have left some trace of their passage and this must be noted in this short narrative.

The only one. The Mesquita

The Arab Mesquita has been described ad infinitum, but we still lack a concise study of the whole - of the mosque and its addition, the Christian cathedral.

The Arabs built the Mesquita for two fundamental reasons: religious necessity and political convenience. But it is not alone as an artistic or social subject.

The houses speak

There are many ancient houses in the city. They represent the synthesis of Cordoba, from the fortified manor house to the distinctive styles that evidence the evolution of architecture over the centuries.

Still, they all are proof of a great city; especially during the 16th century when, very familiar with the beautiful Arab styles, those who designed these houses were inspired by these models and created unique buildings.

Our house is, basically, the oriental house, the style that has come to prevail all along the Mediterranean coast, albeit modified as the geographic situation required.

Someone has attempted to classify, in a far too schematic manner, the types of houses according to the influence of the meteorological phenomena, as house of the rain, of the wind, of the sun.

The house of the rain is a Nordic house, with a tiled, sloping roof that protects it from rain and snow; the house of the wind is the typical fortified-looking stone-built house frequently hammered by the north wind in the Segovian provinces; and then there is the open house, the house of the sun, with its classic flat, tiled roof that is both an observatory, breathing space, command post, and private retreat.

The soul of the homes

The Cordoban home is the house of the sun, modified according to the latitude, a little less open, but still the typical oriental house. The patio, especially the patio, enclosed and pebbled in a manner still in use here, is what most confirms this origin. Patios live and throb. They are the Arab soul incarnate.

The Cordoba patios

The different layout of the patios that one sees across all Andalusia is remarkably interesting, especially between Cordoba and Seville. The Sevillian patio is the Roman patio, praised for its furnishings, its marbles, its luxury, where one lives. The Cordoban patio is only the space given to the sun, a place to meditate and to love with jealously.

Join me in the Cordoban patio, which resembles an orchard, to search for the spirit of the city and whisper *the breeze fans the orchard*. You can be certain that you will be accompanied by the lovely whisper of the invisible harps that first echoed in ancient Aeolia.

The Hispanic houses

Cordoba is not the only place where there is a hidden soul in the home. If you come to Spain, look at its houses. It was only there that one found the family strength and where the individualistic spirit had the strength of its columns - the direct line to the *I*, not the possessive *my*.

Have you seen the equatorial line that in the moral plane divides the North from the South? No? Come to Spain and enter its houses. There, every colour on the palette blends under the historic sun (mountain mansions, Basque hostels, farms, Aragonesque Mudejarisms, Burgos wrought-iron, cane, Valencian straw), such beauty! The examples are infinite. Depending on how the winds of love or war blow, they are the flowers of each region.

But let us go back to the subject of Cordoba. Let us take her houses and compare them to epigraphic inscriptions in other regions.

In Castile, I believe it is on the unknown Bishop's mansion in Cuenca that we find this inscription representing the Lord of the mansion's thoughts: *Relicturo satis,* in other words, this suffices he who passes here. On the other hand, on a Cordoban house that represented a high moral order, there is another inscription, also in Latin, which begins *Non nobis ...,* in other words, not for us, but for those who come after us.

Both express a different point of view. The first, seen with some detachment, is somewhat selfish as it implies that the house has no landlord nor longevity, that it is satisfactory but that is not how one builds houses or towns. Our inscription, the Cordoban one, reflects all the serenity and permanence of a man who comes to this world for a reason, one who removes the selfish purpose from his centre of gravity and thinks of himself in terms of what will come after him. *Non nobis,* he declares, for those who come after us, for our sons and their sons, thereby continuously feeding the pure moral, aesthetic and emotive current that will always flow for those nations who so desire it.

This is the everlasting source…
This is Cordoba, a quiet and miraculous fountain.
Come to her!

Close your eyes to the uncertain modernity of its expansion, and with no guide other than your feelings, lose yourself in her. The treasure, like the sensitivity, is delicate but it shows itself to be splendid, and it attracts the music of its bells that peal from the infinite distance… Occasionally, you will sense the mystic prayer in the middle of the street during your evening run, as it leaps from trellises, from grills, and from shrines. The past relives, and you become a grandee and an ascetic, and in the end, you will feel like a discoverer and conqueror, more gallant and more noble, more majestic. You will no longer be a squire of the ideal because an invisible hand, offering you an equally invisible scallop shell, will have placed a heraldic coat-of-arms on your chest.

The beginning

Let us attempt a brief history of a great city.

What is the purpose of knowing the history of Cordoba?

We are aware of the question of the usefulness of History. As we speak of the usefulness of History, let us set aside those advantages that are common to all studies and not address the already futile issue of whether History is or is not a science. It is of no consequence in this case, as nobody doubts the value of History as a means of placing political and social events in their proper perspective.

A nation wants to learn about itself but cannot do so unless we place its deeds in succession and in such an order that its origin appears clear and transparent. Clearly, the knowledge of History contributes to a moral education but not, as some have said, because the destiny of a people has always been justified on the basis of its virtues and vices.

History is useless as a perennial sermon on ethics, although we should applaud the effort. The historian must above all be sincere. His determination to know the truth is an educational strength of its own. Where do we find more morality if not in truth itself? The citizen's civic education is a part of his moral education. It is an obligation of History's and the History professor's fundamental duty.

Spain and all nations need patriots. Cordoba and all nations need citizens. They must not entertain aggressive and hostile attitudes that result in a dislike of other nations; nor can the future neighbour of any city be unaware of its duties. It is the past that prevails when it comes to these obligations, as a lecture on experiences, a source of energy, never looking backwards as one walks forward, but always remembering the spiritual treasure that is one's native land.

When it is studied, History makes men believe in two virtues: resolve and tolerance. All nations are respectable, and when in the course of time the young man of today becomes a governor, artist or educator, he knows his city and loves it, but not in a romantic or an intuitive manner. He knows his country's qualities and defects, the positive conditions and those that were denied it by resolve or nature. Only then, will he be ready to be a conscientious and human patriot because he loves all men, both rural and city dwellers, as he works for civilization's common cause.

The meaning of History

However, in changing in method and even in content, History has radically altered the old aspirations of ancient professorships.

History is no longer a compendium of the external accomplishments of kings, of chronicles, conflicts and battles. The subject of History is not a particular individual nor a dominant political group, but a nation in its entirety and complexity. Economic, artistic and literary facts, religious beliefs, geographic constraints, labour, indeed all of society shapes true History.

This is why its external, bellicose, flamboyant aspect is increasingly reduced as it configures the History of civilization. A short history of the Cordoban civilization is what I am attempting here.

As the content has changed, so has History changed its method, nor is it a subject that is learnt by rote. The History of the memorizer has become comprehensive. As François Guizot said long ago:

> History is not History as long as one does not perceive the relationship between events that succeed each other and as long as History as a whole entity is not presented as the evolution of a people.

A word of warning to those who will use this book to teach

As you shall see, this History is a sincere and simple book, saying things in an ordinary manner, sometimes suitable for presentations. This book does not pretend to be complete. That would be immodest.

The author only desired to put his soul into this book on Cordoba, because he knows how dedicated he is to this effort and how delicate a matter is teaching. There is an authority that will never disappear, that of the teacher over his disciple, that of he who teaches over he who learns. With this confession, he shares with Cordoba's teachers the responsibilities of our authority...Work with me and correct without fear...

Map of Tartessus[viii]

CHAPTER I
Prehistoric Cordoba (From 10 to 200 BCE)

The history of our town really begins with Rome. Practically nothing is known of everything that happened before the Roman occupation of Cordoba and the little that there is, is shrouded in doubts and uncertainties.

There was a time when the origin of peoples fascinated everyone, especially local intellectuals; later this was forgotten by historians. These origins are once again of great interest and accompanied by meticulous scientific research, although they are studied in a very different manner. More than unreliable written testimonials, researchers are increasingly turning to remnants of industry and art, and to the study of linguistics.

Menéndez y Pelayo declared, some time ago, that ancient Greek and Roman texts — texts which legions of writers have been tirelessly discussing and disagreeing over for ages - were insufficient and more interesting than useful for getting to know and for reconstructing the ancient life of civilizations.

As far as the first eras of the European world are concerned, some historians maintain that all the Mediterranean people shared a same ethnicity and perhaps a same language, which would help us understand their history.[1]

Cordoban prehistory in the area surrounding the city

Acheulean period artefacts found in Cordoba are limited to a few stone tools in Posadas, most of them atypical, as Calderón reported. Others have been discovered near Villarrubia, near to an *Elephas antiquus* jawbone. Similar objects have been found in the village of Santa Cruz, near the Guadajoz river.

Artefacts of the same type were found in the Alcolea prehistoric site where the Neanderthal *homo fossilis cordubensis* skull was discovered. Atypical quartz tools have also been found in the Sociedad Asland quarries in Valdeazores.

Neolithic

There are more Neolithic artefacts. Typical flints have appeared in Majano, Peña Tajada, Alcolea, Orive and las Cuevas. These well-crafted knives from material undoubtedly obtained from the southern mountains of Cabra or Priego, have generally been found in Alcor de la Sierra caves or in cracks in chalky soil. Items from the transitional Eneolithic period have appeared in Alcolea. Dolmenic elements in Montón de la Tierra (Alcolea) and Los Cansinos, are preserved by chance.

The Metal Age

As we know, these are linked to the Copper Age, for which we have a top-quality artefact in the form of an axe that was recently discovered in January 1935 in Valdeazores, near the Pedroches arroyo. Casiano del Prado earlier found Bronze Age axes in Cerro Muriano.

These mines and similar excavations in the region around Cordoba have provided a great many artefacts. There are vestiges in Cerro Muriano, Arroyo de Guadalbarbo, Los Villares, Lagar de la Cruz and Trasierra, all in the mountainous divide of Cordoba.

---

[1] Studies of prehistoric Cordoba are still very scanty. They have been promoted by Carbonell and Trillo-Figueroa, who does not refer specifically to our city, but to our district. In his conference for admission to the Academia de Córdoba, he gave a clear summary of the paleogeology of the province.

Samuel de los Santos also wrote a prehistoric summary with a view to inclusion in a magna History of Cordoba that the Municipality had requested. The most conclusive work on the development of the Palaeolithic period around Cordoba was produced by Casas Morales (BRAC, 1964), who gathered an excellent collection of artefacts, beginning in the Mousterian period some four hundred thousand years ago, mainly from the southern bank of the Guadalquivir River in front of the city to a little further downriver near the mouth of the Guadajoz river. As there are multiple findings for all the prehistoric periods, far too many to list here, the reader is referred to specialty literature.

The artifacts provide few details to help classify these beds. Axes of porphyry, diabase and fibrolite, as well as stone clubs and mallets dating from the Eneolithic period, were already found in these quarries when they were exploited under the Romans.

Iron

The Iron Ages are represented by the tools found in Cerro Muriano.

Antonio Carbonell Llaser found a post-Neolithic breastplate in Espiel that he believed was unique in the province and an interesting link with which to comprehend the evolution of the entire age.

You can see how all this data point to the fact that the province was peopled since the first days of Prehistory. More specifically, regarding the city of Cordoba and referring to the Iberian civilization, we have found some small idols on the Ribera and an Iberian stele on the grounds of the Electromecánica,[ix] as well as some clay figurines, one of which is reminiscent of the *Dama de Elche* that was found in the city.[x]

Antiquity

All these findings are proof of the Iberian antiquity of the Cordoban settlement, beginning in the foothills of the Sierra and later spreading downwards to the river. The claim that Cordoba was founded by Phoenicians – a claim accepted and passed on by local academics - cannot be substantiated.

The first human settlement

In our peninsula, the most civilized settlements in the Spain of yesteryear were located on riversides, along the coast or where there were good means of communication. In summary, those which enjoyed better geographical conditions, because Geography, although it has not made history, has served as the backdrop for mankind's historic journey.

The Guadalquivir River always was an admirable waterway and by navigating along it, one could come close to the heart of Iberia.

All the Mediterranean peoples who settled in the south of the Peninsula[2] entered, one after the other, on the *Sagrado Betis*.

---

[2] Setting aside all references to pure prehistory for a moment, it is said that Eastern Mediterranean peoples began to settle along the south-eastern coast since the days of the so-called Bronze Age. It is to them that we owe the first written records, the transmission of legends and the names of the human settlements in the Peninsula. There were three important settlements along the coast: *Tartessians* in the Baetis river valley; *Iberians*, in the Ebro River valley; *Mastians*, in the southeast, and then in the interior, the *Celts*. Nothing is known regarding when and from where the Tartessians came. Later, the Roman conquest led to a better knowledge of the settlements. Strabo, the Greek geographer, stated that Baetica, or Turdetania, is the name given to the basin of the Baetis river as far as the Guadiana river and was populated by Turdetani (thereby identifying the Tartessians) and Túrdulos.

In effect, everything that has been said regarding the primitive settlements is subject to review. Modern bibliography is extensive and revised daily, although all the literature agrees that there was a human settlement called *Tartessus*, connected to the Guadalquivir River (then known as the *Tartessus*) from the earliest days in Andalusia.

Later, a cultured people of primitive Spain established themselves in the land around the river, in the valley and to an extent into what today is the region of Extremadura. The Turdetani were one of these tribes. The name *Túrdulos* which is given to those from the region of Cordoba, is thought by some to be a diminutive form of *Turdetan*.

Camille Jullian, the famous expert on the Celts, believes that this Tartessian empire, the only one in ancient Europe, flourished at the same time as the great oriental empires and should only be compared to these.[3]

Andalusia – The origin of the name

The etymology of the beautiful name of Andalusia was once attributed to the Vandals. This was poor etymology resulting from the similarity between an ancient and a modern name, based on the brief and hurried stay of the Vandals in the south of Spain.

More likely and closer to the truth is that Andalusia derives from *El Andalus*, a purely Arab toponymic expression with which at the beginning the Arabs designated the southern part of Europe, our Baetica.

More recently, there is another theory that makes one think. The name could derive from *End-ent*, the article, and *elus* that the ancient people turned into *elysium*. The direct and very ancient original meaning would therefore be "the extreme" or "the end" and, by inference, the West.

At the dawn of Geography this remote and attractive land, described as extreme, the end and the west, is where the Greek geographers located the Elysian Fields.

---

[3] Can one therefore accept the validity of the somewhat imaginative *theory of the ellipse*, according to which all ancient civilizations can be explained by means of an ellipse whereby one of the foci was the south of Spain and the other the ancient Orient?

According to this theory, the path between the southern branch (north Africa) and the northern branch (from the Caucasus to the south of Gaul and north Spain) was the route of great migrations of people, art and culture, with Greece and Rome in the middle.

In its own way, each of the foci blended with and influenced the others, according to the geometric properties of the ellipse. All the eastern civilizations fused with ours and the historic parallel nature of both foci is such that *Tartesia* first corresponded to the oriental empires and, later, when Cordoba became prominent, its splendour was also reflected at the other end in Constantinople. The current flowed from one to the other, sustained by the migrations, yet both foci faded almost at the same time as civilization acquired another form.

The first inhabitants

Where did the people who first inhabited Andalusia come from? How did they acquire a legendary culture that has been recognized and celebrated by writers and authors everywhere? This is a useless question if one expects an exact answer. Still, the strength of this initial fact, one that has been affirmed since the imprecise dawn of History and based on a highly spiritual genealogy, is extremely important as it describes our province as the oldest settlement in which the culture of our race was forged and Cordoba as one of the foci of this primitive civilization.

Recognition of Cordoba's ancient roots is particularly valuable when downgrading Celticism, the suggestion of a foreign contribution now relegated to a secondary role. It allows us to focus on our indigenous contribution, on the creation of our own spirituality, a culture born in our own towns, with its own characteristics, one that was neither engulfed by Rome nor created by the Arabs. It is in this cultural initiation of Spain, in its threshold, that we find the name of our city, the name of Cordoba and its district. [4]

The original Cordoba

Where was the capital of these primeval Cordoban people located? We believe that aside from its expansion during its days of glory, the city remains in the same place as the original human settlement.

Nevertheless, some affirm that the original Cordoba was located at the boundaries of the western and northern parts of the present-day city. The site is located as being a bit below where the Arroyo del Moro enters the river, where, it is said, one can see vestiges of the original city under the layers of sand and vegetation.

The etymology of the word *Cordoba* has also been the subject of discussions and digressions, almost all of them false. It is possible that the real etymology

---

[4] Perhaps these problems cannot be resolved, other than through the modern philological science and by new studies of Art. Art is such a serene and truthful documental source that it is almost the only light that illuminates these dark paths. Because of it, and this is an ancient example, today we know Egypt better than the ancient populations that were close to it. In the case of Spain, Iberism daily produces better studies. As regards Celt-Iberism that amazed us for so long, nobody remembers anything. It is fiction. Regarding the Iberian alphabet and the Indigenous culture, some have even declared that it is previous to all known civilizations: Babylonian, Assyrian, Aegean, Cretan, and so forth. [Cejador, J. *Alfabeto e inscripciionrs ibéricas, 1926*]. Commenting on this, they have furthermore added:

"Examples of this are the relationship between the Egyptian Palaeolithic and Neolithic with the Hispanic across Africa [Aleg Scharff]; the reliance of Egyptian art on the southeast Spanish foci, expressed in the pictorial group of the Saharan Atlas [Lhim]; the origin of Dolmenic culture [Wilke]; the halberd [Schmidt]. An increasingly more energetic inclination toward archaeological and ethnologcal studies of the Peninsula [Valera, H in R. Ay. Madrid. Archive. 1928]."

is the one given by Humboldt, that it derives from *car* or *cor* (height) and river, meaning elevation near the river.[5]

This seems to be the best. *Corduba* of the ancients, today Cordoba, reminds one of Corduba, the Assyrian metropolis in Kurdistan, that was metropolis or capital of the ancient *Corduene*, according to M. Graetz.[6]

Summary of etymologies

First etymology. From *Cor* or *Car* (lodge in Greek) or from the Chaldean *Kor* (Latin *curia*) and *uba*, meaning city, human settlement, or tribe, in Chaldean, as we see in the names *Salduba, Calduba,* and *Onuba.* I am reminded of the Iberian settlements of Curica, Curnonium and Curunda and the Betic Oba. Also, *Kordofan*, in British Sudan.

Second etymology. *Corduba* or place of gold, from the Hebrew *Kortz*[7] and the Phoenician *Kord* or gold. Conde, in the *Edrisi*, points out that Cordoba is the same as *Karta-toba*, meaning rich city or good city. Remember that Silio Italico, who was from Italy, declared in the *Punica*s that Cordoba was a gold-bearing land. *Nec decus aurifera cessavit Corduba terrae.*

Regarding place names, see Blásquez's sensible suggestions in *La persistencia de los nombres geográficos*[8] where he states that in the days of Alfonso X, the king liked to name towns according to their traditional names. Thus, *Soricia* (from the Latin *soror,* or sisters) becomes the castle of Dos Hermanas, exactly on the site of the ancient Soricia. Another city such as Aspasia or Aspagia (from the Latin *aspicere,* or look) becomes Espejo, the name that it was originally given because it was located on the heights as a look-out point.

Gómez Moreno's writing on the Iberians and their language, is interesting for his conclusions and references to the use of southern onomastics and the complicated and schematic syllabic Iberian alphabet.[9]

The invasions

Phoenicia and Carthage later settled on the Iberian Peninsula. Were there any Phoenicians and Carthaginians in Cordoba? Nothing positively exact is known regarding our city, except that it is presumed that they might have been,

---

[5] Other etymologies suggest a marked Semitic origin. Today, however, according to better studies, the name, which has changed very little, is of Iberian origin. It is even believed, with credible certainty, that this was the location of an Iberian settlement dating before all the Phoenopunic times. as I already pointed out.

[6] M. Graetz. *Monatsschrift,* 1961.

[7] Verse from the Hebrew Bible, (Job., 41-21).

[8] Blásquez, in *La persistencia de los nombres geográficos*, Homage to M. Pidal.

[9] Gómez Moreno y Pijoan, "Materiales de Arqueologia española," in *J. Ampliación de estudios,* 1912.

an assumption that has led some historians to declare that Cordoba was founded by the Phoenicians. Nonetheless, modern researchers say that the Phoenicians never went beyond the coast, neither as invaders nor colonizers, although they may have visited Cordoba as traders. As regards the Carthaginians, Silio Italico notes that Cordobans accompanied Hannibal on his famous expedition to Italy.

In brief, the only thing that can be said about this obscure period is that a new civilization, whose most important centre of operations was southeast Spain, rose from this contact with Greek, Phoenician and indigenous cultures. This civilization endures and although fundamentally changed by the Roman conquest, is not suppressed, so much so that from time to time, noteworthy currents flow from it.

CHAPTER II
Roman Cordoba
(From 200 BCE to the 5th century AD)

Carthaginian rule, significant vestiges of whose presence are beginning to appear in Iberia, was followed in our peninsula by the era of the Roman Conquest.

The Carthaginians defend their empire against the Romans as much as they can, but in the end, Rome wins the bloody battle for domination of the world that both had so ferociously disputed: *delenda est Carthago* (Carthage must be destroyed)[xi].

Praetor[xii] Lucius Marcius' conquest of Cordoba around the year 200 BCE, was no more than an episode in this fight. Cordoba would remain Roman for almost eight centuries.

Historic Cordoba

This is now the beginning of what we could call the true foundation of historic Cordoba, a subject that our ancestors discussed with passion. The fact is that the next Praetor of Spain who came to Cordoba in 169 BCE, Marcus Claudius Marcellus, modifies and ennobles the city, establishing a great Roman colony and laying the foundations for its future grandeur. We begin to hear the name of the Patrician Colony, as the Romans called it, sound with true decorum.

Built as such, "Marcellus's opus" according to Strabo, Cordoba could henceforth be endowed with everything that Rome had to offer: sumptuous buildings, trade, industry, labour and art. The city identifies itself with Rome and it becomes Romanized; it is like a miniature of the great city, lady of the world. Two races merge here: the native and the conquering race. A constellation of illustrious men of the highest calibre will spring from the mutually revitlized Iberian soul and Roman offspring.

The praetor lives in Cordoba, perhaps the town that Romanizes itself the quickest and one of the most famous colonies in the Roman West.

Emperor Augustus would later divide Spain into three regions: Baetica, Lusitania and Tarraconensus. Was Cordoba the capital of Baetica then? Seville has claimed this ancient historic honour and our writers have discussed this at length with Sevillian essayists who downgrade our city to simply the real capital of the legal covenant that bears its name, one of the four regions into which Baetica was divided: Gaditan [Cadiz], Hispalis [Seville], Astigitan [Ecija] and Corduvensis [Cordoba]. Cordoba the city, acquires great military importance as the key to Baetica and as the civil hub of the region.

It is said that when Julius Caesar first came to Spain as a quaestor[xiii], he planted the famous plane tree that Marcus Valerius Martialis immortalized in his poems.

The Romans fortify and garrison Cordoba; they make it their hub, their parade ground, they build barracks for their legions. Rome, the civilization that best understood the geographic value of Mediterranean Spain and who fashioned its own empire according to the dictates of geography, recognizes Cordoba's strategic value.

As a centre of communications, Cordoba is the starting point for numerous roads. This is why it is here, very close to the city, that both Roman praetors fight Viriathus who, from 149-140 BCE, represented the Spanish quest for independence.

In the end, however, all of Iberia becomes a colony dependent on Rome and all the battles fought in the capital of the world and all the unrest have an impact here, as they did in the Spanish colonies when the time came for Spain to have colonies of its own.

Tiberius Catius Asconius Silius Italicus

As I mentioned earlier, Silius Italicus said of Cordoba: *Nec decus auriferae cesavit Corduba terrae*, in praise of its fertility and not its gold, as he has been traditionally translated. In his epigram; Martial also said: *Qua dives placidium Corduba Boetin amat.*

Silius Italicus' words decus auriferae are frequently quoted on their own, but in my opinion, this is too literal a translation. Silius used the word *auriferae* metaphorically as in "the earth is of gold" and this is confirmed in the following verses of his poem. He speaks of the Iberian chiefs of the tribes that live on the Guadalquivir riverside and who accompanied Hannibal. He says, naming the Cordoban and the Sevillian, both of whom are the same age:

> *Genuit quos ubere ripa*
> *Palladic beti,*
> *umbratus cornua ramo.*

Silius then again refers to the fertility of the land, which is what he meant to say when he made the famous auriferae statement that has become so memorable. *Palladia arbor* say the Latins. Ovid frequently did the same when referring to the olive tree, because it was dedicated to Palas.

El nombre del jefe cordobés… Auraricus (the name of the Cordoban leader.) Truth or fiction, this is the first time in the annals of literature that a Cordoban's first name is mentioned.

Cordoba and the civil wars

When the Roman General Quintus Sertorius (81-72 BCE), arrives in the Peninsula to fight against the ruling party in Rome, on behalf of his political party, Cordoba is anti-Sertorius and he is defeated by Quintus Metellus, the Roman government's defending general. In 70 BCE, numerous writers and poets from Cordoba accompany Metellus to Rome, where they establish the Cordoban school I shall speak of later.

The conflict between Caesar and Pompey also has an effect on the city of Cordoba which at first supports Caesar and on his behalf, fights against the illustrious praetor Marcus Terentius Varro.

Once the campaign against the Pompeiian generals Lucius Afranius and Marcus Petreius is concluded, there still remains part of Andalusia to pacify, for which purpose Julius Caesar sends two legions under Quintus Cassius Longinus who was very knowledgeable of Spanish affairs. Soon after Longinus takes Cordoba, Caesar arrives in the city and there he receives emissaries from all of Andalusia who come to congratulate him.

Longinus remained as Praetor, but as his demands were extreme and as he ruled with great cruelty, there soon arose a plot against him led by Lucius Nacilus and Annius Scapula, and several other leaders from Seville and Italica. Although Longinus is seriously wounded, he survives and once cured of his wounds, cruelly avenges himself on his enemies.

Later, during an absence from Cordoba, he relinquishes command of the city to Marcus Claudius Marcelus, a member of the Claudian family. Cordoba again rebels. Longinus returns and finding that the bridge over the Guadalquivir had been cut, sets up camp on the Campo de la Verdad and ravages the countryside in full view of the Cordobans. In the end, Longinus is defeated, and he sails for Italy but perishes with all his retinue and riches when his ship is wrecked at the mouth of the Ebro River.

The political greed of Caesar's representative had turned the Cordobans into supporters of Pompey's political party.

Cordoba is against Caesar

As Pompey's sons renew their fight against Caesar, they rush to take control of the important stronghold that is Cordoba. Faster than ever, Caesar leads the famous march by which he brings his troops from Rome to the heart of Andalusia in only twenty-six days. He meets secretly in Obulco (Porcuna) with emissaries from Cordoba who offer to hand him the city.

Caesar arrives, but finding that the bridge remains impassable, still manages to cross the river. He is prevented from entering the city centre by Gnaeus Pompeius who comes from Ulia (Montilla) in aid of his brother. Caesar returns across the river, frees Ulia that had been besieged by the Pompeian troops, marches against Ategua and a little later, engages in the Battle of Munda.[10]

These civil wars are of a particular importance that must be pointed out. In terms of Rome, they represented a dichotomy between the ruling city and the countries that form the Empire. The wars were to determine just who owned the World, whether the Roman Senate, the seat of the privileged class, or whether all the countries did. Caesar represented the anti-senatorial movement. In those days, Caesar stood for the people's cause, as did the first Caesars. Hence, the great consideration Rome had for them, even Nero, whose true story is apparently now being written – until then, a story now penned only by those whom he had persecuted.

It appears that Cordoba played no distinctive role in these wars; perhaps it was too distant from Rome to appreciate the problem in all its aspects.

Victorious, Caesar returns to battle Cordoba which resists him fiercely but succumbs to him in the end. The most illustrious Pompeian, Cordoban Annius Escapula, heroically commits suicide, thousands of Pompey's supporters die in the streets of the city and Caesar enters triumphant.

---

[10] The fate of Rome is decided on the fields of Cordoba, between Espejo (Ucubi), Montemayor (Ulia, i.e., Montilla, Mont-Ulia) and Ategua (Teba farm, between Espejo and Cordoba), at the famous Battle of Munda (45 BCE). The exact site of this battle has long been debated, but it could only have been in the South of Cordoba province, near the Guadajoz river (Salsum). Both Spanish and foreign researchers have continued to study this (Schulten). Historians are unanimously agreed that Munda is today's Montilla.

This was the third and last time that he was in our city. His harsh words and contempt for the loyalty of the Cordobans may date from then.

The clash of war was over for Cordoba. From now until the invasion of the Barbarians from the North, the city is cosseted by more than four centuries of peace. Our intellectual dominance begins, the era of Seneca follows and with it the vibrant Cordoban School. Of all the Hispano-American writers, the most illustrious come from Cordoba. These are the highly distinguished intellects of whom Sidonius Apolinaris, in the time of Euricus, said were *praepotens alumnis* and *nutrix* of these minds, and who, according to Menéndez y Pelayo, were romantics of ancient times who by carrying the spirit of insurrection deep in the marrow of their bones, aspired to renovate everything, from philosophy to oratory.

Almost all of Spain remained under Roman influence for centuries, especially Baetica, the valley of the Ebro River and along the Mediterranean coast. The Peninsula is rapidly populated; authors of population censuses of Iberia suggest 40 million inhabitants, a number that seems inflated.

In confirmation, Cicero said, speaking of the Romans: *Nec numero hispanos, nec robore gallos nec artibus gracos superavimus* (We do not surpass the Greeks in the arts, nor the Gauls in strength nor the Spaniards in numbers).

Cordoba expanded considerably during this period and other than the fortified Acropolis - the true Roman city, the original nucleus within the walls - the enormous number of farms, country houses, suburbs and villages, such as Cuteclara, Secunda, Tasi, and so forth., grew until the entire countryside was inhabited by a great population.

We will speak about the existing Roman vestiges in the section on Art.

Latin was accepted as our official language. Latin, which over time was the great generator of our national language, although this latinization of Spain is somewhat debated today because there is no doubt that there are a number of native words in Latin that come from the indigenous languages. Luitfrando (a 10th century Italian writer) says that during the days of the Arab invasion, ten different languages were spoken in Spain.[11]

There remain a great many Latin inscriptions from Cordoba, graphic witness to the greatness of the city, collected in the *Boletín de la Academia de la Historia* and in the volume of the *Corpus Inscriptionum latinarum* corresponding to Spain, published by the famous Hübner.

---

[11] The Latin spoken in Spain was so special, that Cicero called it a wandering language. In a play by Aulo Gelio, a Spanish poet says: *Hispané, non romané, memoratis loqui me* [remember that I speak Spanish, not Latin].

According to ancient Cordoban writers, the official centre (was it marked by a building of its own?) is presumed to have been located on the site of the church of San Miguel and the Instituto, in front of the square that they called the Senate, today, Tendillas. This square, Cordoba's true forum, was the starting point of all the main streets that reached the gates of the city, more or less in straight lines: along Calle Jesús María, towards the river or as far as the church of Santa Ana, as we will point out later; Calle Osario, to the gate of that name; Calle Alfonso XIII, as far as the Puerta del Hierro (Zapatería) and the city wall; and Calle Gondomar to today's Puerta de Gallegos. The Praetorium, palatial residence of the proconsul, is presumed to have been located on the site of today's City Hall. The amphitheatre was on the site of the convent of San Pablo.

The port was located below the bridge over the Guadiana, in the present gardens of the Alcazar. The *Telonium,* or customs house, was by the old jail). The *Naumaquia* mock naval combat fairground was upriver from the bridge, city walls and paths, beyond Martos' mill.

The stadium was located outside the city walls, in Victoria neighbourhood. The ossuary for the wealthy went from Tejares to San Cayetano and the one for the poor was near the threshing floors of the Campo de la Verdad.

It is pure fantasy to say that the temples to Apollo and to Bacchus were in the Trinidad. The temple to Augustus was near the Amparo hermitage, the temple to the Household Gods on the site of today's Hospice, and multiple notable and great buildings, such as the Casa de la Moneda (Mint), near where Santa Ana Church is located today. The Tendillas was the geometric centre of the Roman urb and later of the high part of the city and so it remains today.

As you can see from this brief and, undoubtedly somewhat hypothetical, mapping of the city, [12] almost all the ancient locations have been preserved and a future urban plan can be discerned.

---

[12] The writer Narciso Sentenach recently researched the location and layout of Cordoba; his "Historic Map" is the simplest and detailed for a clear understanding of the city map. The map shows the three cities within the city limits: the Roman, the Arab and the Arab-Christian. The Roman (the Acropolis) forms a pentagon: the position of four sides of this figure is undisputed by any author; the fifth side, almost parallel with the river, consists of a wall that must have been built from the Aurora hermitage to a point a little above the Puerta de Almodovar, passing through Santa Victoria, Plaza Santa Ana, Calle Valladres, across Calle Sanchez de Feria, to the city wall. The famous, highly controversial Puerta de la Estatua was on Plaza de Santa Ana. It is said that the nuclear city of Roman Cordoba was within these boundaries.

Over time, new suburbs were added, taking the city down to the river, when it was encircled by the walls that extended from the Puerta de Almodóvar to the Puerta del Puente and San Ferdinand Street and Alfaros to the Puerta del Rincón. The third walled suburb consisted of the Ajerquía, that is the Arab-Christian neighbourhoods. Altogether, they formed the walled city of Cordoba which lasted pretty much the same until well into the 19th century, although it can still be reconstructed along its major lines.

(Reference is made to the paper published in the *Boletín de la Academia de la Historia*.)

The main highways in Beaetica crossed in Cordoba, coming from two directions from Castulo in the north where they met, only to split up shortly after the confluence of the Baetis and Salso rivers as each continued on its way towards Hispalis and to Malaca in the south. (Numbers 3, 4, 7 and 8 on the Antonine Itinerary.) A third highway north (number 11 on the itinerary), lined with tombs, left from the Puerta del Osario and continued across the Sierra towards Merida.

Christianity in Cordoba

This was the great social event that affected Humanity. Everyone knows of the enormous influence that the propaganda and acceptance of the new doctrine had on the world. Donoso Cortés wished to divide universal History into two great periods, the "nearer and further from the Cross".

It is not known when Christianity began to be preached in Cordoba, although it is presumed to have arrived in the early days of this religion.

The first confirmed Bishop of Cordoba was Severus (3rd century AD), but the great figure of this period is Hosius of Cordoba who died a centenarian in 357. He served as Bishop of Cordoba from 294, attended the famous Spanish Council of Iliberis [Granada] of great religious and social importance, and the great Nicene Council. I will speak more about Hosius later.[13]

The end of Roman rule

Cordoba, as did all the peoples in the empire, must have suffered at the end of the Roman rule from the consequences of misgovernment. This is the period of the plundering of the world, when the ancient courts and free Roman municipalities were subdued after Caracalla decreed that henceforth all the inhabitants of the empire were *citizens of Rome*.

This appeared to be a great advantage for the people, but it was, nonetheless, what today we would call a centralist measure that ended the autonomous municipal way of life of the provinces subject to Rome.

In effect, Rome was losing the provinces as there were tentative movements towards independence in the regions that would become future nations when the Barbarians appeared on the scene.

---

[13] This was the time of the first Cordoban martyrs *Acisclus, Victoria, Zoylus* and others (last decade of the 3rd century and beginning of the 4th.)

The *Palestra Sagrada* or *Memorial de los Santos de Córdoba* by Bartolomé Sánchez de Feria, in 4 volumes, 1772, documents, in great detail, the lives of the Cordoban saints and contains a wealth of accessible material in the form of "Notes and critical reflexions on the principal events in the history of Cordoba."

The Roman city

The great transformation of Cordoba takes place after Julius Caesar, at the end of the 1st century, one which can be called the reform of Augustus, when the bridge was certainly built, and which transformed Cordoba into a great city three centuries after Marcelo came to power. The city walls are extended, more land is added to the inner city and the etablished setting of the city remains unchanged until the Arabs arrived.

What was the Roman city like? There are no remaining descriptions. We can construe something, however, by looking at similarities with other Hispanic and Italian cities and studying remaining artefacts. It must have been a great city indeed and, consequently, endowed with all the monumental buildings that its civilization expected.

In the 18th century, Bartolomé Sánchez de Feria who undoubtedly often hit the mark when he sited locations and buildings, said that the centre of the Roman city was the Tendillas, which he creatively called the Plaza de las Legiones.

The entire urban topography is very interesting, since large buildings have continued to be built in the same locations as under the Romans. It is believed, however, that Sánchez de Feria was more inventive when it came to locating the temples.

The temple to the Sun, although much smaller, must have stood where the cathedral is located today. This is proven with the recent discovery of the Stone of Helios. It is interesting that there remains no street or square dedicated to the Sun. There is a faint memory in an old inn named Mesón del Sol and Martín de Roa calls the Cruz del Rastro, the Puerta del Sol. This also appears in some documents.

The temple to Cibeles is presumed to have stood where Calle de Sevilla crosses Calle Mariana Pineda. Nothing specific is known of other temples.

Local researchers have studied the Arabic and Christian times in Cordoba in greater depth than they have the Roman. Research into Roman Cordoba has advanced much less which is why the aforementioned comments regarding the arrival of the Romans linger.

It appears that the Romans arrived around 206 BCE, under Gaius Lucius Marcius Septimius. They found an Iberian city which is presumed to have been located on the acropolis that is part of the Cordoban landscape, in the modern Compañia and Santa Victoria neighbourhoods.

The first Roman town is presumed to have been a campsite extending some 800 meters from north to south and some 700 meters from east to west. Claudio

Marcelo's improvements (169 to 152 BCE) marked the change from campsite to city.

Four outposts, starting from the Tendillas as the centre, went north to south from the Puerta del Osario to the Plaza Santa Ana, and west to east to the Puerta de Gallegos and to the Puerta de Hierro (later renamed Zapateria, then Liceo, then Alfonso XIII in front of San Pablo convent).

The dimensions of the enclosure that was walled in by the Romans and whose general lines are known, have been confirmed by excavations for new construction work. The entire eastern wall, from the Puerta del Rincón to the Ribera, survives in part and is covered by houses that have been built against it. This wall, extended along the Calles San Ferdinand, Librería, Ayuntamiento and Alfaros, divides the city in two, the right and the left town quarters, to use a common expression.

Low quarters in Cordoba are not so called because it is the poorer people who live there; on the contrary, there were many more or less sumptuous noble houses there. Low quarters are those that, topographically-speaking, are on lower ground along the riverside. The others, Tendillas and Compañia squares, on higher ground, remain as the town centres.

A better name for the eastern quarter was Ajarquía, or low quarter because the other side, the one that runs from the Ayuntamiento to Victoria, is on higher ground. The latter was known as the Medina under the Arabs and Vila, for its excellence, under the Christians. When two churches to Saint Nicholas are built in the city, one (which remains) is called San Nicolás de la Villa and the other (which has since disappeared), San Nicolás de Ajarquía (on the riverside).

Roman city wall, next to the Puerta de Almodovar
Photograph Sam Guimaraens 2017

CHAPTER III
Visigoth Cordoba
(From the beginning of the 5th century to 711)

A new era begins for the world: Rome has fallen. The new people, the Barbarians, rise from the spoils to build nations. Since 410, they invade Spain in successive, devasting waves, which do not cease until the arrival of the Visigoths.

Cordoba's situation during the Barbarian invasion is very special and in truth, there is no historic data to prove with any certainty when it was defeated, until Leovigild conquers the city in 672, close to two hundred years after Roman rule disappeared from the Hispanic districts.

What then happened to Cordoba during the entire 5th century and most of the 6th? Very little, almost nothing at all actually, is known. Historians speculate that it put up with the swift and ferocious invasion of the Vandals until they moved rapidly into Africa. Until then, it is believed that at first Cordoba remains in contact with Rome and attempts to remain faithful to the Empire. Then, isolated and practically independent, the city is left to its own devices until finally, it looks towards Byzantium (Constantinople) where the Eastern Roman Empire had remained and on whom the Latin world placed its hopes after the fall of Rome.

This eastern empire, a fragment of the great Empire, had inherited all the classic tradition of Rome, and hoped to restore the political traditions of the great city. It attempted to rebuild all its lost power, a restoration movement that at the time rested on the figure of Emperor Justinian.

Meanwhile, in the mid-6th century during one of the frequent Visigoth battles for the throne, Athanagild calls in the Byzantines and rises against Agila who in 548 had already been defeated by the Cordobans after he encircled the city.

The Byzantines settle in Spain and rule over the land along the southern coast from the Jucar River to the Guadalquivir, extending their influence on districts in the interior where they remain until 621. Their influence was both religious and artistic-cultural, a subject that has not yet been fully studied.

The principal Visigoth ruler, King Leovigild, conquers Cordoba. During the religious-political fighting, Cordoba, because of its belief in Catholicism which prevails in the city, together with a vague inclination towards nationalism, or if this seems to be too modern a word, *Romanism*, takes Hermenegild's side against his father. Hermenegild is arrested in 584 and the rebellion ends. From then onwards, the city is entirely Visigoth.

The most important feature, the great strength of our city during those historic days, is the subtle cultural and Spanish thread that runs unbroken throughout time. We shall see it reappear with the Mozarabs[xiv]. All the historic events that occur in Cordoba exhibit this unique feature, evidence of the continuity of a Hispanic spirit.

Is it not still said that Cordoba is perhaps the most spiritual of all cities in Andalusia? Here is the proof, because despite our undoubted decadence, there always remained something of our forefathers' spiritual impact and it is there that you find the true Cordoba and its true history.

Cordoba continued to feel Roman and looked towards Byzantium, like all cultured souls of the times who saw the emperors in Constantinople for what they were: the direct heirs of Romanism.

Romanism is one of the strong features of the great Hispanic tradition that later surfaces in Cordoba with sufficient force to merge Arab knowledge and Jewish wisdom, for the good of Spain and its culture. I shall discuss this later.[14]

There are very few memories of the Visigoth domination in Cordoba aside from recent references to a duke, Teodofred, who is said to have built a palace on the site of today's Bishop's palace.

The names of bishops from Cordoba stand out as participants in the great church councils in Toledo. Regarding these, two features of great importance need to be highlighted as they contribute to the decadence of Cordoba. The Goths themselves initially prefer Seville and move their court to Toledo, clearly understanding the geographic problem of Spain, a problem the Church had already solved by following the Roman administrative division for its episcopal boundaries, the best such division in Spain.

From then onwards, Toledo becomes a great city and the centre of life in the nation. For this very same reason, over time Toledo becomes the greatest stronghold of renegade Arabs and rebellious Mozarabs against Cordoba.

The city of Cordoba, following its natural topography, spreads towards the river. The main basilica was built very close to the river, there where the cathedral is located today. According to those who still believe that the city wall under Roman Cordoba did not go beyond the present Plaza de Santa Ana, this was on the other side of the city wall. In accordance with the longstanding continuous

---

[14] There is no other way by which we can appreciate the past life of this great city. Not isolated in historic space as with a localist and erudite vision, but closely entrenched in the general flow of History.

opinion of others, Teodofred's palace was inside the wall, close to the basilica and San Acisclo Church, further west into the countryside.[15]

Anything else that one can say about this period is based on legends, as is the case regarding the general History of all Spain.

During this time, Cordoba depended on Seville for its culture. This is the century of San Isidoro, 7th century Archbishop of Seville who, as the principal figure of his age, had a major impact on Cordoba and left a tradition that we shall see appears during the Mozarabic period.[16]

CHAPTER IV
Arab Cordoba – First Period
A. Beginning and rise. The Emirate (711 - 912)

The entire progression of the Arab domination of our city can be condensed in four stages. Stage 1: beginning and rise, from the conquest in 711 until Abd Al-Rahman III; Stage 2: the Caliphate, 912-1002, the flowering; Stage 3: beginning of the decline (death of Almanzor to the fall of the Caliphate, 1002-1031), a short but very turbulent period; Stage 4 and last: rule of the Taifas, 1031-1236, which includes the Almoravid and Almohad Berber invasions.

Conquest and dependent Emirate

The Arab conquest of Cordoba is an immediate consequence of the defeat at Guadalete, or Guadi Weca as it is called today now that the real location of the battle has been established.[17] When the Arab commander Mugueiz el Rumi arrived before the walls of Cordoba, perhaps after a mock battle, he found that the gates of the city had been opened by the political opponents of King Roderic of the

---

[15] Vide *Observaciones históricas acerca de las antiguas basílicas de San Vicente y San Acisclo*. R. Romero Barros. *Revista España*, 1888.

Critics have rejected the existence of the so-called temple to Janus, traditionally built where the Cathedral is today, in favour of a simple 'triumph'. They have further made it clear that the Visigoth basilica was dedicated to San Vincente and not San Jorge, contrary to what others have said. They also affirm, on apparently sound grounds, that another Visigoth church might be buried under the Merced church.

[16] For a beautiful summary of the entire period, consult *Monumentos latinobizantinos de Córdoba* José & Rodrigo Amador de los Ríos. (Vol. 4 of *Monumentos arquitectónicos de España*. Do bear in mind that more recent studies have changed this somewhat.

[17] Still, some affirm that this is a poor and foolish interpretation of R. Dozy's, and that the old location and name should be retained.

Goths, who believed that the Arabs were not arriving as conquerors but as allies. The governor of Cordoba defended himself for some two months, not in San Jorge Church as tradition says, but in the outskirts of the city (San Acisclo Basilica), until he surrendered to el Rumi most likely at the end of 711, perhaps in November.[18]

In Cordoba, the Arabs, began as they did everywhere, exhibiting an admirable tolerance and great political sense which undoubtedly made it easier for them to conquer Spain in two years, an astounding speed still today. The emirs who governed Spain answered directly to the Umayya Caliphs in Damascus; Spain (*El-Andalus*) was a military colony.

In 716, Emir Al-Horr established Cordoba as the capital of Spain and so it remained for more than three centuries, that is, until the fall of the Caliphate. Another emir, Samah, rebuilt the bridge over the Guadalquivir in 720.

This entire period of dependent emirs is replete with never-ending political battles. The Arabs were divided into factions that came and belonged to different clans. The pure Arabs who arrived in the Peninsula were in the minority. The majority, such as the Berbers, came from places that had been conquered, only united by a religious bond but separated by a desire to rule.

Syrians, Medinians[xv] and Berbers fought each other, while the emirs continued with their conquests, overrunning the Pyrenees into France and completing their fantastic cross-country march to Constantinople to ensure the definite triumph of Islam.

For a time, Cordoba was under the rule of the Syrians, under Baldj and then Tsaalaba (742). Abul-jatar at last puts an end to the Syrian rebellion by giving them land and diplomatically persuades them to leave Cordoba.

Yusuf el Fieri who, in 748 beat other rebels at the Battle of Xecunda (a little beyond the Campo de la Verdad), was the last emir.

The fighting is interminable until finally, Abd Al-Rahman I comes to Spain and, with the agreement of the Umayya, members of his clan, takes possession of Cordoba in 756 and proclaims the first independent Emirate. El-Andalus, under Abd Al-Rahman I, begins to become independent from the emirate of Cordoba.

An independent Emirate

The previous emirs did little for Cordoba as they had neither power nor peace. The period of the Invasion ends with them and after breaking with Damascus, El Andalus becomes independent.

---

[18] This specific point regarding the Arab invasion has been considerably amended following Eduardo Saavedra's research. His work, *Estudios sobre la invasión de los árabes en España,* (1892) should be considered. Also take a look at Juan Menéndez Pidal's interesting work, *Florestal de leyendas. Rodrigo, el último godo,* (1928).

In fact, there is no fundamental difference between the political rule of the emirs and that of the caliphs. The Caliphate, which was not proclaimed until Abd Al-Rahman III, is no more than the breaking of the religious link with the Asian Caliphs, which had in fact already become very weak.

Abd Al-Rahman I (756 -788)[19] establishes his throne in Cordoba during a period of fighting and conspiracies, some of which were encouraged by the Caliphs who did not wish to lose their Spanish territories. Mugueit, the Governor for Africa, then Gafir, the chief of the Fatimids, come from Tunis to battle against Abd Al-Rahman, but are defeated.

In the meantime, a great many Umayya come from Africa and settle in Cordoba. In Cordoba, the emir creates a guard of permanent troops (770 men) that some say numbered 40,000, recruited from slaves and people he brought from Africa, and with whom he enforced his power, as previously he had depended upon tribes that were based in the country.

Even Charlemagne, at the time at the height of his power, intervened in Spanish affairs. A son-in-law and a son of the last dependent emir asked the famous French Emperor for his help in 777. Without hesitation, Charlemagne negotiates the support of the Governor of Zaragoza. Charlemagne was later defeated at Ronceveaux Pass.

Abd Al-Rahman begins building the Mesquita. Like almost all Arabs, he is a poet. He lives for a long time in the Ruzafa. Conde, the author who Arabists critize, left us a somewhat free translation of Al-Rahman's well-known poem to the palm tree:

Tú también insigne palma
Eres aquí forastera…

Al-Rahman's compositions are strong, warlike and sentimental. In another poem, he himself says that he came *driven by hunger, frightened by the weapons and fleeing death,* and that it was here that he found *plenty, safety, friends and wealth.*

Next to him, stands the figure of Bedr who had been freed and for whom he came to Spain and who as a symbol of fidelity, effectively helped him.

Hisham I (788-796) is the antithesis of his father. A peaceful ruler and not at all cruel, he pardons his rebellious brothers who were seeking the throne and his is the glory of completing the Mesquita.

The emir of Cordoba's troops reaches Narbonne in 792 and come close to the mountains in Asturias, near Astorga.

---

[19] A delightful synopsis is Eduardo Saavedra's historic essay entitled *Abd Al-Rahman I.* Madrid, 1910.

Hisham, the moralizer, writing his advice to his successor, leaves his thoughts about governing:

Do justice equally to the poor and to the rich. A prince's well-being rests in the love of his subjects. Be kind and merciful with your subjects: they all are sons of God.

Al Hakeem I (796-822). This is the start of the uprisings that almost always appear amongst the Arabs at the beginning of each reign. Led by Obayda, Toledo rebels against and remains independent from Cordoba for ten years.

During the previous reign, the Alfaquis who, with Hisham, were firm believers in the doctrine of Malik, held considerable power in Cordoba. Al Hakeem was not sufficiently devout to control them, and they began to preach against him. Twice, he had to put down an uprising in Cordoba. The bloodiest was the so-called rebellion of the suburbs in 814, when the emir's troops were responsible for a great deal of bloodshed. The emir destroyed Xecunda suburb and expelled 5,000 families who suffered a great deal as they made their way from Cordoba to the sea.

A Cordoban kingdom in the East

The exiles formed two large groups; the largest, consisting of 3,000 families, made its way to Alexandria (Egypt) over which it rules until 826, conquers Crete and establishes a Creto-Cordoban kingdom that lasts for some hundred years until the first third of the following century. The other, smaller, group consisting of some 2,000 families, takes refuge in Fez, in a place known as Adua el Andalus.[20]

Al Hakeem ends the rebellion in Toledo in 808 thanks to the cunning of a renegade Arab from Huesca, Amru, who invites all the citizens of Toledo to a banquet and assassinates 700 of the most notable. This bloody act of treason is known as the *Day of the Pit*.

The independence of Catalonia begins with the creation of the Hispanic Brand and the assistance of the Frankish kings. In 798, a great flood of the Guadalquivir destroys the Cordoba suburbs on the left bank of the river. There is widespread famine in Andalusia in 815.[21]

---

[20] This exodus is admirably described in *Noguari*, by the Arab scholar M. Gaspar Remiro who earlier had only translated the episode of the Cordoban rule in Crete.

[21] The *Abjar Machmua* (collection of traditions), published by the Academia de la Historia contains poems that are attributed to Al Hakeem: *With my sword, I united the country. As he who uses the needle to connect embroideries.* He is softer and less emphatic when he speaks of *How well humility suits the man who becomes a slave to love.* The insincerely gallant spirit of his poetry is very Arab, but these poems, frequently attributed to the work of princes, are often the labour of fawning courtiers, the recourse of the powerful everywhere.

Abd Al-Rahman II (822 - 852). During his reign, the Arab society in Cordoba becomes increasingly refined and more splendid. There no longer are fights for the throne, the monarchy is fortified, Al-Rahman elevates the capital of his kingdom, expands the Mesquita and brings the finest materials to Cordoba. He equips the city with public baths, street lighting, paving, sanitation, and so forth. and creates centres of learning which ennoble the city. He builds an orphanage for 300 children near the Great Mesquita.

Explaining the splendour of Cordoba, Saint Eulogius of Cordoba says: *Divitiis commulavit cunctarumque, deliciarum mundi afluentia ultra quam credi* (As they amassed wealth, the delights of the world flocked to the city in an incredible manner). Toledo again rebels in 829. [22, 23]

The subjugated

The Muslim world in those days was very complicated and Christians who were subjugated by the Arabs did not resign themselves to their fate, protesting as they could. When they lacked strength but had faith, as did Saint Eulogius of Cordoba and his companions, they responded by preaching, writing and, lastly, with martyrdom.

When the Christians are Goth nobles, they attempt to establish kingdoms as did Muza, the son of renegades from Zaragoza, who claims that he is the third King of Spain, or as does Omar-ben-Hasun when he attempts to create a Christian kingdom in the heart of the Arab demesne. All this begins during the reign of Abd Al-Rahman II, and soon proliferates.

The subjugated Christian Spaniards, or Mozarabs, governed by magistrates of their own, were permitted to worship their own religion. In those days, they had three monasteries within Cordoba and three churches and eight monasteries outside the city walls.[24]

---

[22] The Toledo uprisings are extremely significant. Although led by Arabs, they were very nationalistic as they contained many Mozarabs, in other words, subjugated Christians. The rebellion lasted for many years.

[23] The Normans came to Spain during this prince's reign. These men from the North landed in Lisbon and Cadiz. They travelled to Seville by land, conquered, sacked it and were repulsed with great difficulty. This led to the building of the great arsenal of Seville. This was of great importance as it gave the Cordoban emirs a marina which contributed to other emirs' successes in North Africa and the Canary Islands, and who from now on are vassals of Cordoba. Abd Al-Rahman was so prolific that he was survived by 45 sons and 42 daughters.

[24] These were, according to their generally accepted names in Spanish as follows: inside the city walls, the monasteries of San Acisclo, San Zoylo, Los Tres Mártires (Saints Fausto, Jenaro and Marcial) and the churches of San Cipriano, San Ginés and Santa Eulalia; outside the city walls, the monasteries of San Cristóbal, de Cuteclara, Tabanense, Salvador de Peñamelaria, Armilateme or San Zoylo, San Félix, San Martín and San Justo y Pastor. Francisco Simonet, historian and orientalist, disagrees with the above. *Los Mozárabes* (Memorias de la Academic de la Historia, volume XIII).

Mozarab Cordoba

Although the Mozarabs in Toledo were more numerous, the Cordoba group was more famous, as by continuing the Roman tradition and following the San Isidore school of Seville, they collaborated with Arab culture and contributed to the intellectual splendour of Cordoba.

When the Arabs created the emirate, as they became more conscious of their authority they restrict the rights of the Mozarabs. Hisham I prohibited the use of the Hispano-Latin language and required their attendance at Arab schools, a measure that was implemented by Arab rulers everywhere.

As the great Alvaro of Cordoba said, *Christians read Arab books, not to repudiate them but instead to acquire correct and elegant Arabic speech.*

Local essayists of today (Rafael Castejón, Antonio Hernández, among others) have continued these studies in order to locate and re-establish the correct locations of these monasteries.

Mozarabic culture was at its height during the 9th century. The Mozarabic codices are witness to that great culture. There are notable examples of these in Leon and in the Escorial.

Mozarabism represents a great, strong and unique page in the history of Cordoba. The Mozarabs are not just defenders of their faith and, to a certain extent, of what at the time could be considered the Spanish nationality. They also are poets, musicians and linguists. It was their influence, says Padre Fidel Fita, that made of Cordoba the most famous school in the world. Without them there would never have been an Arab civilization, nor would there have been the splendour of the great 10th century with its astounding intellectual excellence, where Arab scholarship is more Hispanic by blood, more representative of Cordoba than it is of Arabia or Africa.

There was very little that was genuinely Arab in the invasion and conquest of Spain: probably Muza's military chiefs of staff, some tribes that sided with the emirs and a few Umayyad clients. In Moroccan Africa today, there are some scattered Arab communities that in reality were not there before the 12th century when they arrived as Almohad leaders.

In terms of blood lines, the invasion of Spain was essentially Berber as the Berber and the Iberian peoples are one and the same. The Berber is the pre-Roman Iberian who lives on both banks of the Straits of Gibraltar.

The remainder were either converted or renegades, members of other faiths and "Spaniards from over there", that is, from North Africa.

It is precisely during the 9th and 10th centuries when all this is taking place, that the great culture flourishes.

Is this looking for an indigenous theory, a self-serving theory regarding our past that disconnects it from all Arab influence? That would be a historical untruth. One thing is the blood that circulates in one's veins, the other is the cultural thread. The Islamic breath arrived, travelling along all the North African coast, stumbling against the great Egyptian abode - Alexandria, leaping across the Straits, finally settling in Andalusia. It is here where Islam makes Cordoba its centre, using a forceful proselytism to impose its religion on the province and impress its language as the vehicle and form of its culture.

Yet in Andalusia, a fertile orchard nurtured by a millennia of knowledge and learning, it is as if a new and marvelous flowering is taking place, one which would not have occurred without this base, one whose most pure and national cultural elements embrace Mozarabism.

Nonetheless, when faced with the historically accurate fact that the Muslims who came to Spain from Africa did not produce anything truly great on their own, one is led to think that it was only thanks to the existing cultural conditions in Spain that such a grand achievement was possible.

Cordoba and Baghdad

There is an interesting point that is worth mentioning. The two great Arab caliphates are Cordoba and Baghdad. Both ended in a similar way.

Baghdad was slaughtered and inherited by the Turks, and it is these people of Asian stock, lacking in Arab blood, who now represent them and who intensify and exaggerate their legacy. They feel intensely Muslim. Even today, the new Turkey (Ankara) presents this image before the world.

The Cordoban caliphate, now without Arabs, is lost with the Almoravids and Almohads. They come from the heart of Africa, they have no Arab blood, yet on their continent and for us, they represent Islam. We call them Arabs without their being so. Their only Arabic feature is the religion that cloaked them all and the traces of that culture among the learned.

Still, our Hispanic culture that was born here but that we call Arab, has some antecedents that are so much our own in its lineage that it is difficult to appreciate what it owes to its creators, the Islamic and the Spanish.

Today, as a reaction to the hyperbole, some say that "one must be very careful not to succumb to the misleading aspect of the flourishing of the Arabic culture, as we have so often seen since we began looking at the Middle Ages with a romantic eye.

From architecture, in which it excelled, to innumerable forms of industrial art, in reality it produces nothing new; it only imitates."[25]

[25] Hans Heinrich Schaeder, 1896-1957, Historian of Oriental religions. British Library Archives and Manuscripts Catalogue: Person : Description : ark:/81055/vdc_100000000618.0x00002e

This flat statement undoubtedly transgresses and errs in its finality.

Still, regarding the great problem of Cordoban culture as the supreme model of Hispano-Arab learning, all this critical viewpoint is of great interest and is directly tied to the golden book of Mozarabism that is found in all Arabic Spain. Cordoba is the typical Mozarab city. Let us return to the people.

The people

Saint Eulogius of Cordoba is the brightest shining light of all. He, together with Alvaro, Abad Sanson and Speraindeo, are the outstanding figures of whom we shall speak later in another chapter. They fought ferociously against the Arab, the oppressor and the infidel. Facing them is a group of more timorous Christians, who declare that *he who incites martyrdom would not be considered a martyr*. In contradiction, Eulogius wrote his famous *Memorial de los Santos*.

There began a violent persecution in the days of Mohammad, when Mozarab churches were destroyed in 852. A great many Christians converted to Islam because they were afraid, and Eulogius, who was perhaps the greatest Christian martyr worldwide in the 9th century, dies.

This period of history is known as The Era of the Martyrs of the Mozarabic Church. It is believed there are no more than fifty martyrs.

The Mozarabs in Cordoba become divided, heresies invade their midst, and the exodus begins. There are some interesting migrations of Cordoban monks to the Christian kingdoms in the Peninsula and who take Cordoban art and culture into the heart of Spain where they establish monasteries such as San Miguel de Escalada, later San Martín de Castañeda, and others.[26]

Abdullah

Abdullah's reign is an unhappy one; there are uprisings all over the emirate. Within Cordoba itself, a Mozarab count, Servando, at first betrays his own people then attempts to reach an agreement with Omar, the rebel, because he believed in the end of the caliphate. He fights the king from Aguilar. In 900, a great famine and widespread flooding, complete the scene in Cordoba.

Abdullah mistrusts his relatives who, little by little, are systematically assassinated. His final days are sombre, as he fears everything and everyone, he builds the passage that connects the Mesquita to his palace (905). Still, it is said that he was the best of all the poet-princes to reign over Cordoba.

---

[26] Other than a few fragmentary studies of this period and of the Mozarabs, one need only turn to Francisco Simonet's book *Los Mozárabes*, which despite later studies, continues to be a fundamental document. Gómez Moreno's research into "Mozarab Art" is now complete.

CHAPTER V
Arab Cordoba – Second and Third Periods
B. Abd Al-Rahman II (912 to 961)
The great century of the Caliphate (912 – 1002)

Soon after he rose to the throne, Abd Al-Rahman II had subjected and pacified the entire turbulent Arab kingdom. Even Toledo, the most formidable stronghold of rebellion, advantageously supported by a democratic regime, surrenders.

At the beginning, Abd Al-Rahman is almost always victorious in his battles against the Christian princes. The Arabic-Cordoban troops reach the Pyrenees and later, the civil wars between Christians in the Peninsula bring almost all of Spain under his control.

He extends his power in North Africa, aware of the great advantages that control of the other bank of the Mediterranean offers the people of the Peninsula. He takes control of a large part of what used to be the Roman province of Mauritania Tingitana, especially Tangiers and Ceuta and Fez recognizes his sovereignty. The Cordoban emir also extends his influence on the borders of Egypt and numerous minor African kings render homage to him, even from black and tropical Africa, such as present-day Ghana which sends goods (gold and ivory) and students. This is Abd Al-Rahman's great moment. In 929, he proclaims himself Caliph, Prince of All Believers.

The Asturian-Christians, engaging in great civil wars for the succession to the throne, ask Abd Al-Rahman to arbitrate.

This is Cordoba's great century; it receives obsequious embassies from kings of all nations. Juan de Gortz, on behalf of Otto the Great, Emperor of Germany, gives an interesting description of this trip in 953.[27] Emperor Constantine's Ambassador had visited Cordoba earlier (949).

Abd Al-Rahman did more than any of his predecessors for Cordoba. His court shines with rare brilliance and - something that is truly noteworthy – it is an extremely tolerant one. Men of all religions co-exist, work and write in Cordoba; a Cordoban, Bishop Recemundus of Elvira, is sent as Ambassador to Germany; Hasdai ibn Shaprut, a Jew and a sage, is Abd Al-Rahman's secretary.

---

[27] Originally published by Paz y Melia in *Revista de Archivos,* Vol. I, 1872. Re-edited in BRAC [*Bulletin of the Royal Academy of Cordoba*], number 19.

The beautifully conceived and developed site of Medina-Azahara (azahara means flower), owes its creation and conception to Abd Al-Rahman. It is from then and during this period that we owe the somewhat exaggerated, descriptions of our city,[28] said to contain more than one hundred thousand houses, a million inhabitants, countless palaces and 28 suburbs.

Abulfeda, the geographer, and Almacari, the historian, have bequeathed magnificent and possibly unequalled descriptions.

Abd Al-Rahman II is the leading figure worldwide during the 10th century and Cordoba, the greatest city. The Arab prince's outstanding politics are responsible for the greatness of his empire. Expressing himself with the melancholy proper to his race, he himself says *I have reigned for fifty honour-filled years, but I have scrupulously counted the days that I have experienced happiness without any bitterness - only fourteen in all of my long life.*

Al-Hakam II (961-976) represents peace and, consequently, culture. The legendary great library of the Caliphate is partly annotated by him and according to Simonet, contains 400,000 books[29], a truly remarkable number for those times. Al-Hakam is a scholar and book lover.

Cordoba was the hub of western learning and the most cultured city in Europe of the time, Rome not excepted. The number of schools multiply, and they attract countless numbers of students, as occurred in Toledo after the fall of the caliphate. Almacari describes Cordoba as the emporium of the sciences and the cradle of Muslim Law.

Al-Hakam is also fortunate in Africa, where general Ghalib affirms the Umayyad power.

More and more Christian embassies arrive in Cordoba and the Caliph maintains good relations with Leon, Castile, Navarra and Barcelona. These

---

[28] *Vide*: *Los Alcázares musulmanes de Córdoba* by R. Ramírez de Arellano (*Boletín Sociedad Española de Excursiones*, XIII, p. 104) and Velázquez Bosco, *Medina-Azahara y Alamiriya* 1912, describing the status of the archaeological excavations.

The Medina Azahara excavations, conducted with various degrees of success, have been greatly developed during these past few years, leading to the discovery of extremely beautiful quarters such as the Royal Hall or Dar al-Mulk, the House of Marble or Dar al-Yund and the mosque, all of which are currently being restored. This work can be followed in the official Minutes of the State Department of Excavations and in general treatises on Spanish Arab Art written by great maestros such as Gómez Moreno, Torres Balbás, Levi Provencal, Terrasse and many others, as well as in the Boletín de la Real Academic de Córdoba, especially in the Arabist supplement entitled "Al-Mulk".

[29] The expression *book* in those days, according to the classical tradition, only refers to the number of folios which grouped, form a book; the latter are believed to number some 70-80,000.

mutual alliances and the reciprocal intervention in Arabic and Christian matters explain the delay in the Reconquista, a struggle that never was a continuous battle to reconquer the Peninsula, rather one that was frequently interrupted. Cordoba continuously receives embassies from all the Courts who come to offer their friendship and to request favours.[30]

Hisham II. Almanzor (976 to 1002) Hisham is no more than a shadow as Almanzor governed in his name. If not Caliph by right, it is really Almanzor who reigns and who lends his name within the Caliphate to a special period known as the Amiridas. He is known as *meluc-carim*, noble King.

Almanzor is the last great figure of the Arabic era. He is not Cordoban, but Andalusian from Algeciras. Beginning as a civil servant, little by little he rises in standing at the Palace where he destroys the militia of the eunuchs.

He needs to be a military man and so he is, beginning in 977 with his famous raids against Zamora, Leon, Santiago, Pamplona and Barcelona, with which he pushes the Christians back to the edges of the Pyrenees. He is elevated to *hágib* in 978 after which there are no changes to his power or status.

In Cordoba, the marked rise in muttered grievances against the Regent, Hisham's mother Aurora, results in a conspiracy against her and her party that is quelled by a cruel repression. Muslim theologians who accused Almanzor of being a non-believer are apparently the soul of this conspiracy. To please them, the authorities burn the philosophy books in the Al-Hakam library which, the Muslim clerics say, give rise to heterodoxy.

Hisham remains happily ensconced in his Medina-Azahara palace. Almanzor, to better affirm his power, reorganizes the army and creates a special standing force consisting almost solely of foreigners from Africa – Berbers - and Christian soldiers of fortune whom he hires in Leon, Navarra and Castile.

The means that Almanzor used to consolidate his power - treason, treachery, cruelty and assassinations - do not flatter the individual whom his contemporaries call the fox and who did not hesitate to slit his own son's throat - Abdullah had rebelled against his father and taken refuge in the County of Castile with Count Garci-Fernández.

In those days, Santiago was the great city in the North of Spain. Very similar to Cordoba, a city of art and pilgrims, of an incomparable grandeur, it is the holy city and end point of the French Way to Santiago. This heavily frequented itinerary to Santiago de Compostela, was the main route taken by pilgrims through Castile

---

[30] Francisco Codera. *Embajadas de principes cristianos en Cordoba, en el reinado de Al-Haquem II*, Academia de Historia, Vol. XIII.

and to a certain extent, the route along which European movements arrived here. Almanzor got this far in 997 and according to tradition, took Christian bells as trophies to serve as lamps in the Mesquita. He also affirms Cordoban Arab power in Africa.[31]

Third Period
C. From Almanzor to the end of the Caliphate (1002 – 1031)

Start of the decline

The thirty years that pass until Hisham III's overthrow represent a very complicated period that can only be described as a period of non-stop hostilities and the dying days of Cordoba as an empire.

The number of uprisings and bloody events that follow in Cordoba is incalculable. The fortunes of the once noble and feared city would very soon depend on its Christian allies who would now not arrive as subjects but as nobles, or on some semi-militarized bands who exalt their fierce Arabic individualism - an individualism which lacked any political thought other than that of an organized tribe, one which through a stroke of luck may rise impressively to the status of empire but which carries within it the seeds of a rapid dissolution.

As far as Almanzor's sons are concerned, Abdel Malek continues to survive thanks to his father's prestige and the praetorian guard he inherited. His other son, Abd Al-Raman Sanchuelo, witnesses the sacking and destruction of Medina-Azahara in 1009, and ends up decapitated.

Next, there is some interest in Count Sancho of Castile's expedition in support of Suleiman's Berbers and in the battle of Javalquinto, where the Cordobans were defeated in 1009, an event that has been widely sung by local poets.

The opposing side also seeks reinforcements from Christian countries on the other side of the Peninsula. They find these with Count Raimundo of Barcelona and with Armengol in Urgel. These Arab-Catalans win a battle in Vacar in 1010 and are then defeated at Alcalá de Guadaíra (?) where they suffer great losses. Finally, they return to attack Cordoba where they slaughter much of the population and contribute to destroying the city.

---

[31] Almanzor's death in Medinaceli in 1002 marks the actual demise of the Caliphate. He was so widely admired that for many years, the popular bards in the Maghreb sang his life and successes in ancient heroic romances while Christian storytellers expressed their delight at the disappearance of their great enemy. *Mortuus est et sepultus in Inferno* [He is dead and buried in hell] it says in the *Anales de Burgos*. Lastly, he is responsible for the last and great expansion of our Mesquita, and he builds another walled city east of Cordoba, Medina Zihira, rival to Medina Azahara.

The Berbers capture Medina-Azahara in 1010, burn it, sack it and almost destroy it: hunger and fear take hold in the city. One Caliph is forced to sell the books in the great library of Al-Hakeem because of a lack of funds. The next sacking in 1013 makes one forget all the previous ones, as the Vandal-like thirst for destruction reaches new heights. Berbers, slaves, Arabs, Andalusians and Christians create a strange world of discord, fights, treachery, assassinations and uprisings, where there is no oasis in which to rest one's soul.

Each pretender claims a momentary victory and suffers certain failure. One, Mohammad, represents a semblance of the restoration of Umayyad power in 1024 and he even attempts to restore the Medina-Azahara ruins.

Cordoba continues without a government until finally, the *Mexuar* agrees to get rid of Hisham III. Historians generally refer to this event as the proclamation of the Republic in Cordoba in 1031.

Was there any such Republic in Cordoba? Sincerely, I believe there was not, although some historians maintain there was, upholding the tradition and because it resonates. This political concept was very foreign to the Arabs as it was a European concept and, if you wish, associated with the ancient word *Arian*.

Finding itself without a government, the city leaders formed an interim Council of State, in the same way that they temporarily assumed power in Spain in 1808 when they found themselves without a monarch.

Yahweh and the Council of State managed to govern well; nothing more.

Alhaquem II's multicoloured naves in the Mesquita
Photograph Sam Guimaraens 2017

CHAPTER VI
Fourth Period
D. Fall of the Caliphate - the Christian Conquest (1031 - 1236)

The Taifa. Almoravid and Almohad

The Hispano-Muslim world steadily declined during these two centuries. The conquest of Toledo in 1085 is the seminal event of the Reconquista, from its beginnings to this century. The reconquest of Spain begins in Castilla and develops along the geographic boundaries. Toledo, under Christian control, represents the expansion of the campaign against the Hispano-Arab world in the north of Spain; it is the affirmation of Castile. It is here that the fight between Arabs and Christians, between Spain and Islam, is decided. Had it not been the continuous reinforcements from Africa (Africa is depopulating itself onto Spain), the division of the Christian kingdoms and other internal matters, the matter of the Reconquista would have been more easily and rapidly settled.

Numerous large and small Taifa kingdoms descend on the shredded Caliphate, creating a unique canton-like state that did nothing more than decentralize its culture. These petty Arab kingdoms clearly desire to emulate Cordoba, and some kings dream of restoring the Caliphate for their own benefit, thus their eagerness to recall all that was Umayyad and Cordoba's great prestige.

The heart of civilization, the Cordoban epicentre, spreads outwards and crumbles and, to some extent, gathers for the Arabs in Seville. Later, during the 12th century, Toledo is the hub of learning in Spain, the meeting place of Jews, Arabs and Christians, all the men of the three religions. Nevertheless, although Cordoba loses control of the empire, its culture continues rooted in the city that will still produce distinguished scholars such as Averroes and Maimonides and other great geniuses.

The great city might no longer have political strength nor display a lyrical courtly splendour, but the purest of its streams will still flow through the clear fountain of its learning.

The interim

There is a period of peace and restorations from 1031 to 1070, during which the Berbers are expelled and Yahwar and two of his sons rule successively.

Cordoba comes under the power of Seville in 1070. Al-Motamid, the most intelligent Sevillian kinglet, a man who at the time of his misfortunes said that intelligence, therefore, consists in stopping being intelligent, a poet king who sang of his captivity in Africa in an unforgettable manner, conquers Cordoba with cunning: "I won the hand of beautiful Cordoba…" he declared.

Later, from 1075 to 1078, Cordoba is a subject of caliph Al-Mamum of Toledo, and once again belongs to Seville.

The conquest of Toledo in 1085, however, disconcerts the Spanish Arabs who form an alliance against Alfonso VI under the leadership of Al-Motamid, prince of Cordoba and Seville. He sends a Cordoban poet, Aben-Zeidun, as his ambassador to request reinforcements from their eternal reservoir, hostile Africa, which sends them the Almoravids to save them.

The Almoravid (1091 to 1148)

It is the age-old story: they arrive as helpers and remain as owners, take control of Cordoba in 1091 and for half a century, the city is again the capital of Almoravid Arab Spain.

The Almoravid is a fanatic, a purist and a reactionary, against the Andalusian Arabs' skepticism. New and zealous believers persecute Christians, Jews and even unorthodox Arabs.

The most notable feature of this period is Alfonso I of Aragon's legendary (not because untrue, but because of its brilliance) expedition to free the Mozarabs. This famous expedition in 1125 also affects Cordoba (the Christians win a battle in Aguilar), and results in the almost total eradication of the national Christian nucleus under Arab control. On the one hand, Alfonso takes some 10,000 Mozarab families with him to repopulate the conquered kingdoms. The Almoravids send the remaining families back to Africa to prevent their expulsion by some of the fearsome kingdoms in the North who were already threatening the safety of the country. This was very similar to what Spain later did with the Moriscos, for identical historical reasons.

Still, the Almoravid effort is temporary, as the Andalusian Arabs cannot stand their power. Furthermore, the centre of their African empire is threatened by a new force as Christian expeditions are frequent and disturbing. Alfonso VII reaches the sea at Almeria in 1146, and controls Cordoba, albeit only for a few days.

A period between the Almoravid and the Almohad is known as the second Taifa kingdoms. Cordoba has no political personality. Its most often mentioned kinglet, Abengania, pays homage to Emperor Alfonso VII.

The Almohad (1148-1229) are the new owners of Arab Spain. It appears that they showed some predilection for the Cordoba intelligentsia. Victorious and omnipotent at the beginning, they are soundly crushed in the famous battle of Navas de Tolosa, a battle that was of an enormous geographic importance for the victor who gained control of the entire Guadalquivir River valley. New Taifa kingdoms appear in Arab Spain and after much upheaval, Aben-Hud is proclaimed Caliph of Cordoba. His Caliphate is a mockery. Harassed by other pretenders to the throne, this last Arab king of Cordoba signs pacts with Ferdinand III in exchange for the payment of an exorbitant tribute.

The *Reconquista*

The inhabitants of Cordoba were not happy with their king. A group of Arabs from Cordoba call for the Almogavars - mercenary light infantry - who make a surprise attack one night at the gates of the city. Alvaro Colodro and Benito Baños distinguish themselves in the fight and in January 1236, assisted by Domingo Muñoz and Pero Tafur, they take the suburbs.

Help comes in the form of reinforcements from Andujar and Martos They fortify the Axerquia and wait for king Ferdinand III, who besieges the city. Aben-Hud abandons his Cordobans who surrender on June 29, 1236. He is assassinated in Almeria.

Thus ended Muslim rule. The conquest of the city, as a military feat, has been widely praised by Christian chroniclers and local writers. This is very natural. However, one must bear in mind that as a military action, it is only one of many such actions of little importance, and that Ferdinand III was the fortunate heir of Alfonso VIII's great battles.

After the battle of the Navas de Tolosa which opens the natural road to Andalusia to the Christians, their seizure of Cordoba, a city under siege, unable to receive any kind of assistance, has been overrated. Only the great importance of the city and its reputation has led people to claim this as a great military success.[32] Still, as we take note of this lack of importance as a military feat, we stress the great importance of this as a Christian victory.

Cordoba is no longer global. A city whose reputation ranked with that of Rome and who was on a par with Constantinople in Medieval courts, comes to the end of a great life cycle: Cordoba is no more than yet another city, another town in Castile, whose importance decreases daily. When it comes to solving Spanish problems, the only ones they act on are those which are close to them,

---

[32] Such is the city's reputation, that French minstrels gave rein to their imaginations when they sing of Charlemagne's siege and capture of Cordoba in the *Crónica de Turpín* and the "Chanson de Roland":
Seignur barun, a Carlemagne irez;
Il est al siege a Cordres la citet.

ones regarding the conquest or reconquest when Arab Andalusia, looking inwards, defends itself against the Castilians from the district of Granada.

On the same day that Cordoba submits to the rightly historic empire of Castile, its name begins to be gradually erased from the list of great world populaces. Cordoba, an inland city, follows the declining march of the nation, aggravated by its distance from the main roads of life.

New cities arise due to the force of the new times, but in Cordoba, which for two centuries served as a bastion against the kingdom of Granada, the march of history has rapidly passed her by.

Summary of Arab Cordoba

History, the splendid reporter of the city during its Arab days, tells us that as regards the city's five centuries under that rule, it was the first two, that is, the entire 8th and 9th centuries, which contribute in rapidly growing stages to the rise of the supreme flourishing of the Caliphate. The 10th century produced the greatest political and cultural movement of the High Middle Ages, not only of the Middle Ages in Spain as in of all of Europe.

It was a unique century for our city which reached its zenith in the millennium of the birth of Christ. These were the days of the millennial terrors that tormented medieval life when we begin to see signs of the great outlines of those which in time will become the great nations. It is during this century that is born the prestige, all the melancholy grandeur of the glorious name of Cordoba.

The 10th century is our citizenship century of gold, and the 11th and 12th are the years which, while sustaining the cultural grandeur, will prepare and facilitate the Christian conquest of Cordoba.

Arab Cordoba is the one which attracted the eyes of the world and from whom we retain a great uniqueness among the historic pile of cities that once were famous.[33]

---

[33] There is no end to that which the Arab writers said about her and that later, in their own way, the travellers and writers from all over Europe reported. The bibliography would be enormous, and around the name of Cordoba there is an incalculable amount of literature, that no one has been able to fully catalogue.

Monumental Christian tower of the Mesquita
Designed and built by Hernán Ruíz
Photograph Sam Guimaraens, 2017

CHRISTIAN CORDOBA

CHAPTER VII
Christian Cordoba - First Period
(From the Conquest to the beginning of the 16th century)

Where has Cordoba, home of talent, gone? Abu-Beka[xvi]

The history of Cordoba after the Conquest can be divided into two separate and perfectly defined periods: the first, the 13th, 14th and 15th centuries, or if you prefer a chronological threshold, up to the end of the reign of the Catholic Kings - Ferdinand and Isabella - and the second, the 16th, 17th, 18th and 19th centuries.

Both periods have something in common; they are years of decline, interminable days of degeneration, only barely interrupted. With each century that passes, we lose something that is ours; there is a blurring of the racial make-up of the country and accordingly, of grievances, as the slumbering city reaches the 20th century.

Cordoba suffered irreparably since the beginning of the 11th century. The 11th and 12th and the beginning of the 13th centuries, with non-stop raids, periodic slaughters and systematic arson by militarized factions, explain why so little is left of Arab Cordoba. Added to this, the fact that generally speaking, Arab constructions are not sturdy, too delicate and too understated to be able to stand up to the elements and aggression, explains why Arab buildings disappeared so quickly. If the cathedral was spared from this, it was due to an artistic desecration that in the long run may have been beneficial.

The beginning

The inheritance that the Arabs bequeathed Ferdinand III's Christians was relatively depleted.

Nevertheless, during the 13th 14th and 15th centuries, the days of the first Christian era, Cordoba retains some importance, for the simple reason, as I have said, that it was a frontier city on the road to History and a bastion against the Arab kingdom of Granada. The Catholic Kings also used it as a strategic position during their last campaigns against the Granada Arabs.

Afterwards, life in Spain revolves around the Court on the one hand and later, following the discovery of America, all life in Andalusia is centred in

Seville. The city is empowered by the marvellous Guadalquivir River and bit by bit, Cordoba is little more than a vague memory of the past. Its resonant and romantic name remains, but nothing else does. History falls asleep when it arrives in Cordoba, her children emigrate and cause her name to resonate in foreign parts. Occasionally, there is a whisper of spirituality, but Cordoba is no more than an enchanted, soothing place of rest, until it is shaken by the turmoil of the 19th century.

The 13th Century

Ferdinand proceeded with the compulsory distribution of land amongst the nobles who had accompanied him, and he elevates the Mesquita to a primary church. He transfers ownership of villas and castles to the city and in April 1241, he approves the town charter legislation which is nothing more than the legal confirmation of the Municipal Law Courts' jurisdiction. He also grants a similar charter to several other cities as there is a clear trend for creating a united jurisprudence against a variety of medieval laws.

Some Moors remained in Cordoba and became the 'Mudejares'. The Jews also remained and lived mainly in a city quarter of their own, the Judería. Gregory IX ordered the latter to wear a special badge by which they could be identified in public; their situation was worse than before under the Arabs.

We know of no details regarding the partitioning of Cordoba by Ferdinand III. The Vázquez Venegas collection of manuscripts, however, contains a file in Vol. 7, folios 53 to 80, that the compiler describes as "Distribution of Cordoba by the Holy King Ferdinand, based on the tithes paid to the City Council". This is a very useful starting point, or pattern, for determining who were the original owners of city property belonging to the Church, to parish churches, monasteries and to private individuals. All the military orders, the Church, a great many nobles and the king owned a substantial amount of property in the city.

The political and economic impact of the Conquest

Conquered Cordoba swiftly attracted an inflow of immigrants from all over the country. As graphically and beautifully told in Archbishop Rodrigo's chronicle *Quasi ad regales nuptias concurrerunt* (People from all the towns and regions of Spain) who were attracted by Cordoba's fame as a fertile and wealthy region. The valley of the Guadalquivir was, despite the small size of the Spanish population, seen as a foretaste of the 'Indies' that were opening to the conquistadores.

An examination of all the available genealogical studies for Cordoba indicates that a great many Cordoban families originated in Segovia and the highlands. Segovia, from which came leaders such as Domingo Muñoz and lower ranks; Navarra (a few) and Castile, and also from the mountains of Santander, whence came many nobles and ennobled individuals with their respective retinues. This overlapping of Spain on the Cordoba plateaux and mountains is no mean feat.

The classical Cordoban character that we describe as Senecan never existed as such as Seneca was barely known in Cordoba prior to the 15th century and then only by the cultured. Senequism, which some have accepted, and others created as an erudite literary creation, is something that came later. Seneca was born 4 BCE in Cordoba, but his spirit is born in Rome.

Nonetheless, he and all the Hispanic group carry within them the enduring strength of the blood, the uninterrupted traditional thread, and in this respect, he is truly Cordoban.

What I see appear in Cordoba after the Reconquista, is a Castilinization process, better still, of a Northern Hispanization, from the central mountain range upwards, which is evident in the character and the history of the people. I do not wish to say, as some people angrily tell us, that Senequism is a topic for tourists. Nonetheless, the soul of Cordoba consists of many nuances that we summarize by describing it as Senecan and I, for one, do not wish to remove this particular image from her spiritual coat of arms.

The great wave, great for this period, arrives in the middle valley of the Guadalquivir, also but to a lesser extent, in Seville.

This process, the stamp of the man from the North, is repeated during the 15th century in Granada. This city was depopulated when it was conquered, and this is followed by a wave of emigration that also includes people from Cordoba and Jaen as well as from Castile. Therefore, Granada is a special kind of Andalusian city. There is a true racial consanguinity linking the cities of Cordoba and Granada (not the provinces of the same names).

To go into greater detail would exceed the modest limits of this humble book. Still, as Cordoba enters a new era, it is not out of the question to ask ourselves: how was our city shaped both ethnically and spiritually? The seed of today might be found in the answer. The demonstration continues.

Why is it that the people from the Cordoba Sierra, particularly the entire Pedroches Valley, speak and enshrine such a strong and pure Castellano? Why is it the countryside is something else and so different from the viewpoint of the geographic landscape, when we speak of it in all its complexity today? Not the simple, albeit beautiful, subjective literary landscape, but the geographic landscape of 'space and time', of 'land and men'.

The countryside

It is in the division of Andalusia by Ferdinand III that we find the lawful charter of large estates and it is there that we find the source of our agrarian problem. Mudejar serfs who continued to be vassals to the king and the territorial nobility who owned the land begin to confront each other. King Ferdinand did not create nor initiate the problem - that was the way of the times. Furthermore, it was a problem he inherited almost whole from the previous Arab lords. For example: the peasants in Jerez who adopted the Arab culture and converted to Islam, go on strike and rebel against the Wise King soon after the mid-13th century, demonstrating how deep the roots were and how they echoed demands that dated back to earlier times.

A new history for Cordoba begins with the Reconquista and vital new elements will produce it. Nobility, royalty, Church: another civilization. New Art and new Letters. Peasants, middle class and hard, semi-feudal property owners create a new historical framework. How did those people live? What did they think, feel, believe? The trends that shape how citizens assert themselves, trends espoused by the royalty to dominate and, in the end, conquer; those are the basis of Cordoba's real history from the 13th to the 16th centuries. The life of its guilds and its craftsmen, its countryside, their beliefs, which is the true Cordoba.

There still are traces of this, although little historical evidence to ensure that we have uncovered the full History of our city. Not yet, perhaps never. Therefore, we must be content with bringing what we can to the surface and emphasize that which is evident, always reminding ourselves that this is not where the history is. When philosophers search for the location of the 'soul', they do not look for it on the surface of the skin. As we search for the History of Christian Cordoba, we have not gone beyond this, although some – many – have reverently attempted to tread its illustrious paths. In truth, what is said regarding Cordoba can be said of almost all the history of Spain which is currently creating or recreating itself along the new horizons; and of the modern sense of history as it affects History, from its very beginning, from the base to the summit.

Every generation has its own point of view regarding History (the past), regarding behaviour (the present) and what to expect in the future.

The Reconquista is, in fact, over and until the days of Ferdinand and Isabella, the internal policy of the kings of Castile represents a constant struggle against the nobility as the crown attempts to reduce the nobility's power and assert its own, as the nobles repeatedly take advantage of the disturbances caused by the frequent minorities of the kings.

These conflicts are both political and social and I will address these later. They arise in all the cities in the Peninsula, and Cordoba is almost always a part of what today we would call the party of the opposition.

CHAPTER VIII
City Brotherhoods and political strife

The existence of the city brotherhoods is very significant – they are in essence what are known in modern terms today as commonwealths.[34]

A Brotherhood Charter is enacted in 1265 by the City Councils of Cordoba, Jaen, Baeza, Ubeda, Andujar, Santi-Esteban, Iznatoraf, Quesada and Cazorla, as represented by Diego Sánchez De Funes and Sancho Martínez de Jódar. Among other things, the charter states: "We celebrate this Brotherhood in order to protect and defend our land". "Signed and dated in Andujar on the 26th day of April in the year one thousand, three hundred and three."

There is another meeting of the Brotherhood Board in Andujar in 1282, attended by the City Councils of Jaen, Baeza, Ubeda, Arjona and Santi-Esteban, as well as Cordoba, whereby they pledge their mutual protection and assistance.

Most especially, in 1296 the City Councils of Cordoba, Seville and Jerez, with unbeatable courage and daring and a profound sense of citizenship, ratify a magnificent Brotherhood Charter. This Charter is of great interest to our social history.

The original copy of this Charter is kept in the Jerez de la Frontera Municipal Archives. The heading of the document states:

Let it be known that this Charter is enacted in response to the many outrages, grave harm to privileges, charters, franchises and freedoms and to accepted conventions and practices, and many other aggravations inflicted upon us by the kings in the past.

This introduction clearly expresses the spirit and the justification for the Charter. It continues with a specific list of individuals in positions of civil and

---

[34] The *mancomunidad* is very ancient in Spain. Julio Puyol y Alonso studied it as regards the centre of the Peninsula. In his book *Las Hermandades de Castilla y León*, Madrid, 1913, he says that the oldest was Valladolid in 1282, and that all the theory regarding Brotherhoods can be summarized in these words: "To attribute their right to be to something higher than a royal decree and on firmer grounds than the capricious whim of a monarch or the individual expediencies of some magnate". He adds: "Although they never ceased to recognize the supreme power of the king and the unity of the kingdom."

military authority, wardens, bailiffs and judges, who might offend the people in this manner.

To defend themselves from any outrages, it further states:

> *After all legal proceedings have been met, when the person responsible for offending the Community or any individual offender is deemed to be a person of property: "his houses shall be demolished, his vineyards, orchards and all other property shall be destroyed, as well as anything else demanded* (by the plaintiff). *If the offender is not a person of property he may be put to death.*

Furthermore, if the offender has fled, all the Councils that are members of the Brotherhood are authorized *to execute him, wherever he may be found.*

All the dispositions – there are twenty-two of them – are noteworthy and written with an iron will, in defence of the freedoms they represent and that the authors staunchly upheld from the middle of the 13th century to the middle of the 14th century.

Some have occasionally doubted that these Andalusian Councils blossomed. Others have stated that this municipal spirit had become extinct by the time that the Reconquista arrived at the Guadalquivir. It had not, neither there nor in the kingdom of Castile. It took the form of mutual collaboration in the shape of Brotherhoods of Councils whose interaction is interesting. These end during the 14th century. However, during the reign of Pedro I, the battles between the king and his brothers and the nobility are more complex than a simple and dramatic fight between brothers, and it is in the light of those hostilities that we must examine the Brotherhoods.

A Brotherhood, according to the laws of the time, always has the penalty of death as an option. If some individual from a neighbouring town brings a letter from the King to its Council, demanding tributes or other outlandish requests, the Brotherhood can 'kill the messenger'.

Brotherhood Charters are signed by individuals bearing such plebeian names as 'Joan Díaz', 'García Alffon', 'García Pérez' or 'Alffon González'. Seville signed one such charter on behalf of the city and on behalf of the Cordoba City Council.

Three important dates

The Brotherhood Charters enjoyed three truly golden dates: 1265, 1282 and 1296. In other words, seventy years at the end of the 13th century when Cordoba, a frontier town which from the beginning had had governors on the border - the first being Alvaro Pérez de Castro - still retains the spiritual leadership of Andalusia.

As time goes by, this leadership is formalized during the reign of Carlos V in the form of the Junta de la Rambla until it ends when for several reasons Seville becomes the capital of Spain and the crown, by now the sole power, acts as a levelling force.

The Brotherhood Charters represent the strong feelings of municipal sovereignty expressed by their citizens who wish to govern themselves and who resist being assimilated into the royal government.

Under Alfonso X [Alfonso the Wise]

During the hostilities between Alfonso X of Castile and his son Sancho IV, the Cordoba Council declares its support of Sancho. Alfonso X is helped by the king of Morocco, in 1283, whose troops besiege Cordoba where the rebellious son had fortified himself; the siege was lifted when it failed.

Alfonso the Wise sends troops from Seville under the command of Ferdinand Pérez Ponce against the king of Granada, a friend of Sancho's. Alerted to their presence, the Cordobans under Ferdinand Arias de Mexia and Ferdinand Núñez de Temes send troops against them. The Cordobans are sorely defeated at the battle of Los Visos in 1283, during which Núñez de Termes, Head Sheriff of the city, is killed. When he comes to the throne, Sancho expresses his gratitude to Cordoba by granting it an exemption from paying taxes, as described by Andrés Morales y Padilla.

Reigns of Ferdinand IV and Alfonso XI

It is written in the Chronicles of Ferdinand IV that there was a great uprising by the people in the city of Cordoba in 1310, and that the king severely punished those he felt deserved it, and that since the city belonged to the Christians there had never been such a rebellion as this one.

In Cordoba, the king received the embassy of an Arab from Fez who came to speak to him about the conquest of Africa on behalf of several African leaders and the descendants of Cordoban Mozarabs who were living in exile on the other side of the Strait of Gibraltar.

Castilla's recurring problem was the question of under-age rulers. One of the most tumultuous cases occurred during the minority of Alfonso XI when four Regents or tutors of the king 'reigned' simultaneously. Cordoba was a favourite with Infante Juan Manuel, the illustrious and restless author of the *Libro de los ejemplos del conde Lucanor y de Patronio* a compilation of stories entitled "The Tale of Count Lucanor".[35]

---

[35] First printed in 1575 when it was published at Seville under the auspices of Argote de Molina. It was again printed at Madrid in 1642, after which it lay forgotten for nearly two centuries.

Infante Juan Manuel in Cordoba

The Chronicles are sufficiently explicit to enable us to appreciate an extremely interesting period in Cordoba. This was the year 1320. The Cordoba Council had been governing the city for a little more than seventy years and one could say that they were establishing a sound municipal regime. There are historical glimpses which prove this.

The redistribution had created a territorial and feudal nobility which, naturally, aspired to Power. The positions of Mayor and Sheriff were in the hands of the nobles. That was not what the spirit of a city which believed that it was great and still was the great leader of the Guadalquivir valley, wanted.

Seville's power came later, particularly after the discovery and conquest of America. The 16th century was Seville's great century.

The Cordoban legislature (the Representatives are its voice) felt they should be entitled to appoint those who would hold municipal positions. They petitioned Queen Maria de Molina – who was Regent for the second time as her grandson Alfonso XI was still under-age – for this right and for the right to remove any irregular officials.

When the queen denies their request, the people champion Infante Juan Manuel, acclaim him as Regent, rise against the throne and ask the Infante for his support. Juan Manuel accedes to the Cordoban demands and he enters the city, personally leading the uprising.

Meanwhile, Payo Arías de Castro and Fernán Alfonso, supporters of Maria de Molina, garrison the Alcazar (the old Alcazar today). They are defeated and flee the city which falls into the hands of Juan Manuel and his army.

The first truly political action

This is perhaps the first truly political action in Christian Cordoba, as the reason for the 1312 revolt is not very clear. Juan Manuel's authority in Cordoba, once he was recognized as Regent, greatly distressed the border towns from Jaen to Seville that had entered into a cooperative agreement, a kind of Brotherhood as described earlier. They received this news with great sorrow, because of the oath and covenant they had taken and signed between them that neither of them would become the others' guardian.

Moreover, all the cities along the Arab-Christian frontier had signed a peace treaty for eight years with Granada that they feared would be broken. Payo Arías had signed this treaty on behalf of Cordoba, without involving the Regents as if he were an independent agent, during a meeting in Baena between the frontier towns and Granada who feared that as Don Juan was on the border, there might be disagreements and disturbances between the people of the various towns.

The union of the Andalusian towns and cities breaks down and hostilities between Castilian nobles spread to Andalusia, where they continued for two centuries until the Marquis of Priego, of whom we shall speak later, surrendered in Cordoba in the last act of feudal rebellion. Juan Manuel's rebellion, although seemingly a popular uprising, was also a fight amongst the nobility: Cordoba supported Infante Juan Manuel and Seville, Infante Filipe.

It is interesting that the hostilities between the leaders of the Andalusian nobility – which it was what they were – began in 1320 and ended in 1508, in Cordoba. The wars for the Regency of Spain continued, especially after Maria de Molina's death. There were three Regents who acted like kinglets, whilst Juan Manuel was Regent for Cordoba. This situation lasted until Alfonso XI came of age. Juan Manuel, who visited Cordoba frequently, died there around 1348.

More civil strife

The 1312 riots, before the arrival of Juan Manuel, a great scholar, also a troublemaker, assassin and thoroughly evil person, embroil Cordoba in the various factions of the Cordoban nobility, as mentioned earlier. Throughout the entire 14th century, Cordoba continues to serve as the arena for civilian uprisings, followed by unrest from supporters of Pedro (few) and champions of Enrique. When peace is restored, the spirit of the City Council has died, and the city is left in the hands of the king's magistrates. They do not personally strengthen the monarchy - any member of the Trastamara dynasty who rises to power, does so less than previous kings. Still, the Monarchy gains in influence and ends up asserting its authority. Political freedom, inherited from the Middle Ages, will end and give way to another form of freedom, individual liberty, the heritage of the Renaissance.

African Invasions

Invasions from Africa continued. The Benemerine (Arabized Berbers) were again setting their sights on Andalusia and had attacked several townships, including in 1318 to Jerez to whom Cordoba rapidly came in aid. A special Brotherhood was formed between the two cities and henceforth, Cordoba always spoke before the *Cortes*[xvii] on behalf of itself and on behalf of Jerez.

Two of Alfonso XI's uncles, Infantes Juan and Pedro, led an expedition against the Arabs of Granada, where they were defeated and where many Cordobans died with them as Pedro led the troops under the banner of Cordoba in 1319. The Cordoban master, Muñiz de Godoy distinguished himself by saving many of the defeated.

The frontier city of Cabra de la Frontera still enjoys considerable vitality and personality. The disaster that befell both princes moved and frightened Andalusia. Pay (or Payo) Arias, Warden of the Cordoba Alcazar, signed a Peace Treaty with the king of Granada 14 June 1320 on behalf of the deputies of the Andalusian towns and cities, as previously mentioned.

Cordoba helped Alfonso XI in his campaigns, particularly when he took Algeciras and besieged Gibraltar, where the king died 26 March 1350, a victim of the famous bubonic plague epidemic of 1348 which caused such great devastation in Spain. The book *Historia de la Epidemiología española*, states that the plague reached its peak at this time and that it threatened to depopulate Europe.

The epidemic reappeared at intervals. Cordoba suffered, especially during the 17th century, when half of the city was annihilated. Alfonso XI is buried next to his father Ferdinand IV, in Cordoba Cathedral; both were transferred to San Hipólito church in 1736.[36]

CHAPTER IX
Reign of Pedro the Cruel and his immediate successors

The much-discussed reign of this monarch left a deep scar on Cordoba. Since 1358, Cordoba had championed the cause of Enrique of Trastamara, the bastard pretender to the throne. Pedro I, the main character of legends and the star of countless romantic tales, frequently visited Cordoba and it is said that it is here that the first child he sired with Maria de Padilla was born.

Pedro I viciously retaliated against the Cordobans who championed his half-brother. In 1367, after his victory at the Battle of Nájera, he ordered that Pedro de Cabrera and Alfonso de Gahete be killed by slitting their throats on Salvador de Cordoba square. He also instructed a Cordoban noble, Martín López de Córdoba[37] to execute other judicial actions (which the latter did not do) and to

---

[36] There is a curious document, *Respuesta que dio el rey D. Alonso XI a ciertas cartas que le escribió el Consejo de Córdoba* (año 1323) [Reply of King Alonso XI to certain letters from Cordoba Council (1323), that clarifies and highlights the uprisings in Cordoba and the individuals involved in the disputes between the tutors.] (Est. 25, C. 14, A. H.)

[37] Master of the Orders of Alcántara and Calatrava, he gave the highest proof of loyalty when he rose in defense of Pedro's daughters. Another Cordoban, Alfonso Ruíz, later known as *Alfonso de los Infantas*, also distinguished himself by taking the king's daughters to safety in Bayona, which is how he earned that nickname.

demolish several houses belonging to nobles (which he did), including those belonging to the Hoce, Argote and Mesa families.

The conflict between Pedro the Cruel, as he was also called, and his brothers took on many aspects. On one occasion however, when the people of Cordoba heard that Enrique had entered Burgos accompanied by foreign supporters, they gave voice to their rebellion. Pedro, helped by the Arab king of Granada, marched against Cordoba in 1368 and ferociously attacked the city, without success. According to the Chronicle, he came prepared to revenge himself without pity with an army of more than 40,000 men.

The Battle of the Campo de la Verdad

The entire population of Cordoba, gentlemen and their servants, nobles and townsfolk, defended themselves under Alfonso Fernández de Córdoba, the military commander who led them to victory in the so-called Battle of the Campo de la Verdad, the name by which this city suburb has traditionally been known since then. As Alfonso led the Cordoban troops against the King of Granada and King Pedro in defence of the city, he ordered the destruction of two of the supporting arches of the bridge across the river so that the enemy could not advance any further.

The Abad de Rute and other authors believe, nevertheless, that the name Campo de la Verdad already existed before that battle. This battle has played a significant role in the Cordoban literary traditions, and it has inspired many local poets. The brilliant actions of the citizens in the low-lying neighbourhoods are legendary, particularly in Santa Marina, and are attributed by some to the command of a so-called Judge Aguilar. Should this person exist, he would have come later. Unless, as others claim, this is a reference to a 17th century individual, a so-called *Jurado* Aguilar - since Jurado could be part of his surname and not the title of his profession, i.e., a judge.

Still,, modern studies based on the complete knowledge of Arab sources that appear specific and correct, attribute little importance to this battle and further indicate that there never was such a victory. Cordoba, besieged and attacked in the neighbourhood of the Alcazar, against an outer wall that likely was very poorly defended, and, as King Pedro declared, owed its salvation to the rain. Very possibly. An extensive section of the wall, which still exists next to the Puerta de Sevilla, owed its existence to the military need to defend this part of the city, and probably dates in great part to the 14th century.

The Battle of Los Visos in 1366, according to Arab sources, was a defeat. History contains many examples of similar contradictory reports.

Enrique II and his immediate successors

Everything went well for Enrique II in Castile after the Battle of Montiel. Pedro Muñiz de Godoy, Grand Master of Calatrava,[38] stands out among the Cordobans who favoured Enrique, given the support he and all his relatives gave him in Cordoba.

Almost all the branches of the House of Cordoba family were supporters of Enrique II. When he still was a pretender to the throne, as a gesture of gratitude, on 6 November 1367 in Burgos, he granted the people of Cordoba several exemptions.

On 22 May 1369, two months after he rose to the throne, Enrique II bestowed an extraordinary honour upon Cordoba. The text of the royal decree states that the king grants this honour "In appreciation for the great damages and losses that you have suffered in our service." This great honour was so widespread that anyone born in Cordoba could travel freely anywhere in the kingdom of Castille without being required to pay custom duties, excise taxes, tithes nor tributes of any kind, regardless of their name.

The importance of this honour is that it covers almost all the wages paid to the Cordobans who endorsed Enrique, as well as those who came to the city from other places in Andalusia to assist him. It is a confirmation of ancient honours, favours and gifts that Gonzalo Mexias, Master of Santiago, previously bestowed upon the nobles of Cordoba on behalf of the king.[39]

The Jews

The enthronement of the bastard king was a milestone for the Jews in Spain. Although favoured by Pedro I, Enrique persecuted them viciously, in accordance with the ideas of the times. This, along with the fact that the Spanish population as a whole was becoming increasingly less tolerant.

During the wars with Portugal between João I of Portugal and Juan I of Castile, the Cordobans fought in the Battle of Aljubarrota, a Portuguese victory. Later also in another furious encounter that pitted the famous Portuguese Constable Nuño Alvarez Pereyra against nobles from Cordoba and Seville in 1385, the Grand Master of Calatrava and of Alcantara, Muñiz de Godoy, whom I mentioned earlier, was killed in a battle in which Alfonso Fernández de Córdoba especially distinguished himself.

---

[38] Godoy was taken prisoner by Pedro after the defeat at Nájera, together with the famous Du Guesclin (French leader of the white companies) and the chronicler Pedro López de Ayala. Freed after paying a huge ransom, Godoy also fought in Montiel with Enrique and with another Cordoban noble Juan Jiménez, who was killed in the battle.

[39] Cathedral Archives; Historical Archives.

The situation of the Jews worsened in Cordoba during the reign of Enrique III in 1391, as Christians attacked and sacked the Jewish quarter in reaction to the preaching of Hernando Martínez, Archdeacon of Ecija. This archdeacon, whom the eminent converted Jew Pablo de Santa Maria described as *simplex in litteratura*, incited the people of Andalusia with violent sermons that cost the lives of countless Jews. 2,000 were victims in Cordoba. The king condemned the city to pay 24,000 gold doubloons as a punishment for this slaughter. Even so, the attack and sacking of the Jewish quarter was repeated, albeit with less bloodshed, in 1406.

The entire 14th century and the beginning of the 15th century are of particular interest regarding the history of Spain and of Cordoba; in addition to the national history that I mentioned so briefly, there is another silent and inaudible history, the history of the true soul of the city.

The medieval townships' sense of democracy, a reflection of which reached Cordoba, was little by little being lost. On the one hand, the power of the Crown was growing in strength and on the other hand, the nobles were becoming more violent. This is why Cordoba asked the king, without doubt a last attempt at citizenship, to "remove the senior town councillors, the Knights Veinticuatro and the main warden, all of whom were appointed by the king, and to allow the townspeople to fill those positions as they wished."

All these efforts ended in 1402 with the appointment of royal magistrates who would bind the cities more tightly to the royal power. The presence in Cordoba of the first such magistrate is an act of major social significance that is notable for its importance and meaning.

CHAPTER X
The 15ᵗʰ century. Other disputes between nobles.
Juan II – Enrique IV

During the minority of Juan II, his uncle Ferdinand who was Regent chose Cordoba as the centre of military operations against the Arabic kingdom of Granada. He assenbled a force of 500 knights on horseback and 500-foot soldiers from Cordoba and successfully captured Antequera in 1410.[40]

---

[40] Later, a royal indulgence granted to all those who live in Antequera "for one year and day", states that Knight Veinticuatro Alonso de Córdoba who killed his wife and the Knights Commanders, was included in this group.

Juan II was in Cordoba because of the war with Granada. A great celebration was held in the cathedral in 1431 to commemorate the Battle of Higueruela, which was of no importance at all.

Juan II's poetic and chivalrous court (the famous poet Juan de Mena was his contemporary) soon lost interest in fighting the Arabs. In 1434, Suero de Quiñones staged a famous tournament, the *Passo honroso*, on the Orbigo bridge, during which the Cordoban, Pedro de los Rios, distinguished himself while attending this great feudal festivity.

As modern times begin, the crisis in Spain greatly affects Cordoba and there is probably no greater period of unrest impacting the inner life of the city than the entire 15th century. Constant battles between nobles under Enrique IV and at the beginning of Ferdinand and Isabella's reign, together with the latters' numerous rules and regulations with which to organize the city, are proof of this.

The nobles' hostility towards Alvaro de Luna kept Cordoba, where Enrique de Aragon, the king's brother lived, in an uproar. Bishop Sancho de Rojas, enemy of Alvaro, unsuccessfully attempted to place the city and the diocese under an interdict in 1443. Thwarted, he ultimately appointed archdeacon Pedro Fernández de Córdoba y Solier, supporter of Alvaro de Luna, as administrator, Bishop of Cordoba and Governor of the city.

The second half of the 15th century was prolific in events, beginning in 1455 when Enrique IV celebrated his marriage to Queen Joana of Portugal and they became parents of Juana of Castile, known as the *Beltraneja*.

During the conflicts that flourished during his reign, the feudal nobles' last struggle for survival divided the people of Andalusia and of Cordoba province into two camps. In order to clearly understand the spirit of these factions, one must remember that they were not popular with the masses who were seldom interested in them. These were matters that only interested the nobility and other courtiers who refused to accept the establishment of a powerful monarch.

Enrique is ousted from the throne in Avila in 1465 and his brother Alfonso is crowned king. Alonso de Aguilar headed the king's faction in Cordoba; the Count of Cabra, headed that of Don Enrique.

The way this aggrieved husband obtained so-called justice was so emotive that it influenced the literature of the times. Lope de Vega, for example, wrote a dramatic play entitled *Los Comendadores de Córdoba*, and the ballads popularized it in each literary age, like the one that says:

Los comendadores
por mi mal os vi.
Yo vi a vosotros,
Vosotros a mi.

Alonso de Aguilar

Alonso de Aguilar was the true owner of Cordoba. He fought against Bishop Solier, whose palace he burnt and sacked. The bishop fled, taking with him a grievance against Alfonso and his associates that would endure for several years.

After King Alfonso died in 1468, Enrique IV came to Cordoba intending to pacify the city. Unfortunately, he offended Alonso de Aguilar by giving the latter's enemy, the Count of Cabra, command of the Alcazar and other forts in Cordoba and of towns under the city's jurisdiction. Alonso regained control over these strongholds by resorting to treason thereby increasing his power, even though this heightened the civil war.

Alonso is so certain of his power in 1472, that he again violently expels the new Bishop Solier. The bishop retaliates by issuing a letter of excommunication that lists everyone allied with Alfonso, as well as details of all their acts of defiance. The list includes the names of almost every noble in Cordoba on the grounds that they had burnt and sacked His Excellency's properties.

If all this were not enough, there is a renewed persecution of the Jews in 1473, in the form of an infamous riot and slaughter of this perpetually tormented people. The rioting was led by Alonso Rodrigues, a blacksmith who claimed that the Jews were guilty of what undoubtedly was an accidental desecration, an event that is mentioned by all Cordoban historians.

Alonso de Aguilar unsuccessfully attempts to control the rioters and the situation gets worse when Alonso himself kills Rodriguez, the blacksmith. Furious, the townspeople shut Alonso up in the Alcazar where many Jews have taken refuge. The sacking and slaughter that followed were terrible and spread to other towns in the province: Montoro, La Rambla, Santaella and Bujalance, among others.

The Jewish community in Cordoba never recover from this attack; and very soon afterwards, they and all the other Jews in Spain are expelled from the country.

El Grán Capitán
GONZALO FERNÁNDEZ DE CÓRDOBA

The Great Captain

Gonzalo Fernández de Córdoba y Enríquez de Aguilar, the *Gran Capitán* (1453 - 1515), was a member of a great Córdova lineage. This Cordoban-Montillano played a minor role in Cordoba where he did little more than support his older brother, Alonso de Aguilar, during the turbulent period of the hostilities amongst the nobility.

There is little of note regarding his youth; he is the satellite of another star. On one occasion during a skirmish between feudal lords and municipalities, he is imprisoned in Santaella.

He later obtains his military education in the wars against Granada: ten years of military university. In Granada, he distinguishes himself for his gallant courtesy, his diplomacy and fighting spirit

It is in Italy, at the end of the 15th century, however, that he becomes famous as the ancient Mother Baetica again calls her vassals to her service!

During the first military expedition under his command, in 1495, the French, Italian, German and Spanish christen him the Great Captain. Rome and the Papacy launch great celebrations, as they did when Caesar returned triumphant from Gaul. Naples, the great Mediterranean beauty on the other great side of the great Latin lake, receives him spectacularly, with even greater enthusiasm.

Gonzalo's name quickly flies around the world. It is his shining glory. Tales of his many battles are recounted in every history book.

Shadows appear later during the twilight of his life, cast by the misgivings of King Ferdinand because Loja, where Gonzalo lives in retirement, is where you find the real Andalusian Court. All looks are upon him. Why? Do some want to make Loja and Gonzalo the feudal nobility's last stronghold? Is this an attempt to resuscitate and recapture the soul of Andalusia? Nobody knows for certain. There, living as if in a secular monastery, he retreats and barely hears the noise from the outside world until death creeps quietly upon him. Granada honours his remains with hundreds of flags that droop in sorrow around his casket.

There were many facets to the Great Captain's feudal talent, many shining lights. He changes tactics and develops a modern military institution, creating an infantry that brought Spain admiration, terror, supremacy and hatred. Gonzalo is great, sumptuous and cultured: the heritage of Seneca and his Cordoban lineage flows in his veins.

Legend and History collected his famous sayings: his celebrated stories that were not invented but serve to interpret his character and to give shape to his true features as a genius of his race.

Although specialists of this period say that there lacks a complete critical history worthy of this figure, such a history began with the *Crónicas del Gran Capitán* collected in 1908 by A. Rodríguez Villa.

Manuel José Quintana, in his book *Vidas de españoles célebres* composed a most beautiful biography about him. Eugenio de la Iglesia, in his book *Estudios histórico-militares sobre las campañas del Gran Capitán* dealt with the military aspect of his life. M. Orti Belmonte, "Crónica del Gran Capitán" in *Granada y su Reino* (a magazine).

There are more assorted references, such as the "Colección de cartas" and "Correspondencia" published in the *Revista de Archivos*, an acceptable handful of essays.

In these Gonzalo, he of the star-studded horoscope, stands out, as time and again he triumphantly and loudly praises the name of Cordoba, its lineage and its city. Always a prey of that uneasy sadness that is so characteristic of Cordobans, he attempts to bury himself in the monastery of Saint Jerome in Loja, Granada, but this melancholy ultimately prevents him from breaking the mistique of his self-imposed jail.

Gonzalo, although born in Montilla, has, more than anyone, extolled the ancient motto of Cordoba as the Home of Warrior People. Therefore, I have included this brief biography of the man, albeit as a footnote to the story of the city.

CHAPTER XI
The Age of the Catholic Kings
Ferdinand II of Aragon and Isabella I of Castile

Enrique IV dies in 1474 and in Cordoba, Alonso de Aguilar proclaims Juana la Beltraneja Queen of Castile, a proclamation that appears not to have been successful.

In 1477, already during the joint reign of the Catholic Kings, there is a resurgence of Alonso de Aguilar's never-ending conflict against the Count of Cabra in which he now also involves his brother Gonzalo de Cordoba.

The kings appoint Diego Merlo Chief Magistrate of Cordoba, and he manages to restore a degree of calm to the city, although when he attempts to punish two murderers, the townspeople rise in anger. Diego seeks refuge in San Lorenzo church where Alonso seizes him by force and imprisons him in his castle in Aguilar.

Finally, in October 1478, Ferdinand and Isabella arrive in Cordoba and pacify the city, forcing Alonso to hand over the Alcazar and other forts such as the Calahorra. The kings banish Alonso from the troubled city, one which he had stirred up so much during his fifteen years of personal rule.[41]

The reign of the Catholic Kings, especially during the ten years of war against Granada, brings a degree of life and vibrancy to Cordoba. There is no need for us to list each time the kings came and went from the city, which they did frequently as Cordoba had been their military headquarters during much of their campaign against Granada.

---

[41] Alonso de Aguilar, related to the Marquis of Villena, is an extremely interesting historical figure. The last feudal lord who lived in Cordoba, he was arrogant and audacious, fought in many of the battles during the wars against Granada and died in 1501 fighting against the Arabs who rebelled in Sierra Bermeja.

The bards of the times wrote many beautiful ballads recounting his death, which were collected by Agustín Durán in his *Romancero general*. *Antón de Montoro*, 'El Ropero', the Cordoban poet, particularly praises this character, lavish protector of the Jews and last representative of a semi-feuda era.

No se tiene por buen moro
el que o le dé lanzada
....
Llorábale una cautiva,
Una cautiva cristiana.

For a decade, the life of Spain happens in Cordoba: Columbus has ambitions in Cordoba and follows the kings to the city where he meets and woos the romantic figure of Beatriz de Arana, mother of Hernando Colón. King Boabdil, captured in Lucena in 1483, is imprisoned in the Bishop's Palace, and Gonzalo de Cordoba begins to rise to fame with his feats in battle against Granada. In a nutshell, this is the city's last somewhat lively and exciting epoch.

The kings resided in the Alcazar but they also spent some time in the San Jeronimo monastery on the hillside above the city. A curious tradition of Cordoban judicial history dates from this time, that of the *holgazanas* (lazy women), which held that women should be denied the right to inherit spousal property.

The kings expelled the Jews from Cordoba in 1492. Today nothing remains of their famous Cordoban School (whose golden age spanned the 11th and 12th centuries) except for a few synagogues and traces of the Jewish Quarter. Going from the Puerta de Almodovar to the Juderia, the neighbourhood in which the Jews lived was demarcated by the city wall, the Campo de los Martires and the Calle Almanzor. Lastly, it was in Cordoba that the kings instituted the Inquisition, a subject worthy of a most interesting heading of its own.

The Inquisition

In 1482, the Church creates the Inquisition in Cordoba upon the insistence of Friar Alonso de Burgos who was preoccupied with the existence of false converts to Christianity.

The first inquisitors were:

- Pedro Martín del Barrio, or Martínez, canon of the church
- Alvar González de Capillas
- Antón Ruiz de Morales, precentor, buried at the gate of the Chapel of the Last Supper
- Friar Martín Caro, warden of San Francisco.

The Inquisition began operating immediately. Diego Rodriguez Lucero, appointed Senior Inquisitor in 1500, is still remembered with loathing. He was responsible for so many outrages that in 1505 the City Council and the Municipality cried out against his abuse of power and demanded justice.

In their complaint, the city authorities beg the king to come in person to Cordoba whose contemptible judges had burnt 107 innocent Christians and then 27 others at the stake. Lucero fled Cordoba to escape certain death, was tried and sentenced to prison in 1508.

The seat of the Inquisition was the new Alcazar but the autos-da-fé took place in various locations. The Quemadero, or main burning ground where the condemned were burnt alive, was located next to the Marrubial barracks. There are indications that there were pyres elsewhere, such as on the island below the bridge. The first auto-da-fé was carried out in 1483 in the Los Mártires convent.

Magdalena de la Cruz, a famous nun held to be a miracle worker, died in the 1555 auto-da-fé.

The most notable autos-da-fé were carried out in 1625 and 1627, when Isabel Alvarez, a blind, crippled woman, was one of those who perished among the flames that year. The Jewish poet Núñez Bernal, greatly lamented by his relatives, was burnt alive in 1655. There were three more such executions during this century and six in the 18th century, the most significant of which took place during the reign of Felipe V. The last auto-da-fé occurred in 1799 in the chapel of the Court and drew great public attention because it was fifty years since such a solemn event was celebrated.

The history of the Inquisition in Cordoba, like that of all local inquisitions, is interesting. Of course, this is almost impossible to reconstruct as the archives were torched in 1810, all the records disappeared, and there are no first-hand sources. We have to glean what we can from general histories. We do know that the first Chief Magistrate was a Cordoban gentleman called Angulo.

At first, the inquisitors were extremely meticulous in their interrogations. An example of this is the case of the Treasurer, Pedro Fernández de Alcaudete, who in 1482 was accused of being a Judaizer[xviii] and burnt alive in the Campo de la Verdad, at the same time as his uncle Luis García.

Executions were extremely frequent during the second half of the 17th century. Pyres were most often erected at the San Pablo convent, occasionally at San Basilio church and at Jesús Crucificado church.

The general autos-da-fé were held in Corredera square but the burning ground was in Marrubial, with pyres also on the large island in the Guadalquivir River.

There are printed and authorized reports of the most important autos-da-fé almost all listed in José Maria de Valdenebro y Cisnero's book *La Imprenta en Córdoba*.

The Cordoba Inquisition's jurisdiction included the Archdiocese, Jaén, Alcalá la Real abbey, the Archbishop of Toledo's feudal estate of Cazorla, Ecija and Estepa.

We do not know how many victims of the Inquisition there were in Spain nor in Cordoba, and to date nobody has written a thoroughly historical history of this institution. Essential references today include Charles Lea's recently published *A*

History of the Inquisition of Spain[42] and for Cordoba especially, Matute y Luquin's *Autos de fe en Córdoba.*[43] These were completed by Ramírez de Arellano.[44]

Lucero's actions, which deserve a full local study, are well described in Charles Lea's book (Vol. I), not just because of what Lea has to say but also because of the many sources in the Cordoba and the Simanca cathedral archives that he refers to. Before Lea, if these references were known, no one appears to have consulted them. Lea also mentions Magdalena de la Cruz. I believe his work has been translated into French; I know of no translation into Spanish.

There was a huge scandal in 1609 involving the Cordoban Inquisitors and Pedro Fernández Mansilla, the Vicar-General, over which of the two had jurisdiction over a particular case. Matters got so out of hand that the inquisitors called all their kinfolk who armed themselves and attacked the Bishop's Palace in an attempt to capture the Vicar-General. Clerics, friends and servants defended him. The outcome was a great fight when the Vicar-General called the clergy to his defence. He was finally arrested, and the matter ended there, with a whimper.

A Jesuit prelate fostered a similar skirmish in 1643, although this time it was the cathedral clergy against the Inquisitors for reasons involving religious etiquette. A great deal was written about these conflicts, the matter was put before several courts and taken as far as the king, to no avail.

The French abolished the Spanish Inquisition in 1810 after Napoleon's troops captured Cordoba. The Cadiz Constitution and the famous debates at the Cadiz Cortes regarding the suppression of the Holy Office. followed later, in 1812.

25 January 1813, the Cordoba City Council debated whether it should inform the Cortes that the people of Cordoba were in favour of the Inquisition. Although quite a few councillors disagreed, the Council's request for the reinstatement of the Inquisition was approved by majority vote.

Compare this with the 5 May 1820 debate led by the Cárceres delegates, Cayetano Lanuza, Juan Labrada, José Gálvez and Mariano Ortega, which resulted in the transfer of the public jail to the inquisition building. Again in 1824, the Cordoba City Council requested the restoration of the Tribunal of the Holy Office of the Inquisition.

The Marquis of Priego

The last major event pitting Cordoba against the Catholic Kings, namely Ferdinand II, was the rebellion led by the Marquis of Priego, nephew of the Great

---

[42] Lea, Charles. *A History of the Inquisition of Spain* (in four volumes), London, 1908.

[43] Matute y Luquin. *Autos de fe en Córdoba*. ("Matute" is Ramírez Casas Deza's pen name).

[44] Volume XXXVIII. *Boletín de la Academia de Historia*, Cordoba.

Captain, whom the king had punished by demolishing his castle in Montilla, thus wiping out the last remnants of noble power in Andalusia. Ferdinand came to Cordoba accompanied by a large army to witness the destruction of the castle.

The king's condemnation of the Marquis of Priego is not just a simple episode of politics and rebellion against the monarch's authority.

The rebellion began with Lucero's actions which incited Cordoba. All of Cordoba - nobles, townspeople, City Council and many members of the clergy – witnessed the excesses of the Inquisition.

The importance of this event

This episode involving the Marquis of Priego affected the history of Cordoba and that of Andalusia. It was the semi-feudal, semi-agrarian and rural nobility's last cry. From now on, nobles become courtiers, which influences the history of the Andalusian countryside where there is noticeable landowner absenteeism.

When Cordoba brings a suit against the association of sheep farmers, the *Mesta*, the city consists mainly of middle-class farmers, forerunners of present-day farmers, whose interesting history deserves a chapter of its own.

The Catholic King did not rest easily following the disturbances in Cordoba. On his way to Cordoba, he considered taking refuge in Jaen and remaining there while he waited for the situation in the city to be resolved.

When the king declared that *The Marquis of Priego must not disrespect us*, the Constable for Castile who accompanied him replied: *Your Highness must choose one of two roads: the road to Cordoba or the one to Zaragoza.*

The king chose the road to Cordoba where the repression was brutal. Numerous city councillors fled the city and the clerk who wrote the letter of protest to the king when he removed the Marquis of Priego from office and replaced him with Herrera, was punished by cutting off his thumb.

The Catholic King appears to have governed as a sort of dictator during his two reigns. There is no other name for it. Furthermore, the Communard[xix] movement was beginning to form during the entire beginning of the century. There were uprisings against the Catholic King, uprisings and complaints against Cisneros, not by the nobility, but by the people in their hatred of Carlos I. The skilled workers in Valladolid, frightened with the taxes that he demanded they pay, grumbled that they would have to sell their sons to pay the taxes. In no book regarding the Communards does one obtain such a popular feeling than in Gonzalo de Ayora's manuscripts to which I frequently refer.

That which one could call the feudal nobility of Cordoba, ends with the episode of the Marquis of Priego. The nobility that interferes and argues with, and contests the king and the City Council, is exiled and defeated. There is no doubt that the nobility was very powerful, particularly during the 14th century when it was very famous. Alonso Carrillo said that it is very well-known in Spain that there are more mansions belonging to gentlemen heirs of entailed estates in Cordoba than in two cities in Spain, and two of the largest and the more densely populated at that - and that the Cordoba nobility is one of the most respected worldwide.

So, it was.

Even though today the best studies have discovered the presence of a sustained movement of agrarian feudalism in the city that is of great interest and that one did not believe existed.[45]

The appearance of the city changes

Many churches and convents were built in Cordoba during the 13th, 14th and 15th centuries. The first and most ancient convent, dating from the days of the conquest, is the Dominican convent of San Pablo (the Dominicans were greatly favoured by Ferdinand III). The last convent during this period is Santa Marta convent, in 1468, which we will describe further ahead.

All the religious military orders: Order of Santiago, Order of Calatrava, Knights Templar, and so forth, were established in Cordoba where they had their seats and residences. The order whose name has lasted the longest is the Order of Calatrava, and a city square is renamed Tendillas de Calatrava.

The appearance of Cordoba changes completely with all these new buildings. It is traditionally held that proof that the queen did not respect the traditional ancient look of the city was Isabella I's destruction of the ancient Arch of the Albolafia.

---

[45] The noble mansions were extremely interesting, not just because of their artistic value. One is reminded of Banuelos' statement regarding the Cordoban nobility, its extreme pride that prevented the nobles from mixing with merchants, no matter how rich these were. How they expelled a merchant who was riding his horse in the parade before Felipe II, and more details about their private life.

Of the noble lineages whose roots were outside Cordoba, the one that best lives on is the one that bears the title Gondomar, beginning with Diego Sarmiento de Acuña, 1st Count of Gondomar. Quite a bit has been known for some years now regarding the great Spanish ambassador to England, a highly respected, eminent political and literary figure. Pedro Bustamante has recently published a beautiful book in which he debunks that occasionally said in the past, that the name 'Gondomar' is nothing more than a transposition of *Don Gomar*. This Diego was never in Cordoba. His son, Lope, however, was and he married a lady from Cordoba named Aldonza Sotomayor y Figueroa. Diego died in 1617 and a street was named after him. Three centuries later, there still is a *Calle del Conde de Gondomar* in Cordoba.

CHAPTER XII
Cordoba and America

I cannot fail to include an explanatory note regarding Cordoba's role in the conquest and colonization of America, and this appears the best place to do so. It goes without saying that this intervention really deserves a separate book of its own.

The Catholic Kings arrived in Cordoba in April 1486, and it is here that they first meet with Christopher Columbus who had been living in the city since January. The kings submitted Columbus' unusual project to a consultative body, the *Junta de Cordoba*, which, according to the old story, was presided over by Friar Hernando de Talavera who opposed Columbus' proposal. The consultations appear to have continued with the *Junta de Salamanca*, which was in favour of the future discoverer's enterprise.

Columbian studies have abolished the myths that the Juntas were hostile to Columbus and the resulting difficulties to him. There was no such thing, quite the contrary.

Columbus had a son by Beatriz Enríquez de Arana in 1488, the equally famous Ferdinand Colón.

J- La Torre magnificently explains the entire episode with Beatriz in his deeply researched book. Columbus paid little attention to Beatriz except when it was time for him to make his will. Ferdinand Colón never mentioned his mother, nor did he want anything to do with Cordoba, nor did he remember that he was a Cordoban. We named a street after him.

The unknown details of Beatriz's life have been novelized. There are, however, many facts in her biography that need to be clarified. What is clear is that Columbus abandoned her, but nobody knows why. In the last days of his life, when he speaks of her to his heirs, he says: *What I do here, I do to ease my conscience, because she weighs heavily on my soul*, and he adds: *"I am not permitted to tell you why."*[46]

Cordoba must always have been in Columbus' thoughts; in one of his letters, he describes an island as resembling the well-cultivated Cordoban countryside.

An untold number of Cordobans went to America for several reasons and with various destinies, in addition to Beatriz' relatives, Diego de Arana, who

---

[46] For the life of Beatriz de Arana, *see* R. de Arellano's fascinating study, *Bol. Academia Historia*.

sailed with Columbus on his first trip and Pedro de Arana who also sailed at the beginning, in 1493. Knight Veintiquatro Alonso Martínez de Aguado also.

Throughout the 16th and 17th centuries there was an endless flow of Cordobans to America. Pedro de los Ríos is Governor of Castilla del Oro beginning in 1526. There is considerable information regarding him, his wife – the restless and ambitious Catalina de Saavedra, and his son Pedro de los Ríos. Juan Tafur, Lope de Sosa, another governor of Castilla del Oro, the scholar Alarconcillo and Luís de Cárdenas, a ship's captain in Alvaro de Saavedra's 1527 expedition, are also famous.

Many Cordobans accompanied Pizarro on the conquest of Peru and fought alongside him in the many wars of conquest and rebellion: Hernando de Carchilón, Alonso Ruíz, Juan de Hoces, Juan López de Córdoba and Pedro Guajardo, to name but a few.

There was a large group of rebellious Cordobans and Basques in Argentina right from the beginning, namely Alonso de Angulo in 1545, Andrés Hernández de Romo, Lope de los Ríos, and others.

Martín de Solier and the Córdobas especially, served in Chile under the orders of the famous Pedro de Valdivia.

Francisco de Valderrama and García Venegas, went to Nueva Granada (Colombia).

At the end of the 16th century, Antonio de Espejo is an illustrious explorer of what was named New Mexico.

When it comes to the American ocean, Lopes de Hoces stands above all other naval commanders. A relatively unknown Cordoban about whom little has been written, he is an equal to the most heroic Spanish mariners, including the famous Antonio de Oquendo.

Even Inca Garcilasco de la Vega, the Inca author of *Comentarios reales,* buried in the Cathedral, is rumoured to be descended from Cordobans who went to America in the early days of the conquest.

To the above we need to add the list of bishops and monks belonging to the various religious military orders who went to America and are mentioned in profusion in their orders' chronicles.

Both Cortez and Magellan included Cordobans in their retinues. Also, as mentioned earlier, the long line of Cordoban emigrants to America continued without interruption, with varying degrees of success, and one notes the great many towns named Cordoba on the continent to this day. Some changed their name, but many have not.[47]

---

[47] A curious bit of information is that it was in Cordoba that Pedro de La Gasta's famous expedition

Ximénez de Quesada

Recent research has contributed information on America of which we are already aware of, some of it almost intuitively. Such is the case of Gonzalo Ximénez de Quesada, one the great conquistadores, equal to Pizarro and Cortez albeit less fortunate historically, the true founder of Colombia. A warrior, cultured, intelligent and compassionate.

He is a Cordoban, and his published genealogy is clearly and unequivocally documented. Almost all historians point to 1499 as his date of birth. This is possibly correct as the church records for his parents, Gonzalo Ximénez, a student and Isabel de Quesada, indicate that they were married in 1496, and that Gonzalo was not their first-born. He was born in his maternal grandfather's, Gonzalo Fernández de Chillón, house in the Fuensanta suburbs of Cordoba.

His father, an attorney who was employed for many years by the City Council, does not move to Granada until 1524, where he is sent to litigate several Cordoba City lawsuits against private individuals before the Granada Chancery Court.

A plethora of famous Cordobans

Some 600 Cordobans of enough repute to leave a historical trail, have left traces of their passage in our Archives. They belong to every social class and position. The nobility sent its representatives; restless and boisterous, they have their defects and virtues. The Church set an extraordinary number of ecclesiastics to represent it, and they focus on the area along the Pacific and establish Peru as the centre of their activities.

Pedro de Moya y Contreras was a notable Archbishop in Mexico, as was Juan de Almoguera, Archbishop of Lima. The latter, educated in Asunción School in Cordoba, was famous for his book, strongly criticized by the Inquisition, in which he especially addresses the excesses and abuses of priests.

The list of Cordoban clergy in America is extraordinary and would fill a book of its own. I mention the following simply as an example of how Cordobans spread out in America:

Pedro de Moya was in Cordoba in 1586 when he returned from Mexico and was immediately appointed President of the Royal and Supreme Council of the Indies. Another Cordoban, Alonso Fernández, succeeded him in Mexico.

---

to pacify Peru acquired its saddles, spearheads, and so forth, and it is from those accounts that one can obtain extremely interesting data regarding Cordoban industry and economics at the beginning of the 16th century. As you will have noted from the brief list of surnames involved in the conquest, all the most illustrious Cordoban families sent members to America: Angulo, Tafur, Valderrama, Córdoba, Ríos, Sosas, Valenzuela, Saavedra, Venegas, Hoces, and so forth. These are undoubtedly second sons who are searching for fame and fortune in the marvellous adventure-land that is America.

Charcas, Buenos Aires, Puerto Rico, Quito, Nueva Granada, in all these and other places, Church leaders were from Cordoba, such as Friar Juan de los Barrios in that which today is Colombia and Friar Tomás de San Martín, whose name is linked to the foundation of the University of Lima.

Tomás de San Martin was one of the most famous Cordobans in Lima. He embarked with Pizarro in 1530 and was involved, with some success, in all the Peruvian conflicts. A close friend of Lagasca's, he obtained a royal charter in Valladolid in 1551 to establish the University of Lima.

Local historians report that he was the great destroyer of the Inca temples in Cuzco and elsewhere. He established the Dominican Order in Peru and is the author of one of the oldest catechisms in the Indies.

The Viceroys

Other notable Cordobans: Antonio Caballero y Góngora, born in Priego, and Pedro Fernández de Córdoba, Marquis of Guadalcázar.

I do not believe Guadalcázar was born in Cordoba although his family was from here. He served as Viceroy of Mexico between 1621 and 1629, where he founded the city of Cordoba, then transferred to Peru as Viceroy.

Caballero Góngora did well in the position of Viceroy in Colombia during the 18th century, a notable intellectual period in Spanish America. He served as Viceroy between 1782 and 1789, after which he returned to Spain as Bishop of Cordoba; he is buried in the Cathedral.

The greatest traveller

This was Antonio de Espejo. All that we know about Espejo is that which he wrote in his report. He must have been born around 1530 as he had already been some time in Mexico and was entering his 50th year when he began his discoveries in 1583: "I am aged fifty years", he writes. It appears that he was wealthy. According to him, he walked about eight hundred leagues. He states that he named these lands New Andalusia in memory of Cordoba, his homeland.

At sea

The history of Cordobans' seafaring exploits is equally interesting. The most brilliant page is written by Lope de Hoces who died in the battle of Las Dunas in 1639 on board the *Santa Teresa*, as he bravely fought the Dutch. This battle, during which 43 ships were lost, was a major disaster and one of Spain's greatest defeats at sea. Perhaps not as well-known as the defeat of the Invincible Armada, but almost equally devastating. Hoces' history comes to us in fragments from Fernández Duro, who also briefly analyses the historic maritime paintings by Juan de la Corte of the school of Velazquez, that still exist, commemorating the Cordoban sailor in America.

Fernández Duro tells of other Cordoban sailors such as the Count of Santa Cruz de los Manueles – whose last name was Manuel y Fernandéz de Córdoba and who had some naval success as Commander of the Fleet until the end of the 17th century when a series of unfortunate events changed the course of his life. He was dishonoured in Oran when he declared for Austria during the War of the Spanish Succession, infuriating his brother Luís Manuel, the Archdeacon of Cordoba, who tore out the page with the entry of his baptism from the parish records 'so that there would be no memory of such a vile individual'.[48]

The history of both brothers is interesting, each in its own way. Both these "Manueles," after whom a street in Cordoba was until recently named, must be a branch of the family of the famous Infante Juan Manuel, who did so much in Cordoba, a branch which has totally disappeared from the city today. There is a new study in 1930 of this illustrious literary prince which ties in somewhat with the history of Cordoba.

CHAPTER XIII
Carlos I of Spain/ Emperor Carlos V of Austria

The martial uproar ceases in Cordoba as the city begins to lose its vitality. Spiritual matters occasionally come to the fore; sons of Cordoba who have not tamed their spirit of adventure, do great deeds, conquer; others write and paint, but Cordoba appears as a poetic place to retreat.

Conflicts between friars, literary gatherings with almost no vigour nor poetry, bloody fights in defence of this or that point of doctrine, pestilences, devastations, misfortunes, not a ray of happiness shines on the city. Cordoba suffers from all the evils that affect Spain and that is how our city arrives at the threshold of the 19th century. Let us take a look.

The Communities

The first rumours of unrest among the Communards appear in Cordoba during the early days of the reign of Emperor Carlos V (King Carlos I of Spain).

---

[48] Orti Belmonte recently compiled his biography in the Boletim de la Real Académia.

These rumours increase following the 15 June 1520 letter from Toledo to the Cordoba Council inviting Cordoba to a meeting

'so that with more calm and agreement we can decide which matters belong to the service of God and which are controlled by the King, our lord for the good of these kingdoms'.

Cordoba replies that it will not agree to anything that Toledo has asked for, stating its intention to always remain in support of the crown.

Despite this declaration, Francisco Pacheco and Pedro de los Rios representing Cordoba at the famous meetings of the Cortes in Santiago, vote against the king's wishes and deny him any funds; their statement to the king is most interesting.

Cordoba, considers itself fervently pro-government and writes to the city of Jaen, scolding it for supporting the Communards, and expressing its concern regarding the disturbances in Seville.

It appears that Cordoba, flattered by the letters it receives from the emperor, takes upon itself the complex problem of maintaining law and order in Andalusia, sending letters and emissaries for this purpose to Seville, Jaen, Granada, Baeza and Ubeda. In the city, the townspeople distrust the Marquis of Comares, the Marquis of Priego and other nobles.

Finally, a Confederation of Cities, actually a counter-communities movement, meets January 1521 in La Rambla. From there, its Junta writes to Toledo and drafts the bases of the Confederation. Seville, Jerez, Sanlucar, Cadiz, Ronda, Gibraltar, Carmona, Arjona, Porcuna, Martos and Torredonjimeno were represented on this Junta; Jaen, Alcala la Real, Ecija and many Andalusian nobles joined later.[49]

This is what Official Cordoba thought of the Communities Movement, in celebrating the defeat of the French in Navarra and the disaster of the communards in Villalar at the same time. The townspeople felt close to the fiery community movement declared in Jaen, Ubeda and Baeza, and for a few days demonstrate their support of the movement stirred by the heated sermons of an Augustine friar, Juan Bravo, a staunch communard like a fellow friar of the same name in Segovia.

The truth is that Cordoba, in emphasizing its loyalty to the emperor and declaring its support in such a decisive manner, prevented Andalusia from becoming a strong supporter of the Communities Movement that was beginning to show signs of life in several places.

The significance of the city

Cordoba settled the conflict in Andalusia in favour of the emperor. Were all the city's governing bodies already conservative and legalistic? A certain number

---

[49] *Córdoba y la guerra de las Comunidades* A. Rodríguez Villa, 1913.

of problems suggest that this was so. There already are peasant and democratic issues in Andalusia although they are not yet detached from the actions of the nobles.

The internal sensitive points recur and become increasingly acute, almost in the same places as today. Therefore, I say that the Cordoban Community Movement needs to be studied from a new perspective, of which this only anticipates future opinions.

I have already said that Cordoba was the capital of Andalusia until the 16th century. Corregidor Diego de Osorio describes it so well: *If Cordoba is serene and peaceful, so is Andalusia.* He later added that as long as Andalusia remained calm, it was unlikely that there should be any kind of commotion in the rest of the country.

One cannot come to too many conclusions and assumptions based on the Corregidor's words, except that he appears to recognize that there is a strong spiritual force that endures in other sources. Even so, he identifies this as the power of the nobility that rests on the townspeople, as when he offers eight thousand Cordoban knights and two thousand horses, and even speaks of arming 50,000 men in Andalusia to serve Carlos V. He asked for weapons for this purpose but did not get them. In truth, Andalusia and Cordoba contributed little to the emperor's campaign against the Communards. More than anything, they helped calm the fearful and prevent them from acting; it was a spiritual haven.

Cordoba flattered Carlos V, and he wrote many letters thanking the city for her loyalty to him.

The Cordoban Communards

Not everyone in Cordoba was a monarchist. There was a Communard seething that caused some problems. Even the religious orders were divided. The actions of the clergy are of some interest as the Communard movement did not involve the Church. In Cordoba, the convents, more specifically, the Dominican Order of San Pablo, interfered in the life of the city almost from the very foundation of this religious community. The most influential preachers in Cordoba came from this convent and there is no moment in the life of the city in which they do not have their say. Thus, in the same way that the Order of San Pedro has the greatest Art studio in the city, except for the Cathedral, it also has the most significant history of a community. The Dominicans were much more influential in Cordoba than the Jesuits, and for much longer. They were there for five centuries and produced individuals for all tastes: literary, political, legendary, mischievous and saintly.

An example regarding the Communities Movement is Friar Gregorio Prado (1520-21) who never hesitates to stand in the middle of Salvador square, once, twice or as often as he deems necessary, and to harangue the people with political diatribes in favour of the monarchy. This Prior of San Pablo successfully gets his listeners to publicly swear an oath of loyalty to the crown. It is the counter-revolution.

Prior Prado, the official speaker for the crown, is protected by Corregidor Diego de Osorio, a native of Burgos who represents the monarchy in the city so that it favours the government. However, if the Dominicans are monarchists, the Augustinians are Communards. Augustinians, Dominican and Jesuits have been the three most influential religious orders in Cordoba, in this order of importance: Dominicans, Jesuits and Augustinians.

Each, in his own way, represents the spirit of his order in Cordoba. In 1521, an Augustinian Friar Juan Bravo arrives in Cordoba, moves into San Agustín monastery and preaches in support of the Communities. He speaks with such dynamism that the City Council offers a 100 ducats reward for the arrest of this friar who bears the same name as the great Segovian Communard. However, as the Augustinians protect Juan Bravo, this is impossible, even though a Knight Veinticuatro suggests that the City Council take the San Agustín monastery by force. The problem is that Friar Juan Bravo, in addition to being a preacher is a political conspirator who prepares a violent protest, conspires with a shoemaker to incite the city's skilled workers and connives with a lesser noble who feels he is a Communard and a man of the people.

The entire movement in Cordoba was quashed and Bravo had to flee the city. So far, there are no documents about his life. The theoretical insurrection was quelled, but with bloodshed. A noble, Pedro de Hoces' throat was slit, another noble was drawn and quartered; others were drawn, quartered, and tried. Pedro de Hoces, the Cordoban Communard who went unnoticed for quite some time, did no more nor less than other Communards whose names we know. He gave his life for a political and military crime, a member of the political left wing of those days.

Attorney Masedo, a city magistrate who wrangled with individuals in Cordoba who accused him of being cruel, and fiercely supported by Corregidor Osorio, boasted of these judicial acts on his Orders of the Day, saying that without them Cordoba would have been lost.

As you see, the problem of the Cordoban Communities justifies this minor digression in this small book. Because there is much more. Corregidor Osorio and the City Council are united. They issue congratulations and celebrate as Francisco Pacheco, the King's representative for Cordoba before the Corunna

Cortes, returns happy at having voted according to the king's wishes and at having the backing of the Marquis of Comares and the Marquis of Priego.

What role were the parties playing in terms of the Cordoban Community? It is not clear. Both "serve Caesar" but each detests the other, each makes threats against the other, each arms their retinues and each provokes the city.

The city occasionally banishes them from Cordoba, and they pretend to dutifully obey. The City Council shakes out the nobles' banners. Each party intends to obtain control of the city on behalf of Carlos I, but independently and excluding the other party, and while adapting itself to the rhythm of the revolt, serve Caesar and themselves.

The entire process of the movement resulted in major upheavals in terms of the governance of the city. We begin to see the Corregidor's total control over the municipality. His powers had previously been frequently controversial. Did not Alonso de Aguilar imprison Merlo in San Lorenzo and almost kill him? Later in 1508, after Lucero's successes, the Corregidores take charge, but the people snatch their prisoners in the streets and disobey them.

That is why many historians have stated that these seventy years in the life of the city, from around 1450 to 1520, are of such extraordinary political interest from which the city did not recover until the 19th century.

The spirit and the letter

Since the Communities, neither Cordoba nor almost any Spanish city, took politics to the streets. There were theorists who almost always spoke softly and obediently, but nothing more than that, and Cordoba begins to become silent. The only voices that are heard are those of the Corregidor and the Church, each one with a clearly defined role. Cordoba's spirit becomes theological, albeit modestly (there is no great theologian) and mystical (there is no great mystic) - where was Saint Juan de la Cruz born? It becomes decently religious, soberly realistic and preaching. Indeed, little by little, the literary fruits of Cordoba's intellectuals are less and less valued. The city's principles become less severe and more futile (18th century).

Góngora is, par excellence, the sublime cedar at the summit; but the cedar stands almost alone during the 17th century.

At the close of the 16th century, the great vein of men of character shrivels and almost dries out.

Those with strong temperaments emigrate to America where they fight and triumph; and not just lay individuals - numerous illustrious religious figures are also a part of this flowing river of tradition. The greatest exponent of all is Juan de Almoguera, whom I have already mentioned.

CHAPTER XIV
The Municipality of Cordoba

Having reached the moment to discuss the actions of the lay members of the Cordoba City Council, this seems the best time to address this interesting time in the evolution of our Municipality, that is, the city's internal governance and regime. The oldest Minutes of City Council meetings are dated 1479.

Cordoba, like all Spanish cities, was gradually switching from a democratic and almost autonomous regime to a centralist regime; those were the theories of the time. At the beginning, during the 13th and early 14th centuries, Cordoba was democratic; the city retains something of the medieval municipal regime, but not the regime in all its purity. Ferdinand III conquers Cordoba at a time that the modern epoch was coming of age, although there still were hints of democracy.

In 1288, the Cordoba Council approves a Municipal Decree and Ruling regarding marriages and deaths in its vicinity and districts under its control. It is of interest for its references to luxury legislation and other customs.

Afterwards, during the14th and 15th centuries, Castile only has one great internal problem: the rise in the power of the monarchy - the battle between the monarchy and the power of the nobles. This is why the nobles' banners appear in profusion in Cordoba, as elsewhere, under the guise of supporting the king or a pretender to the throne. The nobility, however, is campaigning for its own cause which, deep down, was anti-royal in the sense that the nobles fiercely opposed an absolute monarchy.

Consequently, the city becomes subordinate to the nobles and serves as the arena for battles between the various factions. Thus, for example, the supremacy of Alonso de Aguilar over another faction, the one led by the Count of Cabra, is just one of the more notable examples of the many conflicts that occur in abundance in 15th century Spain.

Cordoba is no longer democratic as it becomes the arena of semi-feudal nobles. These are no longer the days when Cordoba celebrated free brotherhoods with other municipalities in several Andalusian towns. However, as these nobles are defeated all over Spain, they abandon their rural and combative nature and meekly attach themselves to the Court and cease to assert themselves. The absolute monarchy rules. These are the days of a Caesar, the days of the all-powerful Corregidores.

The Corregidor

The Corregidor, or king's spokesperson, is the classic type of a Caesar's liege vassal. The Cortes no longer speak out. Throughout the 16th, 17th and 18th centuries the only voice that is heard in our city is that of the Corregidor who speaks for the king, and that of the City Council which no longer opines but implores and always obeys.

Furthermore, if at the beginning the office of Corregidor is a fundamentally convenient institution, the Corregidor himself is always a foreigner who gives orders. Sometimes, we are lucky, as in the case of Corregidores Zapata in 1570 (16th century) and Ronquillo Briceño (17th century) when the 'petty dictator' as he is called in the 18th century, is an enlightened dictator. The Corregidores do not represent the will of the people; they speak for the king and the Church and are the sole seat of power in the city. Another Zapata was Corregidor in 1616, at the beginning of the 17th century. Ronquillo, in 1682 came from Palencia and was later sent to Madrid. Gaitán de Ayala, in 1586 built the new jail in the Corredera.

In 1455, the Cordoba Cortes contented themselves with declaring that if the king insisted in appointing Corregidores, *he should pay them from his income, taxes and duties.* In was unwise, said Miguel Colmeiro, *to relegate the question of jurisdiction to a matter of salaries.*

Municipal bylaws

Since Spain is ruled by an absolute monarchy, the Cordoba Municipal Bylaws of 1481 are issued by Ferdinand V, the Catholic King, to govern justice in the city. These are later extended by other bylaws, also issued by the Catholic Kings. The first Municipal Bylaws are dated 2 September 1482 and the extended bylaws, 24 February 1491. Queen Juana issues others 8 June 1515.

The municipal history of Cordoba is sometimes remarkably interesting. Public meetings of the City Council were occasionally held in the transept of San Pablo convent.

As regards the democratic spirit of the townspeople, there is Alfonso X's reply to City Council requests, in which he comments that the Council is well known for how well it chose the thirteen good men who now represent the city.

Royal meddling

Pedro Sanchez came to Cordoba 12 June 1402 with full powers from Enrique III to dismiss all the major and minor city administrators and replace them with Councillors Ferdinand Díaz de Cabrera, Alonso Martínez Albolaña, Fernán Gómez, Juan Fernández de Castillejo and Alfonso Ruíz de las Infantas. He also got rid of the Knights Veintiquatro.

The Catholic Kings further issued several royal decrees against the Knights Veintiquatro in 1483, on the strictly forbidden grounds that

> *the Veintiquatros in the city have involved themselves in certain vile trades and negotiations by selling and trading foodstuffs for profit and having others do so for them.*

Judges

Management of the affairs of the city is completed with the creation of a body of Jurados, or judges who form the Court, a body which stems from the Cordoban code of law and has its roots in ancient times in the Fuero Juzgo, or codex of laws. There are tremendous quarrels with the Knights Veintiquatro, especially in 1421, over the latters' authoritarian behaviour. Another body known as Caballeros de Premia, a curious local militia that was permanently ready to go to war, complemented the institution; it disappeared with the Reconquista.

The Catholic Kings confirmed the Court Bylaws in Granada 10 August 1499.

During the 15th century judges wore yellow suits and green velvet robes with yellow satin cuffs on ceremonial occasions. Knights Veintiquatro wore white suits and crimson velvet robes with white satin cuffs.

Festivals

In September 1492, whilst in Zaragoza, the Catholic Kings place a curious tariff on goods that also includes a sales tax. This then gives birth to the concept of granting exemptions or privileges for festivals, of which it is said there are two: one on the first day of Lent and the other on the first day of May. Each festival lasts for twenty days. One of the bylaws mentions *any male or female captive taken to Cordoba to be sold.*

Four gates of the city are authorized to operate as customs houses, or toll houses, as one would call them today: Puente, Seville (demolished in 1821 - there is no illustration of this gate), Rincon, and Plasencia, also destroyed, where there was a watchtower. Watchtowers were built outside the city walls and next to the gates at the end of the 14th century and the beginning of the 15th century. The only one of these towers that still exists is the Torre de la Malmuerta; there also was another at the gate that today is known as the Puerta de Gallegos, at the Puerta de Sevilla and the Puerta de Plasencia.

The City Council and the Mesta – Other bylaws.

During the second half of the 16th century, between 1560 and 1590, Cordoba argued in the Court on behalf of its farmers, against the Mesta, the Council of Sheep Farmers, and its privileges, which they considered exorbitant.

The dispute lasted thirty years and, in the end, the city won. The Court ruled that the leaders of the shepherds who guided the nomadic animals were prohibited from holding a public office either in Cordoba or its surroundings. The Cordoba Court ruling, probably the first one of its kind, was later cited by other towns in their disputes against the Mesta.

This is a curious moment in the agro-economic history of Cordoba. It appears in response to a time when the Cordoban countryside is expanding, and we see the beginning of the birth of a class of peasant farmers that was replacing the feudal nobility who had already begun to abandon their landholdings to settle around the Court.

Felipe II ratified the municipal bylaws. One of the rulings includes a statement to the effect that individuals in Cordoba are prohibited from selling wine that is not made in Cordoba or its surrounding countryside. To import wine from outside the region, an individual had to have a license obtained by his swearing that it was not for sale but only for his personal consumption. In 1627, the number of public taverns is reduced to a single one and on 5 April, the City Council decrees that every owner of a winemaking tank may only sell his wine from his home or at the gate to his establishment. The emblem of the taverns was a branch.

During these centuries, the crown issues a profusion of rules affecting municipal life. As we shall now see, none are more remarkable than those governing trades.

Regarding trades

Laws and regulations governing trades continued to be decreed and enforced during the 18th century, such as in 1786, bylaws originally dated 1503 and upheld in 1698, governing Builders and Carpenters.

More were issued such as in 1789, bylaws governing Tanners and Makers of Gloves, a trade that has totally disappeared and another that is almost in the same state. Bylaws for Weavers were published in 1728 when it appears that their Guild was rather prosperous.

The attitude towards work and the nobility and the quarrels between nobles and craftsmen are also interesting.

In 1783, the prosecutor responds as follows to a question from Butchers and Meat Cutters regarding who may engage in other trades:

Neither they nor their sons in these trades are prevented from engaging in arts and crafts, from becoming members of the respective guilds or providing services to the municipality.
He goes on to explain that once upon a time, this trade had been considered shameful, an attitude that may have originated with the fact that it was *engaged in by Arabs, Berbers and mulattoes.*

The Butchers presented their reasons for becoming members of the Royal Guild of Skilled Workers of 18 March 1783, adding that they had assisted in the crowning of the king, in whose cause they held a bull fight at their expense. The prosecutor replied in their favour, stating that their request was fair and because the Valencia Guild had reinstated them. Presumably because this one must have been well organized and wealthy.

That was how one lived in the city until the 19th century and the modern. The life of the municipality returns in a different manner.

In 1820, the people of Cordoba elect a Junta for the first time. The various institutions and political groups that had governed the city, reflecting the way that Spain was governed, had been granting the city more or less power, depending on their political leanings.[50]

Cordoba, centre of emigration

Carlos V visited Cordoba in 1526 and in 1530 the emperor issued two charters in which he decreed that *all who come to live in Cordoba shall be free of taxes for a period of ten years and promise to reside there for at least 20 years.*[51]

---

[50] It would be wrong to assert that there was no reason to include these matters in such a brief history, as that of our city cannot be written from a restricted viewpoint. At all times and on all occasions, that which is most important to highlight, albeit indirectly, is how the History of the City meshes with the general History of Spain in its various aspects and how the city has contributed to or collaborated with the problems of the nation. The remainder, the story of the city as a mere local narrative of events with great deeds in every corner, are minutiae that are remarkably similar to the continuous sputtering of smouldering oil lamps.

[51] These Charters resulted from a very curious interregional emigration from Cordoba and its surrounding districts to places in the kingdom of Granada where the nobles promised great benefits to anyone who went there to live, as they wished to repopulate the towns and villages that were becoming deserted because of successive deportations of Arabs to various places in Spain.

Cordoba City Council's petition was granted because the city was becoming deserted due to the heavy import and sales taxes levied on the townspeople and the attraction of the benefits Granada promised. So many people left Cordoba and its surrounding districts that the councillors became greatly concerned with the depopulation of the city, a situation that was greatly aggravated by the many Cordobans who were emigrating to America, as recorded in numerous documents.

CHAPTER XV
The Days of the Felipes

Felipe II and the Cordoba Cortes

Felipe II, the king about whom the most has been written in the History of Spain, came to Cordoba in 1570 for a session of the Castilian Cortes and to issue ordinances regarding the rebellion of the Arabs in Granada.

The city made an enormous effort to receive the king in an ostentatious manner, in competition with the Duke of Medina Sidonia who came to Cordoba to call on the king accompanied by such a magnificent entourage that one was reminded of a legendary oriental procession.

Felipe remained in Cordoba for two months while the Castilian Cortes met in the Church Council Chapter Room.

The Cortes met from 31 January to April. Of all the sessions of the Cortes, including those held in 1455, this was the only one that met in Cordoba. It concluded its business in Madrid where it was transferred by Decree on 22 April 1570.

The Cordoba Cortes

The 1455 Cortes, the first session of this council to meet in Cordoba, addressed many important issues. It was preceded two years earlier, in 1453, by the Burgos Cortes; there were no subsequent sessions until 1462.

On this occasion, the delegates insistently repeated a petition they had unsuccessfully presented before, namely that the king must not send Corregidores to the towns and cities unless so requested, to which they added that if the king should do so, despite this petition, these authorities should be paid for by the monarch.

However, because of the way in which it was developed and expressed, the petition appears to be based not on the freedom of the cities - it is written in a language that is far from expressing the spirit of the petition drawn up by the Brotherhood of Cities between Cordoba, Seville and Jaen. It claims poverty, burdens and bad farming years that would not justify overloading their expenses with the salaries of the Corregidores.

In Petition 24, the delegates protested against the chicken coops they purchased for the king and the nobles' food stores, on the grounds that the latter exploited the city as they only paid 12 maravedis for two hens when the going rate was 30 maravedis. Furthermore, that they took by force as many as they wanted to sell again and make money for themselves.

In Petition 25, the delegates protested the rates tenants had to pay their landlords, their links with the authorities and how these oppressed the villages.

These complaints and petitions are not unique; they are similar to all those presented at previous sessions of the Cortes.

At the session of the Cortes that met 4 June 1455, there is a concern to ensure that no coinage, neither gold or silver, nor any goods should be removed from the kingdom.

Lastly, Petition 19, referring to depreciated currencies, states that

It is known that in many cities, towns and places in your kingdoms, the people dismiss your old white coins, created in your mints, claiming they are Sevillian, and others from la Coruña, and other names they give them, and they refuse to accept or use them.

Sevillian *duros* were already in circulation in the 15th century.

Felipe II's Cortes in Cordoba

The first session of the Castilian Cortes was held 4 February 1570 in the Bishop's Palace, where Felipe II was staying. The next sessions met in the Cathedral, in the Chapter House meeting room set aside for this purpose. Two delegates represented each city.

Represented were the cities of Leon, Seville, Murcia, Salamanca, Jaen, Avila, Toro, Zamora, Soria, Segovia, Toledo, Guadalajara, Burgos, Granada and Cuenca which, together with the cities of Madrid and Valladolid, had a vote in the Cortes. Diego de Sosa and Pedro Muñiz de Godoy represented Cordoba.

Felipe II's speech to the assembly was of some importance. He spoke of international affairs, of Flanders, of America, of the privateers and the armadas that he was sending to defend our possessions. He informed the Cortes of the death of his son and of his having again become a widower. He announced the new marriage he intended to celebrate, asked for the corresponding allowance and discussed other matters.

The Cortes deliberated. The Minutes of their meetings are not very meaningful. Based on these, the deliberations appear half-hearted and lacking in spirit. The Cortes were a fiction. One of their petitions, a sign of the times, is the one that seeks to prevent sons and grandsons of traders, scribes or representatives of the Cortes, from joining city regiments.

The Cordoba delegates were charged to resolve some complaints against the Mesta. The one who intervened the most was the delegate from Burgos.

Felipe II spent two months in Cordoba. After the Catholic Kings, he is the king who spent the most time in the city where he received the Duke of Medina Sidonia's and his extraordinary entourage's lavish homage.

Ambrosio de Morales has described this tribute in his writings. The level of luxury, some details of which Madrazo published, is of an insolent extravagance and an incredibly interesting page in the History of our economy.

Felipe III

There is little of note regarding the reign of Felipe III, unless it is the expulsion of the converted Arabs: *Serpents that Spain had raised and harboured in its breast,* according to Cervantes.[52]

The Moriscos who were in Cordoba and after whom a street is named, came from the kingdom of Granada. The residents of that kingdom had led their greatest uprising in 1568. Cordoba rushed in with troops to crush this rebellion, contributed to its success and returned several times with large contingents of Arab prisoners. Francisco Zapata Cisneros, Corregidor for Cordoba, distinguished himself in this repression. Felipe II sent the Moriscos from Andalusia to settle in Galicia and in Castile.

On 30 November 1570, the city begged that its Moriscos (very few) be left alone to live in peace, and so they were. This explains why, in the 16th century, there were many, some say 1,500, Arabic families in the several Cordoba neighbourhoods, especially in Santa Marina.

Still, Felipe III banished them and on 6 February 1610 the Moriscos left Cordoba. Diego de Mardones, highly respected Bishop of Cordoba at the time, did his best to protect them and thanks to his efforts, a few eminent Arabs were allowed to remain, especially Felipe de Mendoza, a distinguished physicist.

Felipe IV

The first years of Felipe IV's reign, who also visited Cordoba with the famous Count Duke of Olivares, were uneventful except for an increasing number of royal petitions asking the king for donations and assistance to the city and the Church. These petitions were sometimes granted, sometimes not, and all were

---

[52] There were very few Moors remaining in Cordoba. Their situation was very precarious. as they had been left without money after having been granted nothing more than life and liberty.

Sancho IV, in 1320, decreed that *All Arabs living in the city, whether bricklayers or carpenters or not, are required to work two days each year on the construction of the cathedral,* and all the Arabs, like the Jews, had to wear a distinguishing badge on their clothing. After 1492, until the arrival of the Arabs from Granada, there were practically no Moriscos in the city.

written in anguish as they beseeched the king for help in their putting up with the frequent and even worse, unsuccessful wars. (Petitions are made in 1625, 1629, 1644, 1645, 1647, 1648, and so forth.)

The situation of the townspeople worsened with the scourge of the black death that afflicted Cordoba in 1649 and 1650, the worst epidemic of many that Cordoba suffered. Some 14,000 people are calculated to have died from this plague. This may appear to be an excessive number were it not for very precise documentation from the period which gives these numbers a certain credence.

The hunger riot

The famous hunger riot of 1652 shook life in Cordoba.

The riot began 6 May at the front door of San Lorenzo church where a peasant woman, holding the cadaver of one of her sons who had died from hunger, aroused the crowd's anger and grief. The townspeople armed themselves as well as they could and attacked the house of the Corregidor, the Count of Peñaparda.

The people of Cordoba had been suffering from massive shortages. After the crowd attacked the Corregidor's house, it moved on to the homes of those they believed were hoarders, as we would call them today, and those whom the people felt were responsible for causing and aggravating the shortages. They gathered all the wheat they could find, including that stored in the bishop's granaries, and took it all to San Lorenzo neighbourhood.

Bishop Tapia attempted to calm the crowd, without success. The next day, the rioting increased, until more than 6,000 armed men were rioting. The crowd voted to elect a new Corregidor, a noble named Diego de Cordoba.

A price was set for bread, there was cheap bread, and the townspeople, lords of the city for two days, stopped rioting once they obtained the wheat.

The king pardoned those responsible for the riot. A few of their names, or nicknames, such as *Arrancacepas* (uprooter of vines), survive to this day. This riot is a curious page in the social and popular history of Cordoba, one frequently described at length by all the local writers, and one which deserves special attention.

The "Landlords should not be farmers" petition rang out in anger, calling for *the land for those who work it* as we have heard so often over the ages, to be replaced in turn by another, more humane, call of *in any case, land for all.*

Bishop Tapia's role during the riot was extremely important, although he was strongly attacked by the hoarders who accused him of what today we would call proletarian notions. Tapia, an immensely popular and very fair cleric, defended himself well. The thousands of bushels of rotting flour the hoarders would not release to the market so that prices would rise, were his best defence. The bishop was considered the hero of the city for his actions, as opposed to Corregidor Alfonso Flórez de Sotomayor who, unable to prevent the riot, fled the city across the rooftops.

The years that followed were monotonous and full of misfortune. As if there were not enough calamities to afflict the entire country, in 1680 the *Memorias de la Catedral* record the following in Cordoba: *"Both in the Cathedral and in the other churches, there were endless supplications, processions and prayers, and so forth."*

First, there was a depreciation of gold and silver currency, a violent earthquake on 9 October 1680, a terrible drought followed by non-stop heavy rain and flooding when a flood destroyed one of the arches of the bridge over the river and lastly, a deadly epidemic that lasted for a long time. Clearly, an endless list of disasters.

The end of the century

This, more or less, is the sad story of Cordoba in a sad Spain during the last days of the House of Austria. Still, one cannot end the 17th century without praising Corregidor Francisco Ronquillo Briceño who repaired many buildings in the city and paid her a great deal of attention. He attempted to restore several ancient trades and create some new ones, bringing workers from outside such as weavers from Valencia and France.

Although there is no specific starting date for the attempt to revitalize the city, the building of the Corredera square in 1683 stands out as a significant occurrence.

Façade of San Lorenzo church
Photograph 4th edition of Historia de Córdoba, 1971

CHAPTER XVI
The Bourbons during the 18th century

When the Bourbons were called to the throne of Spain in 1700, Cordoba supported King Felipe V from the very beginning. The city did what it could to help during the war of succession, frequently making donations and other contributions to the King. Cordoba stood out in the fight against the British and when the royal house came to the aid of Puerto de Santa Maria.

During the 18th century, Cordoba is even more gloomy and unobtrusive than in the previous century; the population decreases, and it receives visits from public figures with decorum. Felipe V's children Teresa and Luis visit Cordoba in 1729. Luis later reigned as Luis I.

The same year, the municipal by-laws are expanded and modified. Those set by the Catholic Kings are traditionally taken as the basis for municipal governance.

The expulsions

Although in 1745 the Government orders the eviction of all gypsies living in the city and in the kingdom, a measure that was implemented with many abuses. The decree of deportation was monstrous: the preamble declared that it was *because the name gypsy must be rubbed out and extinguished.* In 1749 Cordoba accepts the return of those who had a good reputation and were living respectable lives.

There are some extremely interesting books for the study of this remarkable ethnic group, namely Juan Solórzano's work: "Treatise regarding the orders given to the Valladolid Council to the effect that some gypsies who had been ordered to pay back the church should be branded on their faces with the word thief".

4 April 1767 marked the general expulsion of the Jesuits who lived in Cordoba, an action that shocked the city. Elderly Father Ruano was the only one left.

Because of a general change in Carlos III's policy towards the emperors of Morocco, in 1768 the city received the visit of Hamet-e-Gacsel, the Moroccan Ambassador, which curiously disquieted the townspeople. Luis de Borbón and the Count of Artois later arrived in 1782 and, finally in March 1796, King Carlos IV and Queen María Luísa who were received in an excessively obsequious manner.

The idle wives of Cordoba

Carlos IV abolished the famous *Lei de las holgazanas*, or half of the multiplicand as Dr. Morales correctly said. As reported in *Novisima Recopilació* in June 1801: "We abolish, as far as necessary, the supposed law, custom or method that has so far prevailed in the city of Cordoba, whereby married women cannot share in the property and goods acquired during their marriage". It continues: "This Royal decree does not abolish any previous rational law, order or custom; it establishes a right that until now the women of Cordoba have been deprived of by a presumed custom, better said, malicious abuse".

This is basically all that is known of a law that many Cordobans violated by going to Alcolea to marry. According to legend, this was a punishment from Queen Isabel the Catholic Queen against Cordoban women. Frankly, that this was a punishment is pure fiction. There are indications in documents that something of this kind already existed during the 14th century.

Nonetheless, if the 17th century had been disastrous, the 18th was even worse:

- The old Bishop's Palace burnt to the ground in 1745.
- 1750 was such a barren year that the city had to resort to extraordinary charity.
- 1 November 1755, Cordoba was hit by a great earthquake that is still mentioned in all local histories, and which is the famous earthquake that destroyed almost all of Lisbon that very same day.
- There is renewed zeal in the devotion to Saint Felipe Neri, according to a curious brochure by F. Villalón.

Life in Cordoba, as far as a bit of vitality is concerned, revolves around the Episcopal Palace and the Cathedral and one hears of the names of Bishops and their prebendaries in the limited literary and artistic life of the city that I shall discuss in another chapter.

Comedies were banned and cancelled several times during this period, sometimes violently. The figure of Father Posadas and his manner of thinking rules the entire city. Brother Diego extolls Father Posadas' religious principles in his sermons when he visits Cordoba from Cadiz.

The City Council

There is a sense that the City Council would like to be reborn, as it withdraws in contemplation of life in the past. Several times it attempts to begin the difficult task of writing an extensive and complete History of the City.

These are the days of critics and historians of 18th century Spain. The Council, driven by monarchist squabbles, examines Cordoba archives, ignoring particularly useful documents and materials.

In 1804, after again suffering a grave epidemic of yellow fever that kills 1,500 townspeople, the debilitated city is taken by surprise by the grave events following Napoleon's invasion of the Peninsula, which I shall summarize later. What there was of a cultural renaissance at the end of the 18th century, I see as only that represented by Bishop Caballero y Góngora (1723-1796) and by the creation of the Sociedad Económica de Amigos del País.[53] In fact, there is nothing else.

---

[53] Economic Society of Friends of the Country, to promote development.

CHAPTER XVII
The 19ᵗʰ century

The French in Cordoba

News of the 2 May 1808 uprising against the French army arrived in Cordoba on the 7th of that month.

The city began to arm itself under General Echevarria, commander of the regular troops, accompanied by a number of poorly armed and equipped civilians. They set off en masse to defend the capital from the French General Dupont, who had arrived to occupy the city and then continue onwards to Seville and Cadiz.

The Battle of Alcolea Bridge took place 7 June 1808. The Cordobans, faced with Dupont's vastly superior forces, were defeated and forced to retreat to the city. That afternoon, Dupont stormed and captured Cordoba. A patriotic Cordoban, Pedro Moreno, unsuccesfully attempted to attack the General whose troops ransacked the city for the next three days. (Dupont was later taken prisoner at the Battle of Bailén in July 1808).

After Dupont left, Cordoba formed a Governing Junta and assisted General Francisco Castaños in his efforts to establish Spanish Independence, by sending the battalion of Cordoba Volunteers. It further contributed to the national cause with cash donations, equipment sewn by Cordoban women, making rifles and bladed weapons.

Spain suffered a crushing defeat at the Battle of Ocuña and by the end of 1810, French troops had occupied all of Andalusia. Soon afterwards, Maréchal Victor Perrin and Joseph Iˣˣ entered Cordoba.

The intruder king took up residence in the Bishop's Palace and attempted to become friends with the townspeople by showering them with praise and handing out medals.[54] He abolished the Tribunal of the Inquisition in Cordoba and disbanded the religious orders whose members received a pension, although the majority fled to join the national army.

There were Spaniards who accepted the French cause, most because of fear, others because they were ambitious. These deserters were enlisted in the civil militias and in the Rifle Corps.

---

[54] Joseph I, who wrote his *Mémoires*, speaks of Cordoba with particular affection. He says that nobody welcomed him as much as they did in Cordoba and Seville.

In Cordoba, the French authorities ruled with a regime of terror. Executions by firing squad and hangings were frequent in Corredera square and the Campo de la Verdad.[55] The invaders oppressed the townspeople by exacting unbearable extraordinary taxes that were impossible to pay and by pillaging many churches and stealing their treasures.

Only one of the municipal prefects in Cordoba during those times, is worth mentioning. This was the Francophile Badia y Leblich, a traveller and scientists, who attempted some urban and administrative reforms such as building the cemetery and the agricultural gardens, inaugurated 19 March 1811. He also drew the first map of the city.

In those days, the Cordoba newspaper *Correo Politico y Militar* was edited by Prebendary[xxi] Manuel Maria de Arjona, a poet and educated individual, founder of the Academy of Fine and Noble Arts, who had become a Francophile and who was able to intervene and prevent the execution by firing squad of some of Cordoba's sons.

As far as the French generals are concerned, one of particularly despicable memory is General Nicholas Godinot who sent Father Ramirez and Commander Olivaria to the gallows.

At the end of September 1812, the French who had been suffering several defeats at the hands of the English, began to evacuate Andalusia. Cordoba was liberated almost two years after it was captured.

First Constitutional period

The French commotion left Cordoba quite unsettled, as it did all of Spain, and in 1812 the Cadiz Cortes demonstrates the spiritual division of Spain.

The country splits into two parties, Absolutists and Liberals, who are appropriately represented in Cordoba, become active and persecute each other. Their armed disputes and their ideological quarrels were to shape all, or almost all, the spiritual scene in 19th century Spain.

In 1816, with the excuse of the so-called "Napoleon's funeral", Cordoba attempted to sacrifice the Liberals, according to the wishes of the Absolutists, nicknamed 'toadies' by their opponents.

When one of these skirmishes in 1817, Maiquez the famous comedian, escaped Cordoba after being persecuted for his Liberal ideas.

---

[55] There was so much hunger in the city, that wheat reached the price of 800 reales a bushel. Today, we have an excellent knowledge of all that refers to the French invasion thanks to the data in the Municipal Archives, as published by M. A. Orti Belmonte in his article "La dominación francesa en Córdoba", *Diario de Córdoba*, 1916.

The Cabezas de San Juan insurrection led by General Rafael del Riego was a momentous occasion in Cordoba when he arrived with his army 7 March 1820, followed the next day by a column subservient to Ferdinand VII.

The Constitution is again proclaimed

The Constitution was proclaimed in Cordoba 13 March 1820 by a Governing Board presided by Antonio Ramós Romanillos. The constitutional City Council took office 19 March.[56]

On 24 March, the City Council erected a plaque on the Plaza Mayor, solemnly commemorating the Constitution. All of Cordoba was present: Bishop, civil, ecclesiastic and military organizations enthusiastically applauded the event. Riego was highly praised, there were many speeches and Field Marshall Juan Antonio Martinez gave the City Council a clock and an officer's baton as a souvenir.

With a view to informing the people of the general directives, parish priests explained the Constitution to their parishioners every Sunday and Holiday; the same was done in the schools and centres of learning.

The National Voluntary Militia was created and from the beginning had many confrontations and clashes with the military.

The patriotic circle

A patriotic circle that gathered individuals with social and intellectual prestige was founded in Cordoba during 1820.

The circle met regularly in Santo Domingo church, a favourite venue for many Liberals. This was our first political Casino, unusually attended by priests.[57]

---

[56] The first Mayor was the Duke of Almodovar, elected 18 March by the Electoral Board of the Parishes, the day after the news arrived that the king had accepted the Constitution.

[57] This should not be considered so unusual, considering the spirit of those times, the way the Constitution was received, and knowing that the first constitutional City Council elected by the people of Cordoba welcomed such unsuspicious individuals as the cloistered Augustine Father Muñoz Capilla. Antonio Alcalá Galiano, Governor of Cordoba in 1821, left some very interesting remarks and descriptions of this circle and of how the city was a hundred years ago in his book Memorias (1886). Also interesting are his comments regarding the French invasion under General Dupont and the men on the Alcolea roster.

Ramírer de Arellano also warmly described this in his laudable Provincia y diócesis de Córdoba (1922), in which he names a number of individuals who represent an honourable and true picture of the Liberal network in Cordoba in those days.

The circle lasted until 1823. It met in the building that had served as the parish church of Santo Domingo de Silos (in front of the Compañia). Meléndiz, Canon of San Hipólito, belonged to it and was one of its most enthusiastic speakers. Alcalá Galiano mocks him a bit.

Absolutist unrest

Still, Cordoba was affected by considerable Absolutist activism and there even was a minor uprising of little importance, just one of many of our sporadic civil disagreements.

Francisco Valdelomar, Commander of the provincial Cordoba militia quartered in San Pablo, together with some officials, and the brigade of Carabineros stationed in Castro del Rio, led the rebellion.

Whilst the authorities uneasily suspected that something was afoot, one night at the end of June 1822, a rowdy crowd ran out into the streets. The provincial militia was called out and after killing some national soldiers, met up with the carabineros from Castro del Rio. There was a great panic in the city. The City Council, to prevent further unrest, decreed that if the rebels entered Cordoba, the local militia battalion should not resist them and instead withdraw to the Ermitas. Order was not restored in the city until the end of July, when troops loyal to the Count of Valdecañas arrived. The rebellion was quickly crushed in Montilla and elsewhere.

General Riego returned to Cordoba 18 October 1822 where the City Council enthusiastically welcomed him with ceremony, arches of triumph, crowns of laurel, speeches, and so forth.

Return of the absolute monarchy

Nothing of the above prevented the people from noisily declaring their support for the return of the absolute king 10 June 1823, and successfully demanding the reinstatement of the 1820 City Council. The Royal Militia was reinstated and, together with the Absolutists, furiously revenged themselves on everyone who had been prominent during the constitutional regime. Eyewitnesses described it thus:

> *Our fellow citizens conducted the most scandalous attacks against the most respectable houses, ransacking them on the excuse that they were searching for enemies of the King.*

The Duke of Angouleme arrived at the head of French troops sent to restore Ferdinand VII to the throne. The king entered Cordoba, now free from Liberals, 25 October 1823. The king himself wrote in his Diary:

> *That afternoon, at four o'clock, we made a lengthy visit to the Cathedral which is worth seeing for its originality and magnificence: the so-called Patio de los Naranjos is beautiful.*

This political to-ing and fro-ing that leaves Cordoba, as it does all of Spain, agitated and in turmoil as it struggles with different ideologies, is still interesting.

9 May 1814, the commemorative plaque for the Constitution is torn down, the Instituto is raided, and its printing press and collection of engravings are

destroyed. According to Casas Deza, a Capuchin monk appears to have directed the rampage. 24 March 1820, the commemorative plaque is solemnly restored only to be again torn down 10 June 1823.

Ferdinand VII twice visited Cordoba, the first time when he travelled through the city on his way to Cadiz, 6 April of the same year, when according to local tradition, he appeared to attempt to escape by fleeing from the Bishop's Palace where he was staying but a poor and terrified militiaman stopped him. The second time, his entry was a triumphant grand finale. The monarchists highly praised Ferdinand and organized all kinds of celebrations, including bullfights, in his honour.[58]

During his second visit in 1824, the City Council asks him to bring back the Inquisition. Alfaro, Guajardo and others signed the petition 'on behalf of the King's loyal and obedient subjects'.

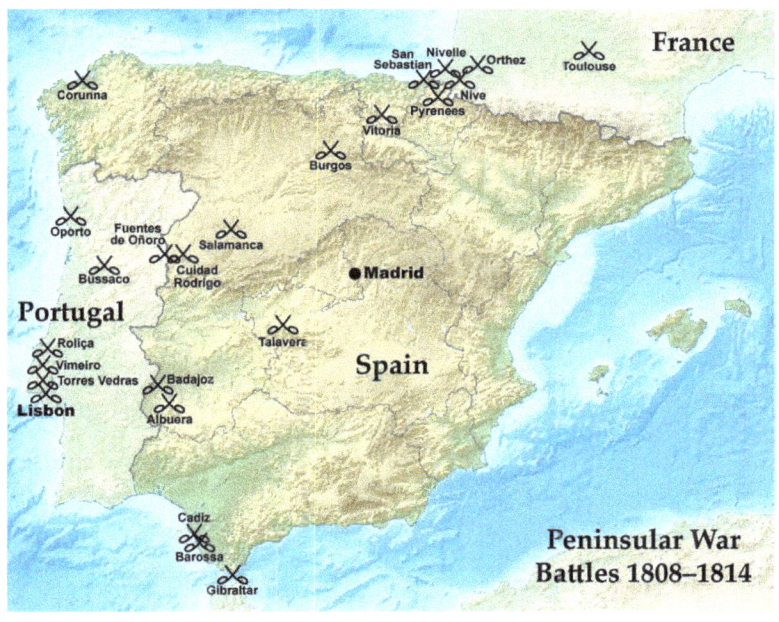

xxii

---

[58] The political hatreds were aired in the bullring with a unique symbolism: all the bulls were black (black is what the Absolutists called the Liberals); all the horses were white and all the matadors who killed the "black scoundrels" wore white. Numerous absurd poems were written to explain the symbolism, that is, death to all the supporters of the Liberal cause at the hands of the Absolutists, and the triumph of loyalty.

CHAPTER XVIII
Cordoba in the hands of the Carlists

Miguel Gómez' expedition

The Carlist invasion of Andalusia led by Miguel Gómez was of greater importance to Cordoba and caused more turmoil in the city.

Spain was again tearing itself apart with civil uprisings. The Carlist party wanted to settle the right to its cause with force and there was civil war in the Peninsula, especially in the North. It was then that a leader, so-called General Gómez, left the northern provinces to lead a daring expedition right across Spain. His objective was to rouse the country in favour of D. Carlos. He joined Cabrera and other leaders in Guadalajara.

Defeated by General Alaix at the Battle of Villarobledo, the rebel army entered the Andalusian provinces in September 1836. Fearing that the Carlists might come to Cordoba, the Nationalist forces in the city and many from the province who had taken refuge here, began to prepare to defend themselves. The Alcazar, the Seminary and the Bishop's Palace were quickly fortified. Many people took refuge there, where they felt they would be safe, taking their jewels and treasures with them.

The rebels, numbering around 6,000 men, entered the city 30 September. The townspeople received them with remarkable complacency. The Nationalists retreated in strength, there is fighting in the streets and Carlist Brigadier Villalobos is killed.

The Carlists attacked the locals who defended the Nationalists, first capturing the Bishop's Palace and then the Seminary, reducing the Liberals to the Alcazar. These finally surrendered, having been given a verbal agreement that they would be free and respected, an agreement ignored by the Carlists.

The Carlists set up their own City Council that issued a decree demanding money from the townspeople. They ransacked the city and according to some calculations, their booty was worth more than fifteen million reales.

The famous General Cabrera was housed or took up lodgings in the house belonging to Count Zamora de Riofrio. Cabrera led some expeditions to provincial towns (Baena and Castro), as did Gómez.

General Gómez' treatment of prisoners was one of extreme cruelty, especially whilst he was being chased by the Queen's army. Many were shot for the most insignificant reason and others ordered on long, painful marches. He wandered around the provinces of Ciudad Real, Extremadura and Seville, going as far as the fields of Gibraltar until finally, safe and sound, together with some other Carlists, he was able to rejoin the army from which he led his expedition. The expedition was a disaster for him and for the Liberals who were unable to prevent the systematic and cruel devastation to which a great many of the provinces were subjected.

Maréchal Alaix's French division entered Cordoba 14 October but showed no inclination to pursue General Gómez who had fled the city hours earlier. The French troops also mistreated the townspeople and like the Carlists, ransacked several houses. The Commanding General promptly punished those responsible for these excesses.[59]

That same year, 1836, there was widespread closure of the convents in Cordoba: Santa Inés, Regina, San Jerónimo and others. This had been preceded by an 1820 decree that ordered the closure of all convents containing less than twenty monastics, including Mártires convent, The last one closed in 1868.

Summary – Between the French and the Carlists

The entire period from 1808 to 1836 is extremely interesting and it was more turbulent than few other times in Cordoba. We have sufficient data regarding this to enable us to study the psychology of the city.

Francophiles and Patriots, Constitutionalists and Absolutists all fought each other. The Francophiles later attempted to apologize for their actions. These include Arjona and Bishop Trevilla, who in 1810 returned the Napoleon eagles that the Spaniards had captured at the Battle of Bailén and that were on display in the Cathedral.

The more direct accusation was levied at Arjona and there is information in Reinoso's books, for example, and later also Méndez Bejarano in *Delitos de Infidencia*, with which to judge this movement and the causes that produced it. Not all supporters joined because of greed or fear.

No great names in Cordoba are labelled Francophile. There are more names of those who support the Carlist cause, which was deep-rooted in the city. This is another study that one can do little more than point out. Not all Carlists were members of the clergy, as one might imagine. Quite the contrary, there

---

[59] Cordoban Diego de León arrived with Alaix's troops, in command of the Hussars. This famous soldier suffered a disastrous end some years later when he was shot by a firing squad (October 1841) in one the most romantic episodes of the civil wars, the assault against the Royal Palace 7 October, an attempt to kidnap Queen Isabel I, defeat General Bartomero Espartero (Prince of Vergara and sometime Regent of Spain), and re-establish Queen Cristina's regency.

were numerous Constitutionalist priests, many of whom were famous in the city. Some held leading positions in centres of learning, such as the Asunción School which in those days and perhaps until 1843, was very Liberal.

General Espartero is celebrated with festivities and studies, possibly following the example of Valencia University which awarded him the title of *Doctor Honoris Causa.*

The quarrels between Constitutionalists (*negros*) and Absolutists (*blancos*) rose to the fore with each shift in Spanish politics, especially in 1814, 1820 and 1823. Persecutions, imprisonments, deportations, beatings, one or another bloody event, all clearly left their mark. There was a rapid turnover in the City Councils and in the discourse of many speakers. Each new cause that triumphed was engulfed by its supporters.

18 April 1830, Carlos IV repealed the Salic Law of succession with great pomp and ceremony, a momentous event in Cordoba as in all of Spain, which divided the city into two camps.

Reaction against the Francophiles in Cordoba is very curious, considering that the entire city had earlier tolerated them. It is also worth mentioning that the Cadiz Cortes had to annul the first elections for deputies. A bad precedent. Politically motivated reactions have always led to excesses, of which some infamous ones in 1823 when the Monarchists predominated over Liberals.

CHAPTER XIX
Cordoba from 1840 to 1880

General Espartero passed through the city 17 July 1843 as he fled to Cadiz after having been deposed as Regent by a military coup, and at the end of 1843 and beginning of 1844, the Provincial de Cordoba troops at the Regina barracks attempted an uprising

In March 1859, there is an event of significant importance when the first train of travellers arrives in Cordoba. In 1861, the city receives the Moroccan embassy, presided by Muley-el-Habbas.

Cordoba warmly received Isabal II when she visited the city in 1862, a trip that the court chroniclers described as triumphant. Poems from the period celebrate the times and the royal visit in very intriguing verses.

Between 1843 and 1868, Cordoba enjoys a period of political calm and there are no major incidents. The 1868 revolution agitates the city and the ensuing propaganda and campaigning stimulate some cantonalism and republicanism. Most notably, there is an unexpectedly strong surge of propaganda on behalf of the workers. In July 1873, General Manuel Paiva's actions end Cantonalist aspirations.

There are two events in 1872 that I believe are more than significant. Agustín Cervantes, a professor at the Instituto[60], sums up the campaigns as "Three socialist speeches." On 25 December 1872, an Anarchist Congress is held at the Moratín theater. According to many, the first such congress in Europe; the second, according to others. The mood in the city takes an angry turn but is calmed down by the Restoration.

The 1868 Revolution

Next, the most famous national event in which the city of Cordoba played a minor role, is the Battle of Alcolea 28 September 1868, which was won by the generals who had rebelled against Queen Isabel II's government. General Serrano Domínguez commanded the rebel forces. In Cordoba, the revolution began 20 September 1868 on Compañia square.

The Battle of Alcolea has been described, judged and commented on in a thousand ways, not so much for its military importance but for its political significance.[61]

The triumphant revolution was proclaimed 20 September in Cordoba, eight days before the battle against the Queen's troops commanded by General, the Marquis of Novaliches. The commanders and officers killed at Alcolea were laid to rest in Cordoba. A simple monument in the meadow at Rivera commemorates the fallen.

Cordoba reacts passively to further events in the country. The city, like all of Spain, acknowledges the proclamation of the Republic in 1873, a governing regime which created no internal problems other than a slight rise in cantonalism. The city accepts the Restoration and is charitable towards all the unfortunate events in the country. Political life in Cordoba becomes slightly more active and as it increases, all the new forms of social life in the city are represented.[62]

---

[60] Professor of Latin. Cobo San Pedro succeeded him.

[61] There is a wealth of literature to consult, from Carlos Rubio's book to the one by A. Leiva Muñoz and the episode described by Benito Pérez Galdós. Articles also are published on the 50th anniversary of the battle (1918).

[62] For documents regarding the worker and peasant political action in the area surrounding the city of Cordoba, today one has the book by Días del Moral, where he uses scrupulous technical methods to examine all the movements, and where he has generously collated the data. This is careful investiga-

Reference to them belongs to contemporary history. I do not wish to speak of any living souls in this book, because to discuss these individuals would be controversial, even though one should never conceal from the young reader that there is a history of today which is evolving in front of him and will develop in time with his collaboration, a contribution that we cannot do without.[63]

The present day

Highly significant is the fact that almost no Spanish city today now has a history of its own. The new centralist philosophy that shaped governance throughout all the 19th century and does so far in the 20th century, means that Madrid sets the rules and guidelines, except for some politically active regions, such as Barcelona which has been determining the course of action for life in Spain since the first days of the Regency. The remaining cities, in general, are content to imitate and obey orders from Madrid.

Furthermore, the history of the early 20th century and the last years of the 19th, has acquired a new quality, one that we can call social history. A great wind has shaken the world as the social classes have all acquired a new appearance, a corporative meaning, the result of several progressions. It appears that a new age is brewing. Who shall be able to write looking at the future?

---

tive research and even if one disagrees with some aspects and some things appear to have been omitted, there is no Spanish province that can boast of such a book to which this one can be compared. Días del Moral, Juan: *Historia de las agitaciones campesínas andalucas, 1929.*

[63] This may be in other books; perhaps *La Estafeta de Palacio* by Ildefonso A. Bermejo; the *Historia de la guerra civil* by Antonio Pirala; A. Leiva Muñoz's *Batalla de Alcolea*; *Historia del siglo XIX* by Pi y Margall; "La interinidad y guerra civil" in Miguel Morayta y Sagrario's *Historia de España*; *Historia del Partido Republicano Español* by Rodríguez Solís; *Historia de la Regencia* by Ortega y Rubio; *La historia filosófica de la Revolución* by Carlos Rubio; *España desde 1868 a 1875* by Serrano Pardo; *De Alcolea a Sagunto* by Villalba Hervás; *Los hombres de la Restauración* by Pongent; *La Republica y sus hombres* by Cruz; *Historia del Socialismo Español* by Mora. Also, Rodolfo Gil's *Córdoba contemporánea*, and local newspapers, a copious source of information for the 19th century. Today I would add Gabriel Maura's study the *Reinado de Alfonso XIII* and better still, Melchor Fernandez Almagro's *Historia del reinado de Alfonso XIII* (1933). These works, together with Pio Zabala's significant *Historia contemporànea de España, 1808-1923,* will enable the reader to better establish the timeline for the events.

The author has preferred to indicate these sources so that, as one used to say in the old days, the *curious reader* might look into them, as they speak of terribly exciting things and events, stopping in time at the imprecise boundaries that separate the frontiers of History when they come so close to the present day.

I do not wish to conclude without saying something more about Rudolfi Gil's work in both volumes of his *Cordoba Contemporánea.* They include authentic remarks regarding the local literature from 1839 to 1896. Many men who lived in those days are mentioned therein. There is a minutely detailed list of authors, books and magazines. It is a grouping of news that alternates with biographies that is most interesting and useful. As time passes by, the book becomes more valuable. I believe that it should be continued in a new spirit.

It is with this major question that we must close this section of our History, as we look to the future and as we think of the present, what is ours, everyone's, that which belongs to us but is so, basically because it is our duty.[64]

Afterwards

This is what I said in 1921. One could almost say the same today. A unique and private matter for Cordoba, there is none for the general History of the Nation. The city has experienced all the national tremors. Its own life and that of its municipality is a history of peasant and worker uprisings. Some of this you will find in the bibliography of Diaz del Moral's book[65]. Everything continues to be too close.

The city's literary life flourishes in the Semana de Góngora and in the Semana Califal, organized by the Real Academia and have led to a rebirth in Cordoban studies. Its social and economic life remains the same although there is a greater presence of industry.Cordoba continues to be true to herself.

The Republic was proclaimed 14 April 1931. In Cordoba, Antonio Jaén Morente was acclaimed by the people as the first Civil Governor of Cordoba Province, pro tem, until he was appointed Civil Governor of Malaga Province a few days later. Eloy Vaquero Castillo was first Mayor of Cordoba, pro-tem for two months.[66]

---

[64] On the other hand, the reconstitution of the historico-patriotic studies, the perfect panorama of our national life must be done and based on local studies that someone will later bring together in a reasoned and complete synthesis.

The historic 1914 Congress preferred to debate the matter of the teaching of local history, because, as they said, "it is a subject that would shape the national soul". That Spring they voted that the Municipalities should favour the teaching of local history, as much as possible.

Truthfully, this is something that we in Cordoba have seriously considered, without excepting the City Council, during the past twenty years.

[65] *Op. cit.*

[66] Five years later, 18 July 1936, Ciriaco Cascajo, Colonel in the Artillery and Military, Commander of Cordoba, officially declared the Fascist National Movement (Franco).

Lucius Annaeus Seneca, the Younger
3 BCE Cordoba – 65 AD Rome
Statue by Ruiz Olmos, next to the Puerta de Almodovar, Cordoba[xxiii]

HISTORY OF CIVILIZATION
A. Literature in its various manifestations

CHAPTER XX
Cordoba's culture - Chapter layout

This portion of the book is broken down into five easily defined sections. Throughout the ages, Cordoba has produced a large contingent of authors. Attempting to cite them all would be a pointless and useless task – many are of little note, others merely scribblers. Let us consign these to oblivion as there are more than enough glorious names to showcase all that our city has contributed to the pursuit of knowledge.

The above breakdown easily corresponds to the literary periods of our history:

1. Cordoban authors under the Roman empire (from its origins to the Barbarian invasions).
2. Christian Cordoban authors (Visigoths and Mozarabs); this is a continuation of the previous school and extends to the 10th century.
3. Jewish-Cordoban authors: principally Sephardic Cordobans from the 10th century to the expulsion.
4. The Muslim culture, represented by Morocco-Cordoban authors (from the beginning of the Emirate to the Christian conquest).
5. The fifth and final section, Christian or Spanish Cordoban (from the Reconquista to the end of the 19th century).

Cordoban authors from the Hispano-Latin period.

The South and the Mediterranean seaboards were the first portions of our peninsula to assimilate Latin learning, adapt it and give it its unique form.

From the origins to the invasions of the Barbarians in the 5th century.

Illustrious names appear early on in Cordoba. One name particularly, resounds in the patrician colony - that of the Seneca family, a family which seems linked to learning.

Lucius Annaeus Seneca, the Orator

Lucius Annaeus Seneca, *the Elder*, thus named for his studies and to distinguish him from his son, is born in 59 BCE in the days preceding the establishment of the Empire. A theorist, enamoured of the tradition of the great Roman public speakers, he composes the *Controversiae* and the *Suasoriae*, which consist of selected portions of the latter's great speeches. He forcibly battles decadence and demonstrates a very Spanish sternness when judging the lack of craftsmanship of bad speakers. He is not simply a critic of the external, as he laments "the absence of the great ideals of the Fatherland and Justice".

Lucius Annaeus Seneca, the Younger 3 BCE to 65 AD

He is the great figure of our land. According to specialists, the Romans never possessed any original philosophical theories. They did not develop a particular philosophy and accepted the concepts regarding life and scientific problems transmitted to them from Greece, with the result that the most important Roman philosopher is a Spaniard and not a Roman. More than a philosopher, he was a formidable moralist who had, and continues to have, a profound and constant influence on Spanish thought.

Seneca's life is disquieting. Seneca's pupil, Nero, appoints him Consul and personal aide, and then condemns him to death. His death has inspired many artists and has resulted in a curious iconography of a man of whom there are no known depictions.[67]

Menendez y Pelayo said of him: "There is no writer from whom one can draw as many beautiful pages, as many noble statements and as many apt maxims".

Seneca is fundamentally a stoic, with many platonic ideas; he longs for virtue and justice and leans as a stoic on the strong rock of the will. He is sometimes a pessimist, at other times a moralist with clear, profound and precise statements; he is also a great teacher. In the history of Spanish education, Seneca represents its strongest foundation.[68]

Seneca inspired the expression *Senequism,* and because of his strong Spanish cast, he is the most outstanding figure of our literature. It is impossible to cite the number of his commentators and disciples, both Spanish and foreign. Throughout the centuries their numbers have been both lost and continue to expand.[69]

---

[67] His death has been a popular theme for painters, even before our school of historical paintings from the 19th century. In Segovia I have seen examples from the end of the 17th century. *Vide*: "Seneca's Head", the interesting bronze sculpture by Villa Amil. *Museo Español de Antigüedades*, Vol. 7. The Berlin Museum bust as an authentic depiction is now again being questioned.

[68] *Vide*: Charles Burnier. *La Pedagogie de Sénéque.* Paris, 1914.

[69] Adolfo Bonilla. *Historia de la Filosofia española*, offers a superb summary of him and his disciples. The bibliography on Seneca is frankly immense. On the occasion of his 19th centenary and the International Congress celebrated in Cordoba with the former as a framework, all of the Senequist values were revalued, which gave birth to an excellent Spanish bibliography on the philosopher and his work. I also note the erection of the statue of Seneca in front of the Puerta de Almodovar, a work by the sculptor Ruiz Olmos, and other commemorations.

Of his ten classic tragedies, written solely to be performed to a limited circle of intelligent friends, only two, *Medea* and *Hippolitus*, are clearly attributed to him. Although they are inspired from Greek theater, there are glimpses of the Andalusian genius.

Much has been said about Seneca's secret Christianity. He undoubtedly never was a Christian, although the magnificent moral treasure of his thoughts led the ancient Church fathers to accept this as a fact.

His conduct did not always match his words. Still, it can be said that never has the Spanish (not the Andalusian) soul spoken as loudly or as clearly. Serenity and strength, disdain and majesty, native integrity, love of liberty, all that is typical and genuinely Spanish, Seneca felt and said.

The following examples, taken from his 16 letters to Lucilius are clear evidence of this as are his essays On Anger, On Consolation and other magnificent books he bequeathed the world:

1. You must act in such a manner as to be master of yourself. (Letters to Lucilius – Letter I)
2. If you are looking on anyone as a friend when you do not trust him as you trust yourself, you are making a grave mistake and have failed to sufficiently grasp the full force of true friendship. (Letter III)
3. If wisdom were offered me on the one condition that I should keep it shut away and not divulge it to anyone, I should reject it. (Letter VI)
4. Thatch is as good a roof for a person as is a ceiling of gold. (Letter VIII)
5. What fortune gave you is not yours. (Letter VIII).
6. Live with men as if God were looking at you. Speak with God as if men could hear you. (Letter X)
7. The oppression by the powerful torments more than poverty and sickness. (Letter XIV)
8. If something prevents you from living well, it will not prevent you from dying well. (Letter XVI)
9. There are more voluntary slaves than forced ones. (Letter XXII)
10. Most people, like objects that float in rivers, do not follow, they let themselves be dragged along. (Letter XXIII)
11. Do not be detained by what people think of you, it is always very doubtful and contrary.
12. My country is the whole world. (Letter XXVIII)
13. A soul like this may be found in a Roman knight just as well as in a freedman or a slave. What is a Roman knight, or a freedman or a slave? Titles born of ambition or of wrong. (Letter XXXI).
14. Speak for yourself, say something that applies to you. (Letter XXXIII)

15. You will find it difficult to find someone who can live with an open door. (Letter XLIII)
16. If we go back to the beginning, we see that all men descend from the gods and that we all have the same number of predecessors. (Letter XLIV)
17. Speak ill of yourself to yourself (Letter LXVIII)
18. Why do some people appear tall to you? Because you add the height of the base to that of the statue. (Letter LXXVI)
19. I accept opinions, but I am not a slave to them. (Letter LXXX
20. What good does it do me to know how to divide a field into many parts, if I do not know how to share it with my brother? (LXXXVIII)
21. What benefit does this older man derive from the eighty years he has spent in idleness? A person like him has not lived; he has merely tarried awhile in life. Nor has he died late in life; he has simply been a long time dying. (Letter XCIII)
22. Remember that your enemy can become your friend. (Letter XCV)
23. Sextius rejected the honour of office, knowing that what can be given, can be taken away. (Letter XCVIII)
24. Everyone has someone to whom to entrust that which has been entrusted to him. (Letter CV)
25. Light sorrows are eloquent; deep sorrows are mute. (Hippolitus, Act II)
26. If you are my judge, listen to me. If you are nothing but a tyrant, give an order. (Medea, Act II)
27. The more power one has the harder it is to abuse it. (Troades, Act II)

Marcus Annaeus Lucanus (39-65 BCE)

A member of the Seneca family, haughty and serene, he ends his life by slitting his veins as did his uncle, the great Lucius Annaeus. Lucanus is a poet and his work *Pharsalia* is notable, particularly for its descriptive strength.

He was perhaps not especially affected by the theme of the poem, but the background is marvelous and in Lucanus' work critics have found all the elements and defects of the Cordoban school of poetry: the Andalusian hyperbole. It is however, rich in eloquence with the brilliant imagination and a certain sentimental tenderness which in time will form the lyricism of this school of poetry.

Junius Annaeus Gallio, brother of Lucius, is also a member of the illustrious Seneca family, as is Annaeus Floro,[70] author of Epitome *de las historias romanas*.

Public speakers with ancient roots have almost all been Cordobans.

---

[70] Mentioned to illustrate the remote ancestry of Cordoban historians who have been so prolific.

Marcus Porcius Latro is the first of whom Quintilian (Marcus Fabius Quintilianus) said: *fuit primus professor claro nominis* (first teacher with an illustrious name), to which Pliny the Elder added *the most illustrious of all the teachers of rhetoric*. Although Marcus Porcius Latro was in fact preceded by Sextilius Ena, perhaps one of the first poets from Cordoba who accompanied General Quintus Caecilius Metellus Pius back to Rome, who lamented the death of Cicero saying, *the language of Latium is silent*, together with soft-spoken Junius Gallio and Victor Estatorio.

They, and others not cited here, make up the Cordoban group within the wider context of Roman literature. Those same accents which characterized Andalusia in the Roman world will later be those of the school's preeminent figures.[71]

The Cordoban group in Rome. A synthesis.

The Cordoban group's importance and great standing in Roman literature began with Latro, whom Pliny said was *clarus inter magistros dicendi*. Contemporary and posterior authors and critics have always singled out this group and nuanced its characteristics. Seneca may represent the pinnacle, his thoughts may be overwhelming, but Lucano, with his great poem *Pharsalia* against Caesar, tyrant and dictator, is the most appealing.

In Marcus Annaeus Lucanus opinion, Pompey the Great represents the Republican model. Although he recognizes Julius Caesar's genius and great worth, modern studies concur with the Cordoban's spiritual opinion. He loves Cato the Elder's severe austerity, and he pens a wonderful phrase in defence of the vanquished Republican cause. It is almost the Hispanic 'it doesn't matter' tinged with a nobility and dignity which is pure Senequism.

Victrix causa deis placuit, sed victa Catonis (the triumphant cause pleased the gods; the vanquished, Cato). The victorious cause will always please the eternal slaves, those who have been previously subjected in spirit; the vanquished cause will please those of indestructible rectitude.

Worth noting is the historical fate which led to the suicide of the three great Cordobans, Seneca, Lucanus and Porcius Latro. This is not mere coincidence: it is a doctrine, whether good or bad, which is not defended here, but about which Seneca said: *To live? What does that matter? Your animals and your slaves also live.*

Education

Regarding Roman schools and teaching in Cordoba, there is reference to Asclepiades, who taught grammar in Turtetania (modern Andalusia).

---

[71] The work of H. de la Ville de Mirmont, Les *declamateurs espagnols au temps d'Auguste et de Tibére*, published in the Bulletin Hispanique, is most interesting.

Grammar studies consisted of art, poetry and history. Cicero stated it clearly: *In grammaticis poet arum petractatio, historiarum congnitio, verborum interpretatio, pronuntiandi quedam sonos. (De Oratore).*

His literary memorandum is extant. Of his *Domicio Esquilino,* only an epigraphic proof remains. He dies aged 101 years and was, according to his epitaph, a teacher of grammar:

D.M.S.

DOMITIVS - ESQUILINUS

MAGISTER – GRAMM.

GRAAECUS – ANNOR.

CI

H.S.E * S.T.T.L.

Perhaps the Teacher Training College should dedicate a plaque in memory of the oldest teacher of whom there exists a record in Cordoba.

CHAPTER XXI
Visigoth and Mozarab writers (3rd to 10th centuries)

The school of Roman scholars began a marked decline. A new literature emerges which both imitated and was inspired by it but which had a new form, particularly a new frame of reference: it was Christian. From Africa, Spain and Roman Gaul names appear whose works link the classical culture of Rome with those of the great names of medieval culture.

The age of the apologists begins, an age which will produce an encyclopaedic sage such as Saint Jerome and later the learned genius, Saint Augustine.

During this period, or rather preceding it to a certain extent, Cordoba produces a major figure: Hosius.[72] He attends two major Christian councils and is the soul of each. Inspired by him, the first ecumenical synod at Nicaea in 325 AD produces the *Nicene Creed.* This is his great moment, as it is ours. It is the spirit of Cordoba, imposing itself on the world, firmly establishing the norms for beliefs which will become universal. [73]

---

[72] Hosius of Cordoba (ca. 256-359), Bishop of Cordoba and an important figure in early Christianity. Likely presided at the first Council of Nicaea. One of Emperor Constantine the Great's closest Christian advisors.

[73] The latest scholarly study of Hosius is the brilliant work by PZ. García Villada in the magazine Razon y Fé, 1916; he also translates and publishes, the famous *Letter to Constantine.* Also, worth noting is

Hosius had attended the Council of Elvira (Granada) in 301 AD, a date which is a milestone in our peninsula as the spirit of the Spanish council travels to Nicaea through the words of this Cordoban.[74] Spain continues to produce scholars during the Visigoth era. All are ecclesiastics and followers of the Hispano-Roman culture.

The major figure at this time is Isidore of Seville (570-636), in whom we can summarise all the culture of an époque. He is a living encyclopaedia who gathers all the knowledge of an era, not for himself, but to share it, taking the teaching to the people. This is his primary distinction and for this, Alvaro of Cordoba will call him *lumen noster*.

For quite some time, a common historical error has prevailed that with one blow the Arab invasions eliminated the previous Spanish civilization and created everything that followed. But civilization continues. The Arabs brought theirs, acquired from multiple influences through contact with the cultured peoples they conquered and the ancient seats of knowledge they preyed upon. Over an extended period, two civilizations in Cordoba lived side by side and in many ways in parallel with each other.

Which had the greater influence? This is exceedingly difficult to determine, but increasing importance is clearly being given to some historians' school of thought regarding the extent to which the foreign Arab culture actually owed to the indigenous culture which found refuge in Cordoba and Toledo.

A historian about whom much has been written may be at the head of this group: Isidoro Pacense, known today as Anonymous of Cordoba, who chronicled the last years of the Visigoth monarchy and the first years of the invasion.[75]

More genuinely Cordoban is Abbot Speraindeo, who maintained a school organized along Visigoth lines, and which perpetuated the Isidorian tradition. Both Alvaro and Eulogius of Cordoba studied there, referring to him as *senex et magister noster*.

Speraindeo writes an *Apologético* and other books and is the teacher of the celebrated Cordoban Mozarabs.

Saint Eulogius, a poet whose poetry sustains him during his captivity and martyrdom. His writings taste of classicism, he is sensitive and eloquent, and pens the renowned *Memorial de los Santos* and *Apologético de los Mártires*. An avid reader, he travels to the Christian kingdoms (Navarra) and brings and disseminates Saint

---

"Hosius of Cordoba" by Tuner, in *The Journal of Theological Studies, 1911,* as proof that this historical figure is still being studied. Other studies have followed.

[74] The two Councils of Nicaea (4th century) and Trent (16th century) frame the grand story of the Church – Cordobans also play a singular and predominant part in the latter.

[75] *Vide: España Sagrada* by P. Flores, and more recently P. Tailhan.

Augustine's *La Ciudad de Dios*, Virgil's *Aeneid*, and Juvenal's *Satires*, to stoke the classical hearth.[76]

Greater than he and all others in the group is Paulo Alvaro of Cordoba (not to be confused with Saint Alvaro), whose magnum opus is the moral treatise *Indiculo Luminoso*. Alvaro represents the strongest protest against the ruling Muslim culture which invaded everything. He is, however, not a classicist in the manner, method and leaning of Eulogius. More exactly, he is a member of the primitive church and of that group which he calls 'strong men' and 'apostolic men'. He stands for the modesty and the simplicity of Christ.

Some have attempted to see a romantic in him, all colour and exuberance, ardent and always full of passion, sometimes violent. He has been the subject of intense studies as some critics see him as the golden link between Lucan and Góngora. Strong and very passionate, he is more Spanish than the others – he has national colour. He wrote *La Vida de San Eulogio, Liber Epistolarum* and *Liber Scintillarum*.

Within the Mozarab group, he is the soul of what one might today call the intransigent party that fights against the victorious Arabs at every opportunity, wherever and however it can.

His quarrel was less with the Arabs than with the division within the Christians in Andalusia - the moderate party and afterwards the heretics, particularly followers of *anthropomorphism* and of *Hostigesis, Bishop* of Malaga. His *Apologetic* is of great interest in the history of philosophy.

Other names follow, but each is of diminishing interest, as their splendour fades in the presence of the glorious culture of the Califate. The 9th century is the century of Cordoban Mozarabism, as the 10th century represented the grand expansion of Cordoban Arab culture.

What is important to remember is that this group of Mozarabs was not just a literary nucleus which provided the Church with martyrs. It was also a national group ensconced in Cordoba, whose point of reference is the Catholic faith and who yearn for independence.[77]

---

[76] In the cathedral, there is a rendition of what he may have looked like, by Bartolome Carducho. There are many iconographic interpretations of Saint Eulogius, who apparently was short in stature.

[77] Mozarabism is a curious topic. With reference to Cordoba, see vols. X ad XX of España *Sagrada* by P. Florez, also those chapters by Bravo in *Obispos de Córdoba,* as well as their joint works.

A brief study by Díaz Jimenéz, titled *"Inmigración mozárabe en el reino de León",* B.A. Historia, number 20 - and the beautiful book by Simonet, already mentioned, as well as *El Glosario de voces ibéricas y Latinas, usadas entre los mozárabes* and *De Schola Cordubae christiana sub gentis ommidiatarum imperio* by *Bourret,* a curious resumé volume and difficult to find in libraries.

In 1958, the Real Academia de Cordoba published the complete works of Saint Eulogius on the 11th centenary of his death, translated for the first time into Spanish by Agustin Ruiz, O.S.B., in a bi-lingual text.

Statue to Maimonides in Cordoba square
Photograph Magdalena Gorrell Jaén 2017

CHAPTER XXII
Jewish Cordoban Writers (10th to 13th centuries)

Before, well before the Arabs, the Jewish people come to Spain. When? Today this poses a historical problem, one that is difficult to resolve. It is almost certain that there already were Jewish settlements here in the 1st Century. The 301 AD Council of Elvira, in Granada, is certain proof of this. They continue in Spain under varying circumstances, but their literary influence is not felt until the 10th Century. What is of interest to us, is that this begins precisely in Cordoba.

In 948 AD, Jewish scholars bring the Jewish academies of learning in the East, to Cordoba. This is an extremely interesting occurrence because it means that all the Jewish intellectual development during the Middle Ages is Spanish.

A Cordoban Jew, Hasdai ben Isaac - physician and counsellor to the great Abderraman and his son Al-Haquem II – who lived in other words, during the glorious days of the Caliphate and used his position to advance his brethren and their culture. He founded libraries and was fluent in several languages. Jews flocked to Cordoba which became the first centre for Talmudic studies.

Their culture is well underway. The Jews focus on education; they are renowned teachers and make education the driving force of their culture. They seek knowledge of all the sciences in order to derive the necessary moral strength with which to succeed and live. They excel in astrology and in medicine, with distinguished names like Abu-Zacaria in the 11th century and Rabbi Moses.

Not all, however, is theirs; their great geniuses emerge from their contacts with the Arabs and Christians and their most glorious names are Cordoban.

Judah Halevi is believed to have been born in Cordoba at the beginning of the 12th Century, perhaps in 1126 AD. He was preceded by the Cordoban poet, Samuel Nagrela (993-1056 AD).

Judah Halevi is considered the prince of Jewish poets. Among his own people, he is known as Israel's foremost poet, whose poetry according to Heine is the *repository of all the tears of his race*. He wrote a *Himno a la Creación* and the *Siónidas*.

Maimonides

Next to him, and outshining him, is Rabbi Moses ben Maimon (Maimonides) (1135-1204 AD), who has been called the Saint Thomas of Judaism. He had an arresting personality, was hugely prolific and is the most dialectic talent ever produced by the Hebrew people. The founder of a rationalist exegesis, he has garnered extravagant praise as the Aristotle of the Middle Ages.

His masterpiece is a philosophical and moral work entitled *Guía de os descarriados o perplejos*. Under its influence, the genius of the Jews expands and diversifies into all the branches of human knowledge. Persecuted by the bigoted Almoravid, he flees to Cairo, where he dies.[78]

Another writer, Abraham ben Hasdai, author of the novel *El príncipe*, is known as the father of famous picaresque novels – a unique chapter of our literature.

Aben Ganach is a philosopher and grammarian.

The literary and scientific decline of the Cordoban Jewish community begins after Maimonides. Its cultural inheritance will be taken up by Toledo in the 13th and 15th centuries.

The roster of illustrious Jews and Cordoban *Conversos,* or converts, is long and extremely interesting. Their thinking, of a perseverance unique in the world, withstood persecutions, influenced us for a long time and did not cease, even with the expulsion of 1492.

Numerous families of the many Conversos who existed throughout the Middle Ages, particularly in the 14th century, continued to live in Cordoba and in Spain. When there no longer were any Jews, but only Conversos, these continue to produce illustrious names who intermingle with the great 16th century names, when we lose trace of them as they blend with the Christians.

Cordoba, which witnessed the birth of this Jewish culture, produced the most sovereign cedar of the Jewish school: Maimonides.

There is no room within the confines of a limited literary study such as this one, to enumerate all the Jewish writers in our province and who, in Lucena, established a school and a group that were worthy rivals of Cordoba.[79]

---

[78] Maimonides, like Seneca and other great figures, has countless commentators and biographers. A book. *Maimonides* by Germán Levy, Paris, 1911, serves as a concise listing and general study. In 1935 Cordoba celebrated his 8th centenary in all solemnity and in 1964, it erected a statue to him and hosted an academic symposium.

[79] *Vide: Estudios sobre los judíos de España,* by Amador de los Rics, a Cordoban author. *Biblioteca rabínico-española* by Rodríguez de Castro and *Diccionario de escritores judíos,* by Kayserling, all sources for more details on Cordoban Jews. Another Cordoban writer, Lorenzo Suárez, translates Maimonides.

The 1935 centenary, celebrated for the first time in Spain and in Cordoba, attracts the attention of intellectuals. Its first task must be to popularize and especially make the works of the great Cordoban easily accessible to everyone in a simple language. For studies of the Jewish civilization in general, always interesting even though they may not be directly connected with Cordoba, the scholar can be directed to books such as *Histoire du Peuple hebreu,* by L. Desnayers, *1930*, as one of the best works of biblical exegesis – forget Renan, he is out of date. Desnayers writes with philology and archaeological discoveries in mind.

This is a new direction with which to abandon, once and for all, de Fleury and other books of this kind which still burden scholars in certain circles. For the past 20 years Desnayers has taught at the Catholic Institute in Tolosa.

Everything which is of interest and refers to the Jews is of the utmost importance to the study of Spanish culture and that of Cordoba in particular. The fine arts owe little to the Jews. Solomon himself had to turn to foreign artisans to construct the great temple of Jerusalem.

This is a culture which must be studied for its profound influence. The *Revue des Etudes Juives* is currently published. Rodolfo Gil's *Romancero judio-español* appeared in 1911.

In the luminous wake of their great culture, they are one of the glories of Spain and honour Cordoba.

For some time now, the standard of hate and disdain by which they were judged has ended and Cordoba, nurturer of their ingenuity, must treat them as does the queen who narrates Count Olinos' beautiful ballad:

Listen, all my daughters

CHAPTER XXIII
Arabic Cordoban Authors (8th to 13th centuries)

Greek, Roman and biblical literature are the sources from which modern literature at least, as well as neo-Latin literature, sprang.

One can say, however, that the direct connection with classic literature had been lost in the 7th century. The romance languages, which gave voice to the new civilizations, do not appear until well into the 12th century.

What is there during this lengthy period? Two literatures: the Jewish and the Arabic. We have just seen the Jewish influence.

Semitic literature exerts its influence on Christian literature and science. Few people, perhaps none, have loved literature as much as the Arabs, to whom to be a poet was everything.[80]

With the ascent of Abderraman II to the throne of Cordoba, Arabic-Hispano-Andalusian poetry and literature dazzle and it is during this first period, until the fall of the Caliphate, that Cordoban literature occupies a prestigious place.

Another book worthy of mention is *Israel* by Adolphe Lodes, 1930, in the same didactic vein, although representing another ideology. The works of the March 1935 Centenary in Cordoba led to an interesting series of conferences which have reappeared; the Organizing Committee is about to publish them.

[80] The Spanish book which contains these poems is *Ensayo biográfico-bibliográfico* by Pons y Boigues, and although written with great care and perfection, does not reproduce them all.

It retains the primitive tradition, but absorbs outside influences with time, and contacts increase. This is the period of supreme culture, a time during which Cordoba was known as the Athens of the Middle Ages. All manner of arts and sciences are practiced, academies flourish, sages from the entire world come to Cordoba to bow to her knowledge, and Cordobans travel the Arab world spreading ideas.

In the 10th century Cordoba is a wise and dazzling court. Knowledge spreads at such a stunning pace that historians commented with awe that it was rare to come across someone in Cordoba who could not read.

The German nun, Roswitha of Gandersheim, says that the city is a *shinning jewel of the world,* a city proud of its ramparts, gleaming, in full control of its possessions.

To be able to fully appreciate this colossal effort, never forget the reality of the co-existence in our city of the Hispano-Roman civilization, Jewish knowledge and the powerful Arab effort. The convergence of these three cultural currents explains the greatness of a civilization, a greatness that no other Spanish city has attained in the past.

In the high Middle Ages, really the Dark Ages, the Arabs are custodians of the treasure of the sciences which they lock up in Cordoba. This is the great unfading glory of our town.

Who would dare list all the writers, or even note the influence of the main ones – except, of course, for the great figures?

Let us, then, simply name the most illustrious and note that until the 11th century because of its position as the centre of Arab Spain, there was a sort of centralization of knowledge in Cordoba. This later spread to the Taifa Kingdoms, formed at the fall of the Caliphate, in whose capitals in particular we find individuals who nurture the sciences and letters in all their manifestations.

Averroes

At the head of all Cordoban authors is Mohammad Ibn Rushd [Averroes] (1126-1198) - a philosopher, astronomer, lawyer and physician. His life is one great adventure; although he rises to the highest positions under the Almoad king of Morocco, his life ends miserably.

Why such extremes of fortune? Averroes is unorthodox, a rationalist philosopher who investigates everything and has the eternal *why?* on his lips; because of this unorthodoxy many of his works were burned.[81]

---

[81] There still exist 28 philosophical treatises, five theological treatises, eight on jurisprudence; four books on astronomy, among them Comentario *del Almagesto de Tolomeo* in which he gathers all the Astronomy of the Middle Ages; as well as many books on medicine.

Although Averroes is an unbeliever, he maintains that religion is necessary for the people as a means of learning, which is why he says that whosoever tries to undermine a person's moral or religious views, deserves death.

He loves and studies Aristotle. Thanks to Averroes, Aristotelian thought, forgotten by all, once again becomes known in the Middle Ages.[82]

In the history of philosophy there exists the most glorious trinity of Cordoban authors; *Averoism*, as there is *Senequism* and the doctrines of *Maimonides*; each one representing a different culture.

The famous painter Rafael, in a gesture of generous and eternal homage, included Averroes in his great fresco in the Vatican, The *School of Athens*.

Chronologically before Averroes, though below him in prestige (but on a par with him and Maimonides according to Dr. Miguel Asin) is the great Ibn Hazan (994-1064) who flourished in the days of Almanzor. He possessed an encyclopaedic knowledge and was a prolific writer. In his works, which encompass 400 volumes, he dwells on history and moral philosophy, as well as being a great poet. In his book *Diferentes sectas y religiones* he proclaims the great virtue of tolerance.[83]

Ibn Hayan (987-1070), known by his nickname "el Cordobí", is another prolific writer, but one who specialized in history - so successfully, that essayists do not hesitate to say that he is "the Prince of Arab historians".

According to the orientalist Reinhart Dozy, he wrote history with erudition, wisely, and skillfully, there are very few who can be compared to him and none who can surpass him. Both he and Ibn Hazan mark a new era for the historical sciences of Arab Spain. Another name is Ibn Masarra (878-931), much studied today, who lived as a hermit in the desert.

Abu Obeid el Bekri (1012-1098), who has been called the best geographer produced by Arab Spain, also delved into other scientific fields with great success.

Prolific and famous, Ibn Pascual (1100-1182) wrote, among others, El *libro de As-sila* (a biographical dictionary) in which he continued the work of another famous author, also Cordoban, Al-Faradhi (killed in 1013 by the Berbers), titled *Historia de los Sabios de España.*[84]

---

[82] Ernes Renan is the author of the famous doctoral thesis Averroes *y el Averroismo.*

[83] *Los caracteres y la conducta,* translated by Dr. M. Asin, 1916. His 9th Centenary was celebrated in Cordoba in 1963 with examples of world Arabism. His works have been studied and reappraised and a statue of him by the sculptor Ruiz Olmos, was erected in front of the Puerta de Sevilla.

[84] These works by these illustrious Cordobans were published by Codera in *Biblioteca Arabicohispana* (volumes I, II, VII and VIII). Codera also published *La Tecmila,* a companion piece to the work of Ibn Pascual, by the Valencian *Alabbar,* in volumes V and VI of this famous collection. However, Takmila-*t-essila* or the complement to that which was lacking in the Escorial manuscript, edited by Codera, 1887-89, was published in 1920 in Algiers by Alfred Bel.

For two centuries Cordoba is not only the largest bibliographical centre of Spain, but in the entire West; the list of names and books is endless. Among others, we note Abu Omar, who was notorious for his literary productivity. Another is Ibn Zeidun (1003-1070), a famous poet in Arab Spain, whose name is linked to Wallada bint Almustakfi, the most famous literary figure among educated women of Cordoba during the Arab period. Daughter of one of those caliphs who briefly succeeded the great Caliphate, a queen among intellectuals, her home is a meeting place for literati – an academy of the arts, where the only cult is that of the spirit and knowledge.

Counting all the poets in Cordoba would be like taking a census of Arabs in the city. This is not within the parameters of this book and would anyway be impossible: according to literary critiques, it is the first case of "a people who are all poets." [85] There is no literature that will predominate forever, nor one that can lay claim to exclusivity in its roots. All literatures are mutually dependent and borrow from one another - culture evolves among all men.

Spanish Arabs occupied a unique position in the great stream of human knowledge. The cause of history is neither Arab, nor Jewish, nor Protestant nor Catholic – it is human, simply and completely human, and from the 8th to the 12th century Cordoban Arabs earned the enduring admiration of posterity by writing this brilliant and glorious page.

Much has been said about this period and how to assess it. A very short time ago, in the prologue to *Al Aljoxani, Los Jueces de Córdoba* - a book which according to its translator Julian Ribera "puts us in the middle of the Cordoba of the Caliphate" and describes life there. Ribera says: "I am daily more and more convinced that the scientific, cultural, literary, artistic and political life of Europe will not be able to be explained without the in-depth study of the culture of the Moslem countries and in particular, that of Spain."

Educated in Cordoba as so many others Muhammad Al Idrisi (1100 to 1165), is a geographer and an adventurer who shines in the Sicilian court and writes the noteworthy *Descripción de España y Africa*.

More than 100 Cordoban are cited as outstanding and described in Pons' *Diccionario de Historiadores y Geógrafos*. According to others, the famous authors in Arab Spain were distributed as follows: 150 in Cordoba, 71 in Murcia, 53 in Malaga, 52 in Almeria, in Seville and in Valencia.

---

[85] In a book which is a classic among us (*Schack, Poesía y Arte de los árabes en España y Sicilia*) ore can see an attempt at such a listing and the poetic urge that seems incomprehensible to us.

Also, though somewhat aged, are the speeches of Simonet and Equilaz, titled, respectively, E *siglo de oro de la literatura arábiga* and Poesía. Clement Huart has published a summary, Litterature *Arabe*, which may serve as a general background, as can Carl Brockelman's great work.

The Arabs were always celebrated physicians – including the famous Abul Kassim (936-1013), who was born in Medina Azahara and died aged almost 100 years. In the history of medicine, he is considered the greatest physician of the Middle Ages, having been the first to separate surgery from other fields, basing it on anatomical knowledge.[86]

Because of his standing as a Hispanic Goth - he was a distant descendant of Witiza king of the Visigoths - there is the historian Ibn Alcutiya (10th century), whom Spanish chroniclers called 'the son of the Gothic woman'; and Mohammed Al Razis' dynasty (the Arab Rasis of our chronicles), as both are sons of Cordoba.

Again, this would be an extensive list and it is a shame to shorten it. It is rich in all the fields of knowledge - particularly in one field into which their fertile imagination led them: tales and novels and accounts of voyages.

All this attests to the cultural superiority of this Spain. There were innumerable schools in Cordoba located next to the mosques, and their teaching was based on grammar and the Koran. Later, higher education was offered in the *madrasas* that have been compared to our universities.

Overall, education seems to have been free and not attached to any government organization, although the state often protected it.[87]

The level of culture among women in Cordoba was extremely high, perhaps the highest level ever reached in Spain.[88] *In just one suburb of Cordoba, 170 women were dedicated to copying the Koran.* In the school of the Beniz-Hazam, a famous family of teachers, and one of the most prestigious schools in Cordoba, female members of the family taught classes.

The Arabic-Cordoban libraries are legendary. Modern historians appear to confirm their number and kind, such as the famous library of Caliph Al Hakam II and that of the bibliophile Aben Fotais, which brought millions when sold at public auction, among others.[89]

For a variety of reasons, discussions regarding Spain's contribution to culture were once very strait-laced but today this has become less so and it is possible

---

[86] His books were extensively translated and commented on and begin to be printed as early as almost the infancy of printing; one was already printed in 1471.

The University of Liege preserves a Latin manuscript of a work by Abul Kassim, written in Cordoba in 1415, that is unusual as it is perfectly illustrated; the miniatures are an artistic depiction of the faces and life in Cordoba at the beginning of the 15th century. It has been reassimilated into Cordoba by Rafael Castejón's translation.

[87] *Vide: La enseñanza entre los musulmanes españoles,* Julian Ribera, reedited by the Real Academia de Cordoba.

[88] *Poetisas musulmanas de España,* Luis Gonzalvo, R. Arch. 1915.

[89] *Vide:* Julian Ribera's brief treatise, *Bibliófilos y Bibliotecas de la España Musulmana,* also reedited by the Real Academia de Cordoba.

that other viewpoints are now being entertained. Nevertheless, it is good to remember certain books, such as *La Ciencia española* by Menendez Pelayo; the work of Felipe Picatoste; *Apuntes para una biblioteca de escritoras españolas* by Manuel Serrano y Sanz; and *Cultura científica española en el siglo XVII* by A. Fernandez Vallin. These books serve as an arsenal of data with which to appreciate Spanish - and to an extent Cordoba's - cultural contribution.

Pertaining to our town and regarding this literary chapter, consult *Colección de Estudios Arabes,* first published in 1897, not just for the works it contains, but also for what else it brings to light The Biblioteca Arabicohispana first published in 1882, consisting of 10 volumes and unfortunately discontinued, was headed by the illustrious D. Francisco Codera.

A group of Arabists, Julián Ribera, Miguel Asín, Gaspar Ramiro and Ambrosio Huici, followed his example and their extremely modern translations are a must for anyone desirous of more information on the studies that have only been sketched here.

The magazine *Al-Andalus* from the Escuelas Arabes in Madrid and Granada is the national publication that currently publishes studies of our Arabist culture. 1959, the year of the 12th centenary of the Arab independence in Spain with the arrival of the first Abderraman, marks the first publication of an annual magazine entitled *Al-Mulk* (the Caliphate motto) and which contains a great deal of interesting information.

Finally, also worth noting is *Manual de Bibliografía musulmana* by Giuseppe Gabrieli, Rome, 1916.

CHAPTER XXIV
Arabic-Cordoban Knowledge

The Whole Picture

Due to the limits imposed by language, it is difficult to convey, to the general public, all that Cordoba did for Arabic culture and knowledge. There have been, of course, many translations but in the case of poetry there is a drawback: if the poems are rendered into prose to maintain the spirit of the poem, they lose their embellishments and fail to touch a chord with their audience.

If, on the contrary, they are rendered into verse, a good poet who is also an Arabist must do it - and such a poet will without his wishing to become a collaborator. The poems become hybrids.

On the other hand, a list of names hardly appeals to the soul. The only alternative, therefore, is to narrow the focus to the cardinal figures in the various fields of knowledge of the time in Cordoba – to persons we could call archetypes.

We are aided in our selection today by the modern studies cited in the bibliography.

Averroes as always, heads the list. His work continues to be studied, as are the peculiar events of his life: condemned as a heretic in the Mesquita, he is banished to Lucena, dies in Morocco. His body is carried to Cordoba on a beast of burden whose load is balanced by the coffin on one side and his books as a counterweight on the other.

Today, Carlos Quirós, Nemesio Morata, and Miguel Asín are his main commentators.

Ibn Hazan, the great sage, has gained in fame. Asín's study of *Fisal o Historia de las Religiones* and his book on love *Collar de la Paloma,* is stunning – this is the only word possible. The Cordoban heart leaps when reading Hazan's magnificent axioms:

- "He who wrongs his relatives, or his friends, is more vile than they; he who returns the wrong done to him is the same as those who wronged him; he who does not return a wrong is superior to them, he is their master, better and more noble."
- "The first to be on his guard against a traitor is precisely the one against whom the traitor acted."
- "The first to despise a false witness is the one who benefited from the false testimony."
- "The honourable man values honour more than riches; he will defend his body at the expense of his riches, his life at the expense of his body, and his honour at the expense of his life."

The reflections continue. Islam, particularly Cordoban Islam, produced these beautiful and magnificent thoughts. But were they all his? One is reminded of Seneca; the tradition remained unbroken.

Ibn Hazan, who flourished in the days of the so-called Cordoban Arab Republic, was ahead of Christian Europe by many centuries. *Fisal* and other works confirm Hazan as a fount of knowledge. In *Fisal* he sets forth and analyses the principles of human reason versus religion. Asín says of him:

In the light of his pages you can detect the golden thread of philosophy; and the Arabs, who held the strand because they were the last to arrive, had little difficulty in getting ahead of the Christian thinkers of the West in the use of synthesis and method which the scholasticism of the 13th century stood for.

Asín's work has been commented on and made popular - with more care than perhaps anyone else - by Gonzáles Palencia. For Cordoba, just knowing about his works is not enough. By expanding the awareness and the boundaries of Cordoban thought, Asín has done as much for our city as those great men who glowingly proclaimed the name of Cordoba throughout the world. If any city owes a debt of gratitude, it is Cordoba to Asín, and the debt is a large and thoughtful one. Repaying it is our duty.

There is another group of Arabists whom we could call Augustinian, centred on the resources of El Escorial; names such as M.R. Blanco, Melchor Antuña, Juan Lazcano, N. Morata, and so forth.

One must also not forget that the Order of Saint Augustine is the order with the longest tradition of studying the history of the country. A short survey of the contributions of the various orders is found in Father Antolínez's speech of acceptance.

Another name which resonates is Ibn Quzman. Julián Ribera is responsible for the study of his poetic works and for his popularity. As studies of his *Cancionero* have shown, Ibn Quzman anticipated many of the themes of Provençal poetry.

Ibn Quzman's school of poetry, the *Zahal*, spread throughout all of Spain and beyond, reaching as far as the East to the tents of Saladin and those of the Crusades. The Zajal also influenced European poetry. It consists of an initial stanza or refrain, with internal rhyming, followed by three mono-rhymed verses, the fourth stanza returns to the rhyme of the refrain The Zajal rhyme is: A, A, a, a, a, A.

In Adolf von Schack's book, Juan Valera presented examples of Zajal poetry which von Schack translated. Keep in mind what was said at the beginning about translating poetry.

En balde es tanto afanar,	(A)
amigos, para pescar.	(A)
En las redes bien qusiera	(a)
prender la trucha ligera,	(a)
mas esta niña hechicera	(a)
es quien nos debe pescar.	(A)

The Zajal is the great folk poetry which Ibn Quzman employed in his attempt to fuse both folk and scholarly poetry. The latter, which is ponderous by nature, worsens in translation.

We have shown how in Cordoba and Islamic Spain, Arabic coexisted with another Latin (romance) language which was used in daily life. Through this, Julian Ribera detected traces of a translated Andalusian epic from the 9th and 10th centuries *and* searched for remnants of this legend in the chronicles, though not in poems.

Not in poems because Reinhart Dozy had already stated that Arabic poetry is "exclusively lyrical and descriptive." In this trenchant comment of Dozy's, perhaps predominantly is a better substitute for exclusively, as his own work, *Conquista de España,* attests regarding Al Ghazali's narrative poems.

This popular epic which Ribera expertly analysed, demonstrates the continuity of a European element within Andalusia. It recalls the Slavs of Cordoba who had such an influence on the history of the town. But it also illustrates something else, that which was perennial, basic, the indigenous element that maintained tradition and understood this epic and created it. It also displays the great fiction surrounding the way in which we speak of the Arabs, in effect mistaking things which are unmistakable.

To begin with, there were very few actual Arabs in Spain; this is a proven fact. There was an African element from *the other side of the river* – the river being the Mediterranean in the Straits - but more than that, there was the Hispano-Roman population who accepted the invaders and became Arabicized. One can almost say, even acknowledging the injection of Berber blood which itself appeared in prehistory, that the great civilization of this period was made by Spaniards when they were Arabs.

The originality of Ribera's thoughts is accentuated when one notes that this popular literature which dates from the 9th century influenced French and Spanish epics which are born several centuries later.

The Zajals were a lyrical system which invaded cultured Europe, transmitting the metric forms yoked to Arabic music and taking, says Ribera, the same path as other classic fields. His studies of the *Cantigas* and *Cancioneros de Trovadores* are the analytical basis for this opinion.

Cordoba thus transformed itself into a splendid home for art, one which creates and disseminates, as the first Provençal troubadours used the lyrical forms of the Andalusian school.

There have been many other studies following Ribera's work and attempts at using this lyrical system. The *Cantigas* are for the most part, Andalusian Zajals. In 1330 Juan Ruiz, Archpriest of Hita, composed the following poem which has the same structure as the Zajal:

Sennores, dat al escolar	(A)
Que os vien demander	(a)
Dat limosna óracion	(a)
faré por vos oracion,	(a)
que Dios vos dé salvacion	(A)
quered por Dios a mí dar.	(A)

The New Aspect

We can draw a historical conclusion from the above. Dozy saw a large and rapid decline after the fall of the Caliphate as, in all our tales, both major and minor, the Almoravid was only a barbarian. However, as he studied Ibn Quzman and his followers, Ribera encountered a known fact, one that has often occurred in the history of literature. That a magnificent literary flowering can indeed coincide with great political decadence. As he said, the Andalusians were one of the peoples who contributed most to the rebirth of philosophic, artistic, scientific and literary Europe in the 12th and 13th centuries.

It is precisely during this period that non-Christian Cordoban thought reached its zenith. Of the four cardinals, Averroes (1126-1198) and his school are from the middle of the 12th Century and Maimonides (1135-1204) dips into the 13th century. They not only represent the pinnacle of Cordoban thought, but of Arab and Hebrew thought as well.

This major contribution of Cordoba to the Renaissance is a key point as it is necessary to better understand Cordoba, the object of this brief study. Universality has always permeated Cordoban thought.

Of the three philosophic schools of thought, Senequism, Averroism and Lulism[90] which flourish in Spain or were promoted by Spaniards, two, Senequism and Averroism, have their roots in Cordoba.

Maimonides, who wrote almost exclusively in Arabic, impresses with the strength of his personality and the extent of his influence which make him supreme among his brethren.

Cordoba continued to flourish intellectually during the 12th century and certainly with respect to knowledge, was even greater in her thoughts than in the 10th century. Furthermore, there was also no such decadence in the city when the Caliphate died. The height of Arab medicine corresponds precisely with the 12th century. Almost all the great philosophers also are great physicians.

Aben Pascual (1100-1182) is an excellent example of a disciple of Averroes. He is noted for his very Arabic biography, study and style. The history of all the Spanish-Arabic scholars is contained in his *Asila*, which remains a living source and has been held up as a model. The *Biblioteca Arabicohispanica* contains much of Pascual's work.

Historians

Aben Hayan (998-1070) stands out not only among Cordoban historians, but also among all Islamic historians. He belongs to the period of Almazor,

---

[90] Philosophical school of thought developed by Ramón Llull (1235-1315), writer and philosopher from Mallorca, which combines mysticism with rationalism in an attempt to convert unbelievers.

and even more so to that of the disappearance of the Caliphate. His major work, not very well known today, dealt with the period from Tariq bin Ziyad and the conquest of the Iberian Peninsula, to the fall of the Caliphate. Dozy gives him extraordinary praise, saying that few can compare with him, and none can excel him.

Preceding him chronologically, though not in merit, although praiseworthy, is Ibn al Alqutiya, a direct descendant of Witiza. His *Historia de la conquista de España* extends to the beginning of the 10th century (912). In his accounts he reveals his Arab roots with the introduction of the basic Andalusia component.

Al-Razi (10th century), known in our histories as Rasi the Arab, completes the list. Often cited, he is less valued today as a historian by traditionalists, although they still praise him as a scholar and a poet.

The anonymous historical chronicle *Akbar Machmuá*, which has recently been more thoroughly studied and is now believed to have been written around the mid-10th century, reveals another cache of Cordoban historians.

Dozy maintains that Al-Bakri (11th century) who lived in Cordoba was the greatest geographer of Arab Spain.

Iben Masarra (888-931) was, according to Asín, the first original thinker that Islam produced. He led a curious and interesting life: fleeing from Cordoba, he returns to the city to retire as head of a small community in a hermitage he founded in the Sierra of Cordoba. At first his school flourished. Eventually, although the school continued, its members were persecuted, fled or were jailed.

According to Asín, who reconstructed Masarra's philosophic and theological doctrine, the school's members believed that all property was illicit thanks to the liberty of man. They were almost atheists who scoffed at the idea of hell, eschewed fatalism and the causality of all acts.

The most renowned physician of the 10th century was Abulcasis, born in Medina Azahara. His book *Tasrif* is considered a medical encyclopaedia.

What was the Arab civilization?

One of the latest essayists, Louis Bertrand, says that the Arab civilization is such a Spanish reality that Spaniards can be as proud of the Cordoban 10th century, as they are of the 16th century, the one they call their golden century.

His conception is clear and in its way is the antithesis of Dozy, whom he considers blinded by Arabism.

Bertrand expresses his thesis thus: "The least one can say is that the Muslim domination was a disaster for Spain."[91] But his work cannot be judged simply

---

[91] Louis Bertrand, *L'Espagne Musulmane. 1932.*

by this statement. With reference to Cordoba and her exaggerated size - houses, mosques, baths, and so forth – Bertrand thinks that Cordoba was, like all ancient cities, small. Arabs preferred the country. Although he accepts the chroniclers' reports of the 28 neighbourhoods which surrounded Cordoba and extended for many kilometres into the Sierra and along the river in a series of rural buildings, he thinks a figure of 500,000 inhabitants is an exaggeration. He therefore maintains that he finds it impossible to accept the incredible numbers advanced by Arabic scholars, figures which Dozy reproduces with eyes closed. Although not all the author's conclusions are valid, it is a beautifully written book with a praiseworthy didactic and artistic vision.

Arabic studies in Spain followed a grand trajectory. There are several notable names among the disciples of the illustrious Arabists, such as García Gómez, García Palencia and Gómez Moreno.

Cordoba has not yet produced a famous Arabist, although there are many who successfully engage in the subject matter. In 1934 for the first time, in order to encourage this tradition, the Colegio de la Asunción de Córdoba inaugurated its short-lived Arab and Hebrew Departments.

* * *

To complete this initiation, the chapter on Arabic writers should be extended to include notes from the *Historia de la Literatura arabíga by* G. Palencia. It includes a great many names, especially that of the famous poet Ibn Quzman, who was if not discovered, at least made popular by Julián Ribera. He also cites a great many popular poets, authors of Zajals. A careful and ample bibliography enhances the value of Palencia's work.

The notable characteristic of these music and poetry studies is the discovery of a large aesthetic source in Arab Spain which influenced all aspects of art (poetry, music, architecture) and from which the wisdom and knowledge of Cordoba became a creative and expanding home rather than a closed preserve.

Asin's much discussed and now accepted work, *Dante y el Islam,* has been one of the best advocates of Arabic-Hispanic culture.

Several beautiful bibliographic sources are available for further reading on Arabic life, almost all from the learned pen of Rodrigo Amador de los Ríos: *Costumbres mahometanas en entierros y funerales, Notas acerca de la mujer, De creencias y supersticiones, Fiestas entre los musulmanes, and so forth.*

In *España Moderna* (1898 and 1900), Miguel Colmeiro with his *Examen de la flora hispanolusitana* remains the unsurpassed expert on plants cultivated by the Arabs. There are others who came after him. Incidentally, there were no orange trees in the Patio of the Oranges, as the Mesquita-Cathedral patio is called today, but there were myrtles.[92]

All the centres of population near Cordoba were annihilated between 1010 and 1013. Cordoba is one of the cities in the world which has the most ruins within a perimeter of various kilometres of its boundaries, especially to the west of the city as far as Medina Azahara and to the east as far as the arroyo of Rabanal, the limits of the urban development under Almanzor which he named Medina Záhira.

CHAPTER XXV
Post-Reconquista Writers

There is a very clear evolution of the literary history of the city of Cordoba during the Christian period. One cannot truly speak of a Cordoban school of thought, except during the period of Góngora. As to poetry, Miguel Gutiérrez denies its existence in his study of the poetic school.

Many names need to be added to the general study of this period since they do not appear in the major works, whether histories or manuals on Spanish literature, as most are considered very second rate. Generally speaking, and as a preliminary study, let us accept this general criterion but with the following exceptions.

The Men of the Renaissance

Illustrious names appear in the second half of the 15th century. The rise of the sublime and powerful Ferdinand de Cordoba connects the Middle Ages to the Renaissance, and from what is known about him today, he is one of the extraordinary greats of the 15th century.

The 16th century produces great names such as Hernán Pérez de Oliva, Francisco de Toledo, Ambrosio de Morales and Francisco del Rosal. The whole school of thought of the period revolved around them and what they represented.

As they were to follow the latter, let us include Martin de Roa and Dias de Rivas, although they were of lesser standing and not known nation-wide.

---

[92] But what was Cordoba like in the 10th century? Consult the works of Rafael Castejón regarding this interesting question.

Poets

Poetry contributes the names of Juan de Mena, Juan Rufo, Carrilo de Sotomayor, Góngora, who represents the pinnacle, and Pablo de Céspedes.

There are many names floating around, but already in Góngora's time, the raw material is less impressive, talent is in a decline.

Vaca de Alfarca is a typical poet from the second half of the 17th century. His work demonstrates the beginning of the decline, the beginning of coldness and a lack of inspiration. His *Lira de Melpómene* or the *Festejos del Pindo* (1662-67) say it all.

History, for example, is represented by Alfón García de Morales. There is a great difference between Ambrosio de Morales (with all his shortcomings) and him. The Abad de Rute - Francisco Fernández de Cordoba - means well but shows no spirit. As the century progresses, the local historians loose sight of their horizon and lack the expansive flights of the great chroniclers. They descend into genealogy or expand more intimately, as does Páez de Valenzuela in *Relaciones,* into manuals on acceptable social behaviour.

History then loses its way and dies in Fray Girón's the *Memorial Estrellado.*

Literary panorama at the end of the 17th and the mid-18th centuries

By the end of the 17th century and the mid-18th century there is no poetry and barely any prose. These are the days of *Ladridos espirituales* (Posadas), *Brisas Sagradas* and *El Nilo de la Iglesia,* (Padre Bustos) and others. The *Relaciones*, a refuge for poetry and a patchwork of poets, demonstrates the ultimate decadence and the most ghastly lowering of taste.

There is a brief Renaissance centered on history in the 18th century, also in Spain, during which everything is erudite. Ruano y Gómez, each in his own way, represent this modest rebirth, as do the brothers Mohedano.

Also during the 18th century the scene was dominated by Gonzalo Antonio Serrano's curious almanacs full of riddles and predictions, whom a kindly local critic said was an astronomer.

Oratory

Sacred oratory is characteristic of this age, although not in Cordoba. Who best represents this? There are so many that it is difficult to select any one in particular, even more so through the leaden medium of written speech.

The great Alonso Cabrera, from the 16th century, seldom preached in Cordoba. There are many examples from the 17th century. The best, perhaps the strongest, is Alvaro Pizaño y Palacios, a canon who although not from Cordoba wished to be associated with the city and who managed to become Pablo de Céspedes' great friend and executor. Within the style of the genre, his oratories have a certain sympathetic charm not seen in other works.

The best way to understand the literary spirit of the end of the 17th century is to bravely read the five sermons, rather, conferences, which Francisco de Posadas gave during Lent in 1696 before the City Council in the Chapter House. They dealt with these themes: Peace, Science, Justice, Love and Patience.

Posadas is marginally palatable. But when it comes to the vertiginous oratory of a Padre Bustos, for example, adjectives and patience fail one.

In Cordoba, judging from the examples at hand, the quality of the sermons was not very high, that is until the arrival in the 18th century of Fray Diego de Cádiz whose oratory was a welcome change and captivated his audience.

Physicians

Physicians like Leiva Aguilar, who writes in 1653, or Alonso de Burgos, add nothing new. Just look at their books: they fight, argue, exaggerate, horrify us with epidemics. Later, with Sánchez de Feria, they are lost to History, which, when some of them write it, is another kind of epidemic.

On the other hand, it must be said that there are those who believe that Alonso de Burgos' book is excellent with regard to Hygiene and one of the most interesting. Daza de Valdés, who wrote in 1623 in the early days of the early 17th century, is considered a skilled optician by modern standards.

Thus, we arrive at the 19th century. We shall speak of this century and its men later, all reflected in the splendour of the Duque de Rivas.

Literary Sources

I have by no means mentioned everyone. I will do so later in greater detail and in a more orderly fashion, but first we need to speak of books, to get to know and classify them.

Which books are these? Two, which are fundamental: *La Imprenta en Córdoba*, by Valdenebro, and the *Diccionario Biográfico* by Ramirez de Arrellano[93].

Both are extremely useful books. Valdenebro compiled everything printed in Cordoba up to 1896. Between books and pamphlets, he found 54 for the 16th century, 243 in the 17th century and 576 in the 18th century.

The value for mosthe most of the works from two centuries ago has already been noted. Valdenbro did not fail to include the copious collection of "novels"

---

[93] Ramirez de Arellano, R., *Ensayo Catálogo biográfico de escritores. Provincia y diócesis de Córdoba, 1922.*

which seem to be a hallmark of Cordoban printing, and which appear in high numbers in his bibliography.

Arellano's book, *Diccionario Biográfico*, is partly based on *La Imprenta*. The first volume consists of 2,226 bibliographic entries, reaching 3,458 entries in the second volume with the addition of those that could be Cordoban.

The book is, naturally, very uneven. It contains very polished, perfect literary biographies (especially those which coincided with the very specialized research subjects he enjoyed spotlighting); others are lightweight, incomplete. Some are total failures, especially those with reference to anything Arab.

Are both of these valuable books literary history? No, but they are the path, the landmark that says, "this is the way to History" and along the way, with what they say, they themselves make History.

The *Relaciones* before Newspapers

Along the way, the *Relaciones*, or chronicles, represent a genre which is prolifically Cordoban. Think of Mexía de la Cerda with his *Relaciones de Fiestas (1651);* better still, those by Páez de Valenzuela for his *Fiestas de Santa Teresa (1615)* or his *Honras* to Margarita, wife of Felipe III (1612). In these very numerous accounts one discovers, expressed in great detail, all the historic and literary history of the city over nearly two centuries. Local writers should study Páez de Valenzuela as he perfectly chronicled life in Cordoba at a given moment in 1624 (festivals, auto da fés, names, customs), and equally well at other moments.

It would be worth turning to these chronicles to organize and collect a number of names which might be of interest in our local circles. We already know the famous names.

The Spirit of the 17th Century

To better understand life in Cordoba in other epochs, let us look at some local statistics: in 1650, there were 15 monasteries and 18 nunneries in the city, inhabited by 740 monks and 1,212 nuns.

There were, therefore, 2,000 members of the professed clergy, not including the regular clergy and the religious chapters, which together with their dependents likely numbered around 1,000.

Add to these those who lived from the Church, either in a charitable capacity (hospitals or workhouses – both innumerable in the city), or people dependent on the church (choristers, guards and so forth). Now add all those who depended on the Inquisition for their livelihood and the picture is almost complete.

Cordoba had about 50,000 inhabitants at the time: some 10,000 families. More than half of them probably lived from the Church or in some capacity, connected to the Church.

Furthermore, these are only the economic ties, not the spiritual ones which embraced everyone. There was no sign anywhere of any literary heterodoxy, except for the very spare notes of the Conversos. The Inquisition punished very few offenses that were directly against the faith.

Judging from the references, the most famous Cordoban preacher of this period, aside from the curious Pizaño, mentioned earlier, was the Dominican Juan de Rivas (1612-1687). He seems to have had a great deal of influence in the city. The influence of the Dominicans emerges more in history than that of the Jesuits, and many examples from the 15th to the 18th century can be cited.

CHAPTER XXVI
Cordoba's Secret: *Los Romances*

Just as the Relaciones lead us to erudite poetry - poetry almost non-existent as such - the innumerable and inexhaustible romantic novels, or *Romances*, are a remarkably interesting study. There are all kinds, types and categories of novels. They represent the popular mood.

The romantic novels were Cordoba's great literary genre. No one in all the literature of Spain's golden age wrote them as well as Góngora; nor has anyone since written them as well as the Duque de Rivas. Cordoba still has famous authors of romantic novels today, such as Juan de Castro and Blanco Belmonte. These are the great novels, and they occupy a position of honour in literary history.

The other novels, however, are more popular and they cater to every taste: sometimes religious, sometimes legendary, sometimes involving heroes, outlaws and saints, sometimes the common man.

The popular novels did not educate - they entertained. Until very recently, these rough and sometimes vulgar stories such as *El Ganso de la Catedral* (The Goose in the Cathedral), recited in wineries and farmhouses, were the spiritual bread of the poor classes. They progressed from this dull and coarse fare to newspapers, and from there to books with totally different themes and which created a different world as they travelled from farmhouse to farmhouse and from winery to winery.

The romantic novels are another field of study, not just literary but also social, open to the Cordoban researcher as they cover all subjects, not only topics of local interest.

Published stories provide the themes. They put the masses in touch with El Cid and Bernardo del Carpio, for example, and they do it in their own way. They summarize plays and present them to the general public in their own simplified style and with a rather naive vulgarity.

In the *Romance del marqués de Vilar* for instance, they versify a murder which occurred in the 17th century. And there is the story of Pero Mato, the physician who avenges his honour too late, but well. Or - and quite as interesting as the topic of riches and poverty - there is a stab at class struggle in an 18th century ballad which was put to music and was received with much applause.

There is also the Coloquio de la mujer famosa from *La montaña de los ángeles*, a book which was written under a pen name in the 17th century. This legend appears again in the *Romance de la mujer penitente* and may also have been adapted and turned into a literary jewel in *Don Alvaro* by the Duque de Rivas.

The Legends

Legends are extraordinarily important in Cordoba where they have taken on a national character and occupy a place of honour in Spanish literature. Angel de Saavedra highly praised Hispano-Arab legends. Even legends which are specific to the city, and which die within her walls are of interest.

There is a useful book with regards to the legends: *Casos raros de Córdoba.* Of no value historically, it is nevertheless useful in literary criticism, not for what it says but for the themes it brings together. It goes well with another book which, though not from Cordoba, was also very popular: *Casos raros de vicios y virtudes* (18th century). Their sources are legends which reappear transmitted in the so-called *Romances de cordel* (gutter press), the prolific popular press in Cordoba.

What was the importance of the legend of *Lisardo, el estudiante cordobés*, a character in *El Tenorio* who watches his own funeral go by, and where did that legend come from? In which Cordoban romantic legends - romanticism is eternal – did the Duque de Rivas find his first inspiration for his works? At times he drew directly from them but at others, less obviously so.

Regarding the chapter on legends and traditions as they were compiled in the 17th century, it's worth mentioning a book which has often been cited: *Diálogos entre Colodro, Escusado y Osorio. Casos especialísimos de Córdoba.* Fragments of this book are to be found in various libraries.

The most complete seems to be the manuscript of *La Colombina* which deals with a message copied by Alfonso Josef de Ayora who died on Holy Friday 1760.

His nephew, Manuel Josef Díaz de Ayora, states that D. Pedro de Villa-Ceballos had assured him that according to ancient tradition, the author of this book was Pedro Díaz de Rivas, about whom he had read somewhere in a book by an author whom he neither knew nor could remember. However, B. J. Gallardo states, written in his own hand that "The wise and elegant Díaz de Rivas was incapable of writing such nonsense. Signed in the year 1823. B. J. Gallardo". The manuscript contains a dialogue between two traders at an inn during the Daimiel fair, Colodro and Domingo Escusado, who had gone there to seek lodging. The dialogue consists of three parts. The first part takes place in the inn on the day of the meeting; the second, also in the inn, after dinner, when they return from the fair; the third, on the road at the end of the fair, in the company of a soldier they had bumped into.

At the end of the manuscript there is an index of what is in the book written by Manuel Josef de Ayora. There are eighty or ninety plots, all of them picturesque (violent deaths, encounters with nuns, abbesses, monks and gentlemen; ghostly apparitions, visions, divine punishments, strange and impossible occurrences, weddings, and so forth).

The Inquisition is seldom mentioned, although there is the tale of an English cleric who had retired to a hermitage in Cordoba. Imprisoned by the Inquisition, he was later set free after having penned, while in jail, magnificent poetry and prose in praise of the cross. He returned to the hermitage and died a saint. There is also a reference to a rivalry between The Inquisition in Cordoba and its Vicar General and how the latter was incarcerated, and other "special occurrences which took place".

A typical example of the contents of this manuscript, entirely written in an entertaining but infantile style, is the story of a spinster daughter of a Cordoba council member, who went astray. Fearing that her father would find out and would, at the very least, "fling her from the peak of Cabra", she sends a note with a key and a signal to a priest who lived next to her house. The priest came on the agreed night and helped the girl who gave birth to a child in the garden. He wrapped the child in his cloak, took it away and brought it to his sister. The woman gave him gold jewelry to sell to provide for the child's upkeep.

There also are historical plots involving the Gran Capitán, Ambrosio de Morales, and others. They are of almost no historical value, but they do preserve the city's legendary tales.

Cordoba has always been an attraction and a literary inspiration, particularly in the 19th century. I will not attempt to even sketch it. It is a very thought-provoking subject. Aside from Cervantes, Lope de Vega is perhaps the one who was most attracted by Cordoban themes – think of his famous drama Los

Comendadores de Cordoba; or *Fuente Ovejuna* which has a Cordoban flair but, as everyone knows, takes place out of the city. *Fuente Ovejuna has* been viewed from the aesthetic and social aspect but not from the historic one, as it seems to involve a mutiny which clashed with a violent judicial response encouraged to a degree by the authorities in Cordoba.

Salas Barbadillo wrote *El sutil Cordobés Pedro de Urdemalas.* Lastly, *La vida y hechos de Estebanillo González, hombre de buen humor,* by an anonymous author, sets its mark as the archetypical picaresque novel of 18th century Cordoba:

I arrived in Cordoba to perfect myself in the waters of El Potro...because after having been a student, a page and a soldier, I lacked only this rank and distinction to achieve my degree in Law, my profession today. Estebanillo.

Alfonso X, 13th-century manuscript illumination.[xxiv]

CHAPTER XXVII
Synthesis of Literary History (9th to 20th Centuries)

This last chapter of our brief literary history of Cordoba, a history which is easily understood from the days following the Conquista to the onset of the present age, becomes more difficult and complicated when attempting to make an easy classification. There are many names, not all of which can be included. I shall attempt to classify them in four large chronological groups.

The first group consists of the forerunners of the Renaissance, from the 14th century to the end of the 15th century; the second, the Renaissance group, the Golden Age, the flowering of the school (16th century and first half of 17th century); the third, which goes from the second half of the 16th century to the end of 18th century, is characterized by the predominance of prose and the decline of the Cordoban group; and finally, the fourth group consisting of the entire 19th century. I will highlight the significance of the authors who represent each group, in each section.

First Period
Forerunners of the Renaissance
14th century to the end of the 15th century

El vergel de nobles doncellas, and *De casso y fortuna* by Fray Martin de Cordoba, initiate the computation of books worth mentioning. The first is dealt with as belonging to the trend in the past which defended the rights of women.

Fray Martin was born at the end of the 14th century. His book was published in 1562, as was *El compendio de la fortuna* which he dedicated to Don Alvaro de Luna. As a historical-literary note with regard to Penafiel's epitaph (already noted by Ambrosio Morales, who was mistaken in the date which was subsequently corrected), one can mention the medieval author, Infante D. Juan Manuel's, who died in Cordoba in 1348.

Also noteworthy is the famous Pero Tafur, author of *Andanças e viajes:*[94] as well as *Cancionero, by* Alfonso de Baena the Jewish author so often mentioned in our literary history, a most interesting compilation of almost 600 compositions in verse.

Juan de Mena

Juan de Mena (1411-1456) is the name that fills the entire period. It has been said that he was not only a Cordoban poet but that he represented the entire Cordoban school of thought, and that all the darkness and twisting of the second Góngora period was presaged in his work. His major work is *El Labyrinto o las Trescientas.* While retaining his own personality, he remains a devotee and

---

[94] We include him among Cordoban authors. He is highlighted in the interesting biographical study by R. Ramírez de Arellano under the heading "Pero Tafur," *B. A. Historia,* 1892. He belongs to lineage of the first Conquistadores from Cordoba. Probably born at the beginning of the 15th century and died at a very advanced age. A curious traveller, one of the most interesting ones of this period, he deserves to be mentioned in the geography previous to the discovery of America.

an imitator of Dante. He is a nationalist, and his works paint a clear vision of a greater Spain.

Cordoba's major epic poet, he was the most impressive and most commented poet during the 15th century and beginning of the 16th century. It is important to note that two trends – one scholarly, one popular – were shaping our Hispanic literature.

Of Cordoba, Juan de Mena said:

> O flor de saber y caballería;
> Córdoba madre, tu hijo perdona
> si en los cantares que agora pregona
> no divulgare tu sabiduría.

Gómez Manrique sang his praise:

> Esta muerte que condena
> a buenos y comunales,
> me levó a Juan de Mena,
> cuya pluma fue tan Buena
> que vi pocas sus iguales.

The poet Antón de Montoro (1404-1480)[95] was a master of satire and epigrams. Lope de Vega even compared Antón, a Jewish Converso, to Martal.[96] Antón's satirical poems are a defence against his competitors and those who censure him because of his Jewish origins. His light style becomes bitter when dealing with the outrage perpetrated against the Jews of Cordoba in 1473. His poems, experienced and drawn from real life, have a strength and an intensity which make them stand out against previous satirical compositions.

When speaking of Antón de Montoro we left the city limits to some extent. We should now return to a poet previously mentioned, Alfonso de Baena, who lived a bit earlier than Antón de Montoro.

Alfonso de Baena is famous not because he penned verses like the one that begins

> Yo nasci dentro en Baena
> do aprendy facer borrones...

but because he was the author of the famous *Cancionero*, an anthology of poems from the reign of Enrique II to the minority of Juan II. His *Cancionero* was published by Emilio Cotarelo in Madrid, which is rather curious. This light-

---

[95] Uncertain dates. Menendez y Pelayo believed he was born around 1440.

[96] *Vide:* Ramírez de Arellano, *Antón de Montero y su Testamento. El motín de 1473 y Las Ordenanzas de los Aljabibes.* (R. Archivos, 1900).

hearted flatterer penned some very interesting verses and reached heights of flattery with an irreverence criticized by Menendez y Pelayo. He wrote these verses to Isabel la Catolica:

Alta Reina soberana,
se fuérades antes vos
que la fija de Santa Ana,
de vos el fija de Dios
rescibiera carne humana

With these writers we enter the full dawn of the Renaissance, into the new artistic, literary, scientific and social life, and we discover the continuity of culture documented in Cordoba by names salvaged from the past. Names such as Andrés de Córdoba, a physician who wrote and practiced near the Pope in 1417, Alfonso Hispalense de Córdoba, author of *Tablas astronómicas* dedicated in 1484 to Queen Isabel, and Martín de Córdoba, date unknown, who wrote about History.

Clearly, our literary talent although seemingly much diminished in numbers, at least from what data we have, had not been extinguished.

Ferdinand de Córdoba

Ferdinand de Córdoba is particularly noteworthy. Adolfo Bonilla wrote a wonderful study of him.

He is all Renaissance; a lively and sharp encyclopaedia whose genius touches all subject matters. Held in high esteem by Popes, he triumphs in Rome, after having astounded the University of Paris who think he is a sorcerer. He is one of the strange persons produced by our city. This Cordoban with his enigmatic and always interesting life, parades the bright flame of knowledge throughout the world. Fernández Bethencourt calls him the second Seneca.[97]

Was he of Jewish origin, as has been said? He undoubtedly belonged to the noble house of Córdoba and was the son of Ferdinand Alfonso Carrillo.

Ayora

Bringing this literary period to a close is another famous Cordoban, Gonzalo de Ayora - military writer, wise organizer of the Spanish troops and precursor of the military reforms of the Gran Capitan who, as is well known, left his mark on military strategy.

Ayora is a restless man who along with writing, wages war and travels; he studies History and Religion; at the end of his life, he becomes a *comunero* (a

---

[97] Volume VIII *Historia Geneológica.*

member of the Communities of Castille who rose against Charles V); he was a chronicler of the Reyes Católicos.

His *Cartas* to D. Ferdinand and the *Relación de todo lo sucedido en la Guerra de las Comunidades* must be singled out with praise. His life spans the second half of the 15th century and the first third of the 16th century.[98]

CHAPTER XXVIII
Synthesis of Literary History
Second Period
The flowering of the Cordoban School.
The Renaissance and the Golden Age of Spain
(16th century and first half of the 17th century)

The Renaissance in Spain was bursting with major players, including Cordoban authors. This intellectual movement, common to all of Spain, occurred for a variety of reasons and culminated in the magnificent flowering of the Golden Age of Spain. Cordoba's role during this major period cannot be viewed out of context but as it relates to this larger movement.

Hernán Pérez de Oliva

Cordoban Hernán Pérez de Oliva (1494-1531[99]) unlocks the century. A skilled crafter of the Spanish language, he continues to appeal through his books and his teaching. He was rector of the University of Salamanca where he held the Chair of Philosophy.

---

[98] *Gonzalo de Ayora, R. Ramírez de Arrelano (B.A. Historia),* has new data to add to the biography *Essai sur a vie et les ouvrages du chroniqueur Gonzalo de Ayora.* E. Cat. 1890. He later added more details when including a better chapter on the subject in his *Diccionario.*

Ayora has received little prominence in Cordoba, and not because many writers (Salvá y Capmany, among others) have not mentioned him. His experience as a soldier in Italy and Africa seems remarkable. He is an excellent writer. A friend of Ferdinand I against Felipe el Hermoso, he later becomes a daring and active *comunero* at an advanced age. Charles V never forgave him, at least not in his heart; in 1536 he called him a "fickle and roguish *comunero*". Manuel Danvila used his manuscript, although only very superficially. It is definitely worth publishing.

[99] Date confirmed in E. Esperabé's *Historia Universidad Salamanca*, 1918.

There are various references to Cordoban writers in the history of the University of Salamanca, as well as in the Universidad of Alcalá. The latter called Ambrosio de Morales *Rarum Corduba patriae sue decus et splendor*. Morales was a professor of Humanities at the University of Alcalá.

His major work is *Diálogo de la dignidad del hombre,* in which he discusses transcendental doctrines as well as moral and social ideas. In him, Cordoba has no better exponent of Humanism. Also, a poet and a philosopher, the Inquisition censured his work.

Ambrosio de Morales

Ambrosio de Morales (1513-1591). Morales (who has a modern and pedantic biographer, Enrique Redel) was an erudite and curious investigator, though not always discerning nor fortunate. It is not fair to flatly state, as some critics have, that he was just another chronicler, since he possessed an archaeological and documentary curiosity which enhances his image. He was a great writer at times. A more enlightened study and biography of Morales have yet to be written.

Of his numerous works, one must note: *Discurso sobre la lengua castellana, Las antigüedades de las ciudades de España, Crónica general* (a continuation of the one by Florián Ocampo) and *Viaje Santo,* which were reprinted in the 18th century. It is possible that the printing of his *Crónica general* led to the founding, in Cordoba, of the first serious printer in the city when Gabriel Ramos Bejarano established himself in the town.

He spent his last days placidly retired as an honoured guest in the San Jacinto Hospital in San Sebastian, seeking peace and receiving his well-deserved chronicler's pension. In 1591, he named the foundling children as his heirs. The Archbishop of Toledo, Bernardo de Rojas y Sandoval, a disciple of Morales, ordered a tomb for him in 1618. Bernardo de Alderete and Tomás Tamayo de Vargas composed the inscriptions.

Morales' style of writing is clear and attractive. On occasion, as when he speaks of his disciples, he is so human that one cannot but like him. His preface to Las *antigüedades de las ciudades de España* is considered a masterpiece.

Art was the great chronicler's weak; Díaz de Rivas corrects him with respect and restraint.

The best summary of Ambrosio de Morales appears in Ramirez de Arellano's *Dictionary* – and is far superior to Redel's book. It gives a much better picture of the man and the writer. Arellano undertook his historical work "for the honour and authority of our Spain," as he himself states, and in 1563 Morales was named Chronicler of the Kingdom.

Studies of Pérez de Oliva have increased in the last ten years (see bibliography). His reputation is growing. Ferdinand de Córdoba, Hernán and Francisco de Toledo who occupied half of the 15th century and the first part of the 16th century all continue to contribute to the literary prestige of Cordoba. Hernán is a great humanist. As has been said, he is worth much more than his nephew Morales who inherited sources, books and doctrine and who often copies him without always acknowledging the fact. His complete works appeared in Cordoba in 1596. He deserves and requires a popular inclusion in our historical literary heritage, not only for his local origins, but for being an outstanding figure in Hispanic literature.

His archaeological pilgrimage through much of Spain, particularly in the North (Leon, Galicia, Asturias), and many other places (Salamanca, Burgos, Toledo, Jaen, Valencia), collecting books and studying documents, is the first recorded major mission of study undertaken in our country. By royal decree and through Morales, El Escorial was enriched with a large number of Arabic codices, a great many of which were gifted them by the Cathedral in Cordoba.

Franciscan friar Antonio de Córdoba from this period has left many works which have been amply catalogued by Nicolás Antonio. A religious writer, he is certainly the only truly prestigious literary figure produced by the Franciscans in Cordoba. Another, Antonio de Cordoba y Lara, a specialist in law and professor in Salamanca, wrote around 1574 - as did Antonio Ruiz Morales, nephew of Ambrosio's who, following in his uncle's footsteps, wrote *Historia de la Orden de Santiago*. Antonio Ruiz Morales who died in 1554, also wrote *Agustin de Sbarroya* of the Order of Preachers. Domingo Soto praised him for his extraordinary natural gifts.

Ferdinand Colón (1488-1539) as well as being his father's chronicler, was the most important bibliophile of his age. His library was famous.[100]

Pedro de Soto 1563 had a noteworthy intervention in the Council of Trent in 1563.

The Cordoban Jesuit Juan Fernández, a member of the missions to the Far East, was the first Spaniard to write accurately about Japanese matters: *Cartas japonesas*, *Gramática japonesa* and *Diccionario* (1567).

Francisco de Toledo

A highly prestigious spot is reserved for Francisco de Toledo (1532-1596), one of the first Cordoban Jesuits. He is better than another Cordoban Jesuit, Martin de Roa, although Roa is more attractive because he lived in Cordoba and wrote about the city.

Toledo was born October 4, 1532, though some say he was born October of 1533.

Antonio Astrain says that master Francisco de Toledo descends from well-known Cordoban Jews of very humble lineage – son of Alfonso de Toledo, public scribe. Some speak badly of him because under orders from the Pope, he scrutinized certain of Archbishop Carranza's proposals.[101]

He authored the highly praised *Instrucciones de Sacerdotes y Casos de conciencia* printed in Rome in 1692 and later translated into Spanish. Orator, Latin poet

---

[100] The *Historia del Almirante* is found in volumes 5 and 6 of the *Libros raros de America* collection and in *Descripción y Cosmografía de España,* volume 46, of the Sociedad Geográfica.
[101] *Vide:* Antonio Astrain.

with his *Sacrarum concionum* and theologian, he left many books on these subjects. He never remembered Cordoba, nor probably Spain either.

In Rome he was involved in politics, but against Philip II. Though his works are no longer interesting, his opinions regarding the temporal power of kings may have influenced Father Juan de Mariana in the latter's frequently mentioned work, De *Rege et Regis Institutionem*. More Cordoban is Diego Simancas (16th century), whom Bernardo de Alderete said was a very learned person.

Toledo's heritage was Jewish, and his family suffered heavily under the Inquisition. The Inquisition persecuted and burned his father and his grandfathers at the stake, as it did innumerable illustrious Conversos during the 15th and 16th centuries.

Another Cordoban Jesuit, Ferdinand de Jaén, one of the first of the group of professors at the Society of Jesus school in Cordoba (1519-1567), had an illustrious career in Rome and died in Vienna.

Astrain does not ignore the criticism of Father Antonio de Córdoba's scrutiny of the Jesuit school when, at first, he was critical of the faculty who knew little and were surpassed by the Dominicans. He subsequently changed his opinion and even entertained the idea of transforming the school into a university.

Martin de Roa

Father Martin de Roa (1561-1637) is a worthy example, along with Cardinal Francisco de Toledo. He belonged to the Society of Jesus from a young age and dedicated a great deal of his time to teaching.

He not only wrote about Cordoba, but also about Jerez, Malaga and Ecija – places where he occupied positions within his Order. An extremely learned humanist, he is known as one of the elegant speakers of the Spanish language.

Of his many works, one must cite De *las antigüedades y excelencias de Córdoba (1624)*, *Antiguo Principado de Córdoba en la España Ulterior*, *Historia de la Compañía de Jesús en la Provincia de Córdoba*, *Flos Sanctorum*, and more. He was a professor at the Jesuit Colegio de Santa Catalina in 1617 and for many years. In other years, he was the energizing spirit and real rector of the Colegio de la Asunción.

Roa is very Cordoban and his defence of Cordoba, of its prestige and antiquities is very erudite and charming, although perhaps somewhat extreme at times.

During the 16th and 17th centuries a great many Cordoban are connected with and members of the Society of Jesus. Worthy of mention is Tomás Sanchez (1560-1634), a notable writer who wrote excellent works on ethics and other affiliated themes, none of which were printed in Cordoba nor translated. A Cordoban Jesuit, Pedro de Soto, an important player during the Council of Trent, died in 1563.

Francisco del Rosal

A name worthy of great praise is Francisco del Rosal (ca. 1537-1613)[xxv]. A Cordoban physician who studied in Salamanca and lived in Castile, he is above all a linguist who skilfully mastered the neo-Latin and classical languages. Many of his works as a writer are known, but his fame rests on *Origen y etimología de todos los vacablos de la lengua castellana,* which in his time represented a huge philological feat. He remains unpublished to date but is one of the Cordobans who have helped to make the name of their city illustrious.

Greatly praised by our local historians, the eminent humanist Pedro de Valencia, was considered a Cordoban as he was from Cordoba, as was his father. The most recent modern study of him was by Serrano Sanz: *Pedro de Valencia,* R. Arch. 1899. Alfonso de Bárcena, born in 1598, was an illustrious grammarian. Andrés Angulo, born in 1545, was a notable lawyer. There are also those who could be considered minor historians, such as Damián de Armenta, born in 1596, Felipe de Sosa who was also a poet and was praised by Morales, and Juan Páez de Valenzuela

In 1605, Luis de Bañuelos writes the curious *Libro de la Gineta,* which contains some very interesting chapters such as "De la manera que en Córdoba se hace fiestas de plaza", and others.

In 1625, Alonso Carillo Lasso de la Vega pens Caballería *de Córdoba.*

Let us close this aside with a mention of Martin García Cereced's *Tratado de las campañas del emperador Carlos V* about a charming adventurer who wanders the world for 25 years. As an archer in Pavia, in three bulky volumes he recounts the military life of the Emperor and life during that agitated period.[102] A heavy book, which occasionally stirs some interest.

Alonso de Cabrera

Lastly, Fray Alonso Cabrera (1546-1598), considered the best public speaker of the century, was included in the *Catálogo de autoridades de la lengua castellana* for his famous sermon in honour of Philip II.[103]

According to Miguel Mir, among our 16th century scholars, Fray Alonso Cabrera is the one who has best spoken and best wielded the Spanish language. Antonio Nicolás has this to say of Cabrera: *clara vox et suavis* and *pura dictio.*

Cabrera preached occasionally in Cordoba, but the foremost preacher during these years was Juan de Avila, the spiritual founder of the Colegio de la Asunción. Cabrera lived between Cordoba city and province for 20 years, from 1549 to

---

[102] Both these books have been published by the Sociedad de Bibliófilos and are part of their collection.
[103] *Sermones de Fray Alonso Cabrera. Predicadores de los siglos XVI y XVII,* Nueva Biblioteca de Autores Españoles. 1906.

1569. Another contemporary of Cabrera's was Fray Luis de Granada, who lived in Cordoba between 1548 and 1555.

The Poets

We now arrive at Juan Rufo (1547-1620), about whom Ramírez de Arellano[104] has recently written a modern and complete biography. He practiced as a judge and lived a stubbornly adventurous life (bohemian, in the meaning of years past). He chronicled the life of Don Juan de Austria and wrote a debated poem, *La Austriada*, also *Los seiscientos apotegmas*, *La Carta a Luis Rufo siendo niño*, romances, sonnets, quatrains, and so forth. He was cultured, elegant and tasteful in his serious works.

La Austriada often lacks epic force, although there are passages which have an admirable simplicity and vigour, and the characters of some players are perfectly drawn. His short verses are graceful and even sometimes exquisitely refined.

Rufo had an interesting life. He went to Lepanto with Don Juan de Austria in 1571. El Greco is said to have painted his portrait and portrays him in the Entierro del conde de Orgaz (Burial of the Count of Orgaz).

A great many of the sonnets in *La Austriada* are dedicated to Don Juan de Austria's battle against the rebellious Arabs (they almost constitute a history). According to Cervantes, *La Austriada*, *La Araucana* by Alonso de Ercilla and *Monserrat* by Cristóbal de Virués are the best works in heroic verse written in Spain.

Luis Carrillo de Sotomayor (1583-1610) is regarded as the importer of *Gongorismo* and Góngora's immediate predecessor. His "untalented verses," according to Gustave Merimée, appeared in 1611, and were little known by his contemporaries.

Luis de Góngora y Argote 1561-1627 Córdoba[xxvi]

---

[104] R. Ramirez de Arellano, *Juan Rufo. Jurado de Córdoba*, Madrid, 1912.

Góngora

Luis de Góngora y Argote (1561-1627). His name spans the entire second half of the 16th century as he steps firmly into the great Golden Age of Spanish literature.

There is nothing new to be said here about Góngora. His uniqueness which gave a name to a certain style, Gongorism, has led to his being studied by all literary critics. Adolfo de Castro's assessment, before the celebration of Góngora's centenary, is probably the most accurate. Attempts have been made to physiologically explain Góngora's style - twisted, restless, disjointed, excessive use of learned words. Nowadays, however, beautiful studies defend, admire and explain it.

When he follows the royal road of good taste, he is unsurpassed. One only needs to read him to admire him. *Angelica y Medoro, Amarrado al duro banco, El español con dos lanzas,* and so forth., all his ballads are priceless gems. For them, Cordoba has garnered the praise that no one has written ballads like the Cordobans. Góngora represents the summit. Below him, you need to search for the one known as the Duque de Rivas (1791-1865).

Despite the above, is there a comprehensive study of his work and his influence on Spanish literature? A literary study, yes; but not a biographical one, certainly not in the sense that there is one for Rufo, for instance, and certainly not an amply documented one. Góngora still reserves many surprises, and his influence is so strong that it reaches the present.

He did not introduce the excessive use of erudite words, which reaches its peak in *Las Soledades.* This was already occurring, as is clear in Ferdinand de Herrera's (Góngora's teacher) *El Divino* and in Cordoba's Juan de Mena.[105]

Other Poets

There are other poets around Góngora who do not approach his level by a long shot. Poets such as Diego Pérez de Castillejo and Rufo's son, Luis Rufo (1581-1653), author of *Quinientas apotegmas.*

---

[105] It has been often said that one cannot write a rough, unadorned and isolated History. The renewal of the Renaissance was necessary before the literary movement of the 16th and 17th centuries could take place in Cordoba. The same is true with Góngora. *Gongorismo* is a style, the Spanish version of a trend which invaded all types of literature and which eventually created another style – conceptism, in other words, the decadence with all the vacuity and twisted heaviness of the 18th century, where one finds neither a poet nor an artist. The brilliant imaginative difference of Góngora easily lent itself to this poetic deviation.

As a curiosity, see *La vida inédita de Góngora* by José Pellicer de Salas, published by Aurelio Baig in 1918, "Góngora et le gongorisme" by Thomas Lucien Paul, *Revue Hispanique,* 1918, "Testamento de Góngora, Lucas de la Torre", *Revue Hispanique, 1912.*

Best of all is the biographical summary not only of Góngora but also of other Cordoban authors, found Fitz-Maurice Kelly's second corrected edition, Madrid 1926. The edited edition of Góngora's works is by Foulché-Desbolc. The centenary enhanced Góngora's Bibliography.

Pérez de Rivas Tafur (from the beginning of the 17th century), figured in the group which celebrated the *Fiesta Poetica* of 1617, in which we find the names of other poets who took part, some of whom were notable, but in other literary fields.

Gonzalo Cervantes de Saavedra, praised by his relative, the great Cervantes in *Caliope*. *Saavedra Torreblanca* is author of the novel *Los Pastores del Betis,* an interesting citation because this literary genre hardly caught on in Cordoba, which never has produced a great novelist. His son, Martín Saavedra de Guzmán also wrote.[106]

Pedro de Cárdena Angulo, poet and something of a historian, Juan Antonio Calderón, who collected *Flores de poetas ilustres de España* in 1611, the Aguayo brothers, Diego and Juan, and finally, Juan Fernández de Córdoba (1646), second Count of Torres Cabrera, are the most well-known, although there are others.. Also, Francisco Aguayo, the mystical poet.

A Great Didactic Poet

A separate heading is reserved for an author who will often be referred to: Pablo de Céspedes (1538-1608). He is a didactic poet whose *Poema de la Pintura,* fragments of which only Pacheco, the erudite painter from Seville, has preserved. These fragments contain spirited royal stanzas, some of the most sonorous and dashing stanzas produced in the Spanish language and gallant verses such as *El caballo cordobés* - an unsurpassed painting in words.

Didactic Writers

Separate from the didactic style of Céspedes, who above all was a teacher and perfectly positioned to transmit his knowledge, there is a group of didactic writers who focused on moral questions and good government.

There is a great deal of this type of literature during the 17th century, which could be considered a criticism of the Spanish state. Examples are Alonso Guajardo y Fajardo, who writes *Proverbios morales en redondíllas* at the end of the 16th century, and a comedy of morals, *La Dolería del sueño del mundo*, by Ferdinand Paéz de Castillejo and *Tratado de lo que debe ser un caballero prudente.*[107]

---

[106] The study of these Cordoban Cervantes by Gonzáles Auriles was interesting. *Cervantes en Córdoba, 1914.* A much better study was done by Rodríguez Marín, and in modern times, there is a well-done and perfect biographical study of the Cervantes family ties by J. La Torre. It is worth noting the luminous literary skills of the Saavedra name, which shine in varying degrees throughout the entire literary history of Cordoba, until they burst into splendor with the Duque de Rivas.

[107] These books are very curious and of great interest for the new focus on the governing of the people and the teaching of the populace. They are in a sense forerunners of another well-written book into the 17th century by Count Fernán-Nuñez, Francisco Gutiérrez de los Rios, a semi-Cordoban. *El hombre*

The most famous of all is Juan de Castilla y Aguayo who prints *El perfecto regidor* in 1586 for his own use, and Alonso de Carrillo, who writes *Soberania del reino de España* and *Importancia de las leyes*. Cervantes is not to be trusted in his generous praise of Aguayo. In *El passagero*, Cristóbal Suárez de Figueroa also heaped extravagant praise on the Cordoban poet, Luis Carrillo.

There are other writers of prose such as Francisco Torreblanca Villalpando (1580-1645) a disciple of Roa's, who occasionally writes well on legal subjects and very curiously on others such as *Epitome de los Delitos* in which the devil intervenes *per appellatio vel oculta invocatio*. This was not uncommon for the age and there are many examples of similarities with the *Sermonarios* of the period.

The Value of These Didactic Writers

This group of Cordoban writers remains in tune with the severe moral tone, another of their attributes and one which was already put to the test in our remote literary days. It has always been there, sometimes it has degenerated, become preachy and has neglected to teach by example. Nevertheless, there is a serious emergence of morale nuances which deserve to be studied. Where these are perhaps best compiled is in the works of Tomás Sánchez, el Latino, although there is no pagan influence.

Senequism

What we call *senequism* is most clearly illustrated in this group of prose writers and is that which I have referred to in another section of this book. We speak of senequism as an imitation of or being of the Seneca school of thought – not *Senequism*, which alludes to a moral tone, conjuring an image of Seneca as its most universal representative, thereby reaching people at a deeper level. One does not have to be cultured to profess senequism. It is a point of view vis-à-vis life, reached by some through education, surfacing in others instinctively and managed with no more effort than that which allows a well to spring through an act of nature. Closer to Seneca, is the unlettered man whose only moral principles are based on a handful of sayings or a few proverbs, or maybe not even that. One who only requires an instinctive noble attitude towards life, as opposed to the pseudo-educated man who seeks all answers in books.

---

práctico, as his work is titled, is written to teach his children and in it he included all of his personal experience. Undoubtedly, the best book of its kind written in Spain.

> Cual suele estar de variadas flores
> adorno y rico el más florido mayo,
> tal de mil varias sciencias y primores
> está el ingenio don Juan Aguayo.
>
> Cervantes: *Canto de Caliope*

This is not an attempt at tracing a moral regionalism nor depicting Cordoba as a moral province, separate from the rest of Spain. On the contrary, as others have also said, these characteristics are national in their fundamental stamp.

Nevertheless, a serious study of the Cordoban ethic would be extremely interesting. Quite apart from the fact that Cordoba produced the most important philosophical schools in Spain, there is an unbreakable nexus between ethics and philosophy. Its treble philosophies, with Seneca, Averroes and Maimonides as major figures, occurred for a reason and not purely by chance: it was the great crossing of the three great peninsular civilizations.

This produces a certain type of person and eventually creates, refines and sets characters. There is no question of ignoring the Hispanic connection. Cordoba, due to geographic and ethnic laws, has always represented a sense of continuity, a sense of union and parity with Castile, in other words, with History.

Just as Burgos was known as *Caput castellae*, Cordoba has always been the head of Andalusia. Just as Burgos competed with Toledo, in the past Cordoba competed in the literary field with Seville. That is, the city competed in the 17th century and a bit in the 18th century; in the 19th century there were no thoughts nor even enough breath to speak.

Cordoba was never less Cordoba than in the 19th century. In this the city followed the general tendency throughout Spain. Everything was forgotten, or almost everything, and as one didn't think of the present, the soul of the city was far, very far away – particularly in the odious final years of the 19th century and the beginnings of the 20th century.

CHAPTER XXIX
Synthesis of Literary History
Third Period
The predominance of prose.
Decline of the Cordoban School.
Second half of the 17th century and 18th century

The time periods used in books to enable a better understanding are not insurmountable barriers, nor can one state exactly when they start nor when they end. There is always a long transition. This particular period of time, this third Cordoban period, is characterized by erudition and the study of History.

As in Spanish literature in general, after a long flow of creativity and impulsiveness, Cordoba experiences years of erudite tranquillity, maturity and critique.

We have previously seen the study of History culminate in the persons of Ambrosio de Morales and Father Martin de Roa; and with the increasing trend to initiate and expand local studies, there are several names which should be highlighted, if not generically, at least chronologically.

Heading the list is Pedro Díaz de Rivas who in addition to being a distinguished archaeologist, was far shrewder and had a better artistic vision than Ambrosio de Morales. His best work is *De las antigüedades y excelencias de Córdoba* (ca. 1625). He speaks well of the disassembling of walls of Arab origin.

In this archaeological vein, there is the antiquarian and historical investigator, Luis de San Clemente who died in 1621.

Before them is Agustín de la Oliva, brother to Morales, who was a great antiquarian. Also, Manuel Ayora, whom writers refer to as the one from the orchard with the wrought-iron handles. Better known is Bernardo de Cabrera y Gómez, numismatist as well as antiquarian and notable collector, who follows the tradition of the Cordoban bibliophiles and wrote *Sobre medallas desconocidas de España* in the 17th century.

Francisco Torreblanca Villalpando, who died in 1645, wrote *Tratado panagerico de la grandeza de la ciudad de Córdoba*. Also, from this period and recently published, are *Anales* by José Antonio Moreno covering 1236 to 1619. *Casos raros de Córdoba* is attributed to Martín López de Córdoba (17th century).

Alonso Carrillo writes *Las antiguas minas de Córdoba,* Francisco Carrillo de Córdoba, *Certamen histórico* in 1673, Martín de los Ríos, *Genealogía de las familias nobles de Córdoba,* Juan Páez de Valenzuela, who in 1624 wrote the curious description of the arrival of Felipe V, is highlighted on another page.

They do not really constitute a school nor are they in perfect chronological order, although they are united, each in his own way, in their investigation of the origins of Cordoba and in their praise of the city's greatness. Examples are the fantastic *Memorial estrellado* by Fray Juan Félix Girón and *Origen y primeros pobladores de España* (1686) which sounds like the work of someone who is delirious. Jacinto Cárdenas wrote *Advertencias o preceptos del arte de torear* in 1651.

Historians

The above were minor historians. The learned family of the Morales, however, was on another level and continued to maintain the literary tradition of its ancestors. Names such as Alfonso García de Morales and Andrés Morales y Padilla are interchangeable.

The work, *Historia general de la muy leal ciudad de Córdoba y de sus nobilísimas familias,* is the most ambitious effort at compiling a history of the city – at least since the Reconquista.

The final edition was completed on 25 July 1620, as is noted in almost all copies. Of the various extant copies, the most complete and cared for appears to be the one held by the Academia de Historia, though it is possible that these are in fact two different books put together: one on the history of the city and one dealing with the genealogies.

The author of this *Historia de Córdoba* is Doctor Andrés Morales y Padilla who presented it to the Cordoba Municipality or City Council on 14 August 1649, where it became a part of the archives.

Forty years later, in 1689, Juan de Morales removed it from the archives and gave it to Alonso Fernández de Henestrosa, no doubt to do some historical research, make copies, and so forth.

Time passed and it is not known whether any research was undertaken. In 1716, the *Historia* was in Ecija in the hands of Juan de Henestrosa who returned it to the Cordoba City Council where it can still be found today. It is worth noting, however, that the Academia de Historia says that the author was Ortiz de Zúñiga.

The Vacas de Alfaro

Enrique Vaca de Alfaro (1635-1680?) was a renowned physician and prolific author, known for works such as *Historia de Córdoba* and Cronicón. Some attribute *La antigüedad y grandeza de la cathedral and* the Atheneum *Cordubense,* written in 1683, to him. He was a noteworthy author, although hardly as skilled as a poet.

There were three Vacas de Alfaro named Enrique. The eldest, a physician at the beginning of the 16th century. Then, the most well-known Enrique Vaca de Alfaro (1592-1620) was celebrated by Francisco Pacheco and other authors who praise his wit and speak of his death while in the flower of his youth.

The other Enrique Vaca de Alfaro is believed to have been born around 1635. He was more prolific: he left books and manuscripts, among which the aforementioned *Atheneum Cordubense,* a biographic history of Cordoban men of letters that was written in 1663,[108] as well as *La Vida del rabí Moisés, medico* (1663).

The Abad de Rute

Of this group of historians, the most famous and praised is Francisco Fernández de Córdoba, better known as the Abad de Rute. He relates the conquest of Cordoba in great detail and left a manuscript of the Historia *de las antigüedades y*

---

[108] *Manuscrito Colombia,* volume 87.

fundación de la ciudad de Córdoba; as well as a genealogical history of his family, which is being published by the *Boletín de la Academia cordobesa.* He dies in 1626.

The Works of the Canons

We now arrive almost to the days of Sánchez de Feria; but first, because it is the best history of Christian Cordoba and of the Church in Cordoba, one must cite the *Catálogo de los obispos de Córdoba* by Doctor Juan Gómez Bravo in which he mixes the name of Bernardo de Alderete – not a Cordoban, but the famous author of *Origen y principio de la lengua castellana* – and that of Vaca de Alfaro.

Note the persistence of History during this period and that there are very few lay names, the majority are without a doubt names of monks or priests, and the only spiritual home at this time was near the cathedral or the religious orders. Francisco de Posadas from this period (1644-1713) left several works. Pedro de Alcalá wrote a life of this priest.[109]

The amount of mere poetry produced is generally deplorable. In the section on painting, we mentioned poetic painters, the typical example of the literary jousts which occurred so often in the Jesuit schools, as well the *Certamenes fiestas poéticas* in honour of San Rafael in which poetry abounds – they all give an idea of the state of this branch of literature, a subject to which we will return.

Leiva Aguilar is a 17th century (1634) physician and writer.

Ruano

Another Jesuit priest, Francisco Ruano (1704-1768), wrote the *Historia de la Casa de Cabrera en Córdoba.* He wrote his *Historia general de Córdoba* in 1761, of which only one volume was published (the rest remain in manuscript form). When the Jesuits were banished from Spain, he was allowed to remain because of his advanced age. Not very well known, Ruano is the best collector of antiquities produced by Cordoba and a very good historian – not for his history of the city, but for *La Casa de Cabrera en Córdoba* and an addition by J.M. Rey Diaz (1913), Apuntes *para la historia de la Casa de Cabrera.*

The End of the 18th century

Bartolomé Sánchez de Feria (1719-1783) was famous in Cordoba during the 18th century. He was a physician, but his real interest lay in the study and preservation of antiquities. Of all his books, the best is definitely *Palestra sagrada o Memorial de los santos de Córdoba,* which is an overview of the city's antiquities. His

---

[109] The bizarre titles of his works, like *Laaridos del perro* (sermons) and lives of saints, point to his literary tastes. Ramirez de Arellano, when studying Posadas works, disdainfully says: "*he sometimes spoke in Spanish*".

Memorias sagradas del yerno de Córdoba is probably the most complete document on famous hermits.

He writes well, and although today the book must be read with a certain caution as he accepted many known misconceptions and used incorrect terms, and so forth. Still, it is perfectly acceptable. One of his sons, Francisco Sánchez de Feira, was also a writer, as well as one of the pro-French Cordobans during the Peninsular War.

Other Erudite Literary Genres

This will close the uninterrupted list of historians.[110] There are other literary genres but in all, the critical and erudite, not the creative, dominate.

A good example is the Mohedano brothers, as they are known in the general history of literature – Pedro (1722-1785) and Rafael (1725-1783). They are significant for having been the first to make a major study of Spanish literature. Their work, *Historia literaria de España,* remained unfinished. They published 13 volumes in which they were unable to get past the first century

This boasting, this elaborate display of learning is not surprising. Literary criticism and history were the constant preoccupation, the characteristic of the 18th century. The two Cordoban friars lived within this general trend at a time when there were many wise men, but no artists and no poets. After the grandeur of the 17th century, this creative weariness is the natural law.

The Mohedanos were distracted by their own knowledge and perhaps too ambitious. Nevertheless, they were the first to begin a complete study of Spanish literature and to consider Arabs as essential to Spanish history, protecting and guiding these studies. They are probably the first Arabists of Andalusia.

Vicente de los Rios is a very interesting writer and the first to make critical studies of the works of Cervantes: *Vida de Miguel de Cervantes Saavedra y análisis del Quijote.* Mathematician Antonio Blancas published *Efemérides all meridiano de Córdoba.* Regarding astronomy, he was preceded by a physician, Gonzalo Antonio Serrano, of whom much was said during the 18th century (1677-1761).[111]

---

[110] One must note the historical investigation which Vásquez de Venegas carried out in the middle of the 18th century, in search of documents and exploring many archives; he collected a great many which are spread between the Academia de Historia, the Archivo Histórico, and the Comisión de Monumentos de Córdoba – all very useful for the History of Cordoba.

[111] In several conferences, Alejandro Guichot pioneered literary history, or, if you will, the development of the Cordoban thought. It is a useful outline, with which I only partly concur.

Quite true, I have purposely not mentioned all the Cordobans who wrote in a literary style. Occasionally, one or the other stands out, but in general that which was a glorious spirit was being lost little by little. Works printed in Cordoba in this period are clear witnesses to this - slow, sleep inducing, like *Colirio provechoso para las almas tentadas, Los ladridos espirituales.* This does not only happen in

A bit of a Renaissance

During this period, what there is of a Renaissance in the 18th century can focus on a character that is interesting, although not of primary importance. This is Archbishop-Bishop Antonio Caballero Góngora (1723-1796) who became Viceroy of Colombia.

His tenure as Bishop coincided with the foundation of the *Sociedades Economicas*. He precedes and leads up to the establishment of the Academia de Cordoba. He was a patron of culture and the arts, and his school of drawing formed the foundation of these studies in Cordoba. The importance of the bishopric in Cordoban culture, especially regarding the Cathedral, is significant. All the literary history of Cordoba in the 17th and 18th centuries revolved around the Cathedral.

There is no doubt that the Cathedral produced the most illustrious characters. There were many worthy bishops but the significant influence on Spanish culture does not appear until the end of the 19th century with Fray Ceferino González. The canon is superior to the bishops.

As proof there are also, for example, the Alderetes, contemporaries of Góngora, who are superior to all previous bishops, and later Gomez Bravo.

There are two Alderetes, of whom the most important is Bernardo (1565-1645), who, from the moment he came to Cordoba to be a canon at the Cathedral, lived for forty years in Cordoba and died there. His major work is *Del origen de la lengua castellana*. He also undertook a history of the cathedral and its prelates.

It is curious that in Cordoba there has never been an internal study of the Cathedral – there are no names of clerics or lay persons, which must be ferreted out from general histories.

Martin de Roa, of course, stands out as the strongest writer, but he is not the only one. Little has been said about Juan de Almoguera, an alumnus of the Colegio de la Asuncíon and Archbishop of Lima. He is noteworthy for his small book in which he strongly criticizes the colonizers, notably the priests, reviving the spirit of Fray Bartolomé de las Casas.

There is another Cordoban, also a student of the Colegio de la Asunción, Martin de Ascargosta, Archbishop of Granada, who deserves a to be mentioned with praise.

Cordoba; it is the poor taste of the age. There are some, Juan del Pino (1605), for example, who stands out for being the first historian of the *Revelaciones de San Rafael;* Fray *Perez de Veas* (1636), whose *Espirituales fiestas* is interesting for the details about Cordoban customs; the monks *Rafael Leiva* and *Pedro de Alcalá* (18th century), biographers who write about Fray Francisco de Posadas; and Fray *Rafael Leal*, "something of a poet", who praised Carlos IV in 1796. There are many writers during the 18th century. The monk of San Basilio, Jerónimo Vilces (1702-1766), has a certain discretion and seems to be the best one in the Colegio de la Paz.

CHAPTER XXX
Synthesis of Literary History
Fourth Period (19th century)

At the beginning of this century, there was some vitality, some literary activity in Cordoba. Arjona had founded the *Real Academia* and Angel de Saavedra, Duke of Rivas (1791-1865), the last great literary figure that Cordoba has produced, was at his height of his glory.

Manuel Maria Arjona, a talented poet, historian and orator, is not a Cordoban. We can say that he represented Cordoba during the new literary renaissance that began in the 18th century. He had considerable influence here as he participated in our cultural and political life.

Arjona lived between 1761 and 1820. He came to Cordoba at the very beginning of the 19th century, in 1801, to assume the position of Confessor. His involvement in the city is insignificant because until 1808, he is almost always absent, due to disagreements with the Bishop and the City Council.

His work is the founding of the Academia in November 1810, by which time the French already occupied the city. Arjona, more or less spiritual and uninterested, was the most notorious pro-French dignitary in Cordoba although he would later try to defend his opinion. Herein, it is not his political aspirations which are important, but his considerable literary activity during the decade of 1810 to 1820 when he was the Director of the Academia.

Of the many who accompanied him during this period, one of the most praiseworthy was José Manuel Moreno Bejarano (1764-1833), one of the last good Latinists in the city.

Arjona's poems – not all – are collected in the *Biblioteca de Autores Españoles*.

The Duke of Rivas

His life, like that of all the Cordoban intellectuals, was romantic and adventuresome. His activities as a Liberal, during the heated political climate of the period, brought him unique adventures that enriched his excellent poetic muse.

Consider the titles of some of his works such as *El moro expósito*, in which he gave a new look to the fourth saga of the Castilian legend, *Los siete infantes de Lara*; *Un castellano leal*, the eternal prototype of the historical romance, and most especially, *Don Alvaro o ia fuerza del sino*, representative of the romantic school of Spanish literature.

To find worthy paragons of this dramatic writing elsewhere, we have to look at Victor Hugo. *Don Alvaro* marks the birth of modern Spanish theatre.

The Duke of Rivas' romanticism takes one back to the old days of nationalism, a period long forgotten by the pedantic neoclassic school of literature that in Spain scorned Calderón and despised Lope de Vega. The Duke of Rivas advocated the new aesthetic theory of romanticism in his prologue to *El moro expósito*.

All of Angel Saavedra's literary work can be divided into two periods: a first sickly sweet, rhetoric, classical era, in which he has not yet developed his personality. Nonetheless, it is a product of what may represent Cordoba's mediocre literary output during the 18th century, that which is known as the *Palestras*. A second era, the great one, is marked by his personality, during which the glorious crest of romanticism rippled in the wind.

Don Alvaro is a breath of lyricism: the salubrious and fertile lyricism of the Cordoba School, the great school. When all is considered, Saavedra's romanticism could be seen as the dramatic evolution of the romance. His romances are romantic dramas that throb with the soul of the Cordoban. Passionate and imaginatively brilliant, they explode with colour and desire, forming a truly national network rooted in the multiple outgrowths of Hispanic stock that shaped the school. All these have their glorious representative in Angel Saavedra, who reinstates the name of Cordoba and is anointed with all the stature of the ancient luminaries of the school.

It is in Cordoba – the city that through the ages cherished the national spirit since the primitive Tartessian soul, the great primitive culture – that the first Spanish romantic author was to emerge with extraordinary vitality.

Regarding those who support the thesis of the power of Castile, it must be noted that romanticism seizes all, thanks to the impassioned strength of this great Cordoban.

Other Andalusian playwrights were unable to do this, neither Martínez de la Rosa (Granada) nor García Gutiérrez. It is not a question of attempting to create a universal literary movement, one that has political roots all over the world, a totally Cordoban movement. That would be absurd.

Still, even acknowledging all that Saavedra learned and changed during his emigration, we must recognize that his romanticism is rooted in Cordoba.

Why is it that Cordoban writers are considered the finest romanticists in all Spanish literature? It is because that when it comes to the different types of romances, there are none that can equal those written by Góngora or the Duke of Rivas.

Because we, who have never been sensitive to the novel (in the history of Cordoba there has never been a novelist, even a mediocre one, though I know some will argue in favour of Valera), we are receptive to the romance like nobody else, as if in the rhythm of the conquest we had brought it as an old gift of Castile.

We feel this so deeply, that when the romance falls outside heroic hands, we love it and popularize it in such a manner that its topics touch every human condition, and its production is so prolific that the 18th century becomes the century of our romances.

Even today, without wishing to name too many noteworthy individuals, the best romances, although they are no longer fashionable, are written by individuals with Cordoban roots.

All these and other issues, in this brief summary of the literary history of Cordoba, should be addressed even if only as an introduction.

It is also worth repeating that Cordoba has not produced any novelists nor has it served as the setting for any great novel. I know that Pío Baroja wrote one. It is well done, but I do not accept his spirit. The rapid documentation closed the road to this admirable author.

Other writers

In the interval during which the 18th century moves towards the 19th century, mention must be made of Padre José Muñoz Capilla (1771-1840), who in addition to being a writer also was a politician, especially from 1812 to 1820. Writing as a teacher, he produced his *Arte de escribir* and perhaps that which was his best work, *Tratado de organización de las Sociedades*. He had a reputation as a religious speaker.[112] After the Duke of Rivas it becomes difficult to list names.

The two figures of 19th century Cordoba

There are two Cordobans, Rei Heredia and Borja Pavón, almost contemporaries, who are, generally speaking, the only representatives of that which was good during the 18th century Renaissance, the new flowering of studies.

---

[112] He is attributed the authorship of a booklet published in 1819 entitled *Lecciones de enseñanza mutua según los métodos de Bell y Lancaster*, that he published and distributed free to the bishop's teachers. He also left a sermon. Regarding his political activity, it is important to recall what Alcalá-Galiano said about the "innocence" of the Royal Political Society, despite the fact that Alcalá spoke there, as did the one to who was to become the Duke of Rivas.

José Maria Rei Heredia (1818-1861) has already been noted for his importance. He was a teacher by profession, and the few books of his that remain are textbooks or intended as such. Of enduring value are *Elementos de Lógica*, *Elementos de Etica*, which he wrote when he held a professorship in Madrid, and *Teoria trascendental de las cantidades imaginarias*. A philosopher and mathematician in the purest meaning of the word, one needs to go far back in the history of Cordoba and in the pages of the literature of the city, to find a man of such worth as he in the specialty he promoted.

Francisco de Borja Pavón (1814-1904) was born shortly before Rey Heredia. He is the last Cordoban classicist. His education is strongly based on the study of classicism. He also was an exceptional translator of the Latin poets, especially Marcus Valerius Martialis.

A historian and critic, he wrote to many illustrious Cordobans, drawing their attention. His dedication to Cordoba and its culture was foremost in his mind. His extraordinary dedication to Christian Cordoba led him to leave beautiful works that we must always refer to.

Measured, correct, prolific, he filled an entire era. His articles, lying loose and scattered, must be collected and classified. It is not because of his closeness to us that young people today have the right to ignore or admire Borja Pavón.

It is extremely difficult to summarize all of this humanist's abundant work. He wrote about Gonzalo de Ayora, Carillo de Sottomayor, *Cultura intelectual de Córdoba en el siglo XVII*, *Imprenta e impresores de Córdoba*, *La década en Córdoba del 23 al 33*, las *Necrologías*, and so forth., and a thousand more subjects.[113]

History

Luís María Ramírez de las Casas Deza (1802-1874) deserves a special honourable mention in this very brief history. A physician by profession, his true love was Arts and Letters, especially History.

He is the author of *Descripción de la Catedral*, la *Coreografia de la provincia*. *El indicador* (which has served as the basis for all our artistic guidebooks). His *Anales de Córdoba* (1236-1850), stored unpublished in the City Library, has since been published by the Real Academia de Córdoba, together with other works of his such as *Hijos ilustres escritores y profesores de la Bellas Artes* of Cordoba province (Ms. Biblioteca Nacional).[114]

---

[113] Angel M. Barcia published an extensive biographical study, full of interesting information and accompanied by valuable translations from the Latin of the best poets: *D. Francisco de B. Pavón y traducciones de poetas latinos*. R. Archivos, 1906 and 1907.

[114] Always celebrated for his love of the city, his work, although much corrected today, is highly appreciated, especially because it was written at a time when there was little interest in this kind of research.

Although not from Cordoba, the Ramírez de Arellano family[115] were well known during the 19th century for their interesting research into the History of Cordoba. One member of this family, Feliciano, the Marquis of Fuensanta del Valle by which name he is best known, continued the publication of a gigantic work: 112 volumes of *Colección de documentos inéditos para la Historia de España*, unknown in Spain although an inexcusable patchwork of information for the historian and containing many published documents on Cordoba. Teodomiro (1820-1909) publishes *Paseos por Córdoba*. Leiva Muñoz wrote *La batalla de Acolea, Memorias íntimas, and so forth.*

Art Critics and other species

Rafael Romero Barros, a renowned artist and writer, not Cordoban by birth but in spirit, and of whom I have spoken elsewhere, represents genuine Art critics during this period.

His countless, highly praised writings are scattered in newspapers and magazines and need, like those of his contemporary, Borja, to be compiled as they are necessary to complete the History of Art in Cordoba towards which he made invaluable discoveries. An example of these are *Iconografía cristiana, La Mesquita de Almanzor, La campana del abad Sansón, La Custodia de la Catedral, Estudio biográfico de Zambrano,* and so forth.

Alcántara Garcia who left many works that have proved popular during this century when pedagogic works are highly praised, represents the educational aspect better than anyone else.

Of the many storytellers, particular note is made of Conde Souleret who was known for his serialized novels, and Juan de Dios Mora who wrote historical novels.

During the second half of the 19th century and the beginning of the 20th, representing Cordoba with the dignity of writers among educators and treatise writers, we note Angel Avilés, Rafael Conde-Luque (also a teacher) and Angel María de Barcia. Narciso Sentenach, an adoptive son of Cordoba during the same period, successfully cultivated the History of Cordoban Art.

Poets

This is a truly difficult section because one cannot easily omit it, as to do so would be unjust. Still, we cite only the names of those who stood out, and none of the very few present-day poets, even though there is not one Cordoban

---

[115] This family's tradition continues with Rafael Ramírez de Arellano, a Cordoban whom I have frequently referred to in this book. This has been known for years.

author today who has not penned a verse.

Standing above all, Antonio Fernández Grilo (1845-1906) had many advantages that he did not cultivate. He was well-known during his time. He later became a courtier and, to be fair, nothing of his work remains other than the more popular *El invierno* and *Las emeritas*. He also was an admirable reader, a quality that served him well for his poems, the ones that today's critics have panned.

Manuel Fernández Ruano (1833-1888). Cultivated religious poetry, such as: *San Eulogio* and *A la venida del Espíritu Santo*. He also ventured into the theatre without success.

Another poet of great native artistry, Julio Valdedomar, was active in Cordoba. *Orientales, El Albaicín, A la Ruzafa. La puesta del Sol,* for example. Although not a native of Cordoba, he successfully captures the spirit of the city, and he also cultivates the inevitable ballads.

Rafael Vaquero (1846) for his popularity and democratic background, a witty, satirical and occasionally, as in *A la fe*, cultivator of the novel.

Lastly, Enrique Redel, with a sad or imitated romanticism.

In the classical sense that we saw inspired Borja Pavón, we note Rafael García Lovera (1825). An example of this is *La vida del campo*. Also worthy of note are Ignacio de Argote, Marquis of Cabriñana (1822-1895), for his *Canto épico a la conquista de Córdoba*; Teodoro Manuel, *Ensayos poéticos* (1861) and Ignacio García Lovera.

* * *

This brief resume ends here. Does this mean that there were no other authors nor poets? Of course, there were, but I only wanted to mention those who would best represent a trend.

In the *Almanaque del Diario de Córdoba* one can find a true representation of our literary life during the last half of the 19th century and the beginning of the 20th. This is complemented, albeit with an excessively benign critique, by Rodolfi Gil's *Córdoba contemporánea* covering from 1850 to 1900.

I will not enter into the present day, during which we live, as there is no impartiality nor perspective whilst the thread of life is being woven. However, since the shining light of the Duke of Rivas was extinguished, will anyone mind if we acknowledge the unquestionable fact that we have not produced either a great poet or a colossal first-rate writer?

I do not believe this is decadence, but rather a kind of high that, because it is so prolific, has created a school with illustrious followers who represent it with decorum.

That is what they said in 1921. The years have gone by, and we basically continue to think in the same way. The new generation has not yet found a place to shine. Yes, although the spirit has been polished in the city, there has been no great renaissance as far as writers are concerned.

CHAPTER XXXI
Second half of the 19th century and beginning of the 20th century. Synthesis of "now"

Not all the names that I have cited are accompanied with all of Cordoba's cultural and vital emotion during the last century. However, there are notes and men who need to stand out, given that time has provided the needed detachment. One method has been the *Juegos Florales* literary competitions that due to their short-lived nature almost never produced a work that is worth remembering. The first of these competitions was held in 1859; they were almost born from the literary gatherings that Valdelomar (better known as Baron Fuente Quinto) organized during the 1850s.

Other such gatherings were Argote's (Marquis of Cabriñanas), a kind of poet and collector of writings and works of art, and Jover's (Marquis Pontificio). These occasions were generally feeble and weak.

As regards the Cordoban poets (consult the list in *Gil*), the Valdelomares, namely Julio, stand out.

Nevertheless, despite Cordoba's perennial emotions, we produced a great poet, one to whom I would like to draw your attention: Belmonte Muller, recently deceased. I believe he is the most cultured, refined and delicate of all. He is the one who stood out the most in the literary world outside of Cordoba.

The newspapers

The newspapers, with their name alone, have represented all the political parties. I am not going to mention them all, just the most representative.

The *Diario de Córdoba*, founded in 1849, is still lively. Its collection is extremely interesting. All the literary life of Cordoba in the past is found in its articles, and it was distinguished for its moderation and courtesy.

Before September 1868, newspapers bore Arcadian names such as *El Guadalquivir* or *La Alborada*. After the Battle of Alcolea, the birth of a new political movement led to the appearance of several newspapers such as the *El*

Sufragio Universal, La Voz del Pueblo, Los Campos de Alcolea, el Betis Republicano or the satirical *Cencerro*. They are short-lived, with a limited circulation.

The revolutionary press and the freedom of expression brought newspapers such as the *Federación Andaluza-Extremeña*, a significant name, and others that today we cannot envisage such as the Protestant *La Reforma*.

There was a moment when, in the heat of the opposition to the 1869 Constitution, promotion of the Protestant religion intensified in Cordoba opposed by *La Tradición* and other religious newspapers. This was a time of active religious conflicts – the *Unión Masónica* was occasionally published. It was a time of religious and political conflict. *El Pendón Italiano*, attacking Amadeo de Saboya, was announced but not published.

Later of course, the afore-mentioned *Ramillete*; soon gave the literary touch. There could not be a more typical name than this one for a newspaper whose editor was Burell.

Aside from *El Comercio de Córdoba*, the fighting strength of the press was centred in *La Lealtad*, monarchist and conservative, that aimed at being the voice for the movement to restore the Bourbons to the throne. Against it, *El Adalid* (1894-1891), combative, audacious and even aggressive, also conservative, represented another branch.

Truthfully, the best newspaper ever in Cordoba, the one with the most youthful impetus and best understanding, was *La Unión de Córdoba*. Published at the end of the 19th century, it was a liberal paper, during a period of culture, of new people.

This newspaper bequeathed a bunch of names such as Blanco Belmonte, poet and author, absent from the city for many years.[116]

The men

Judging men is more challenging.

Cordoba, during the 19th century, gave us two notables in addition to the Duke of Rivas: Rey Heredia and Borja Pavón. The former stands out for his profound, deep, educational feelings, and his scientific wisdom. This is why his name is not markedly popular, although he, being of the people, should be. Rey Heredia's *Lógica* is, in my opinion, a magnificent book.

Borja Pavón, has a method: he focused on all things Cordoban. Furthermore, he was a classicist, and he shaped his spirit with scientific asides, necessary to complete an entire education.

---

[116] As a rule, this book does not include the study of any living person. Occasionally, some are mentioned in passing. Just to answer anybody who is looking for omissions.

His classical interests took him to History, which is why as a teacher although he overlooked all things Arab, this is not to say that he did not value them. He neglected to appreciate this facet, as he did in part with the artistic one.

Pavón only has one defect as far as I am concerned: he only lived in Cordoba which narrowed his horizon. If this writer had broken the wall of the Cordoban orchard, it is as certain and just as proper, as it was said in his day, that his name would have been included in the list of great writers and researchers, of master creators of literary criticism.

You should not be amazed to note that in terms of power, he was no less talented than any one of the greats that you might care to mention, although I would not be afraid to go as far as to compare him with Milá Fontanals or Menéndez Pelayo. Had his education been different, he would have gone far. Pavón created a school. His was the motivation and he was its teacher for many years. At the end, during the serenity of his old age, he established a patriarchy for which there was no heir.

The *Diario*'s collection contains the names of the entire scramble of thinkers in Cordoba during the second half of the 19th century. The basic features of this generation were their individuality and their lack of a method. Almost all were ex-seminarians, but this is not meant to be disparaging, as I believe that the Seminary produced many men of value. Furthermore, they were rapidly self-taught, which is why the efforts of their innate talent were not accompanied by the cultural instruments of a technicism that could not be improvised.

Vida, Alcalde Blanco, Montis, Valdelomares and Maraver are names that also come to mind.

Special mention is made of Ramírez Casas Deza. He had great historic intuition. He wanted everything to be Cordoban. Less refined, less of a writer than Pavón, he acquired a tool at school, Latin, which he employed. Almost everything that Hübner published regarding Cordoba, is by Casas Deza.

He explained Geography, he desired to write about it, but he never experienced it. True, this failing was not his alone. The teaching of Geography is still disregarded in Spain today with a carelessness that demeans us. I particularly refer to Universities where Geography remains absent from the curriculum. This lack of judgement is a tragic legacy we continue to suffer from.

Ramírez Casas Deza, with an independence that he was unable to attain during his lifetime, was undoubtedly possessed of excellent conditions and he gave all that he could.

Criticism of Art

The name of Romero Barros stands out in the criticism of Art and the teaching of the subjectI have already spoken of his significance. His disciples are well-known. They are Hidalgo Cavieda, Villegas Brieva, Muñoz Lucena, Serrano Pérez and, lastly, his sons Rafael, who was ruined – a great draftsman – and Julio Enrique, a pillar of the Museum of Fine Arts, who published a great many works on Archaeology and Art by the time of his death.

The Ramirez de Arellano family

This family is linked to local History. Carlos was not a writer. He published a *Diccionario* and was appointed Mayor. Feliciano worked hard to create and complete the gigantic 112-volume *Documentos inéditos en España*. Cordoba stands out in this work, particularly in volumes 107 and 112 of this great piece of historical research.

Among other things, Teodomiro produced *Paseos por Córdoba*. He carefully concealed his sources, and he mixed the divine and the human. The book is confusing, incomplete (he left out the Cathedral), and contains nothing personal. The redeeming feature of his work is his great love for Cordoba.

More than all the other Arellanos, Rafael was the best prepared, although he failed in part as he lacked an aesthetic literary sense. Still, he was the one who did the most for Cordoba.

I do not want to know whether some modest anonymous person generously contributed to his output during his research, or not, but until he arrived there were no first-hand local studies, just copies of others. His *Diccionario de Artistas, La Platería Cordobesa* and all his research of all that local history had to offer at the end of the 19th century and beginning of the 20th, is seriously authentic.

I would not say that his *Historia de Córdoba*, also incomplete, was a failed project, but he erred in that he did not write it in Cordoba, but some distance away and based it on out-of-date research that he did not update in time. Furthermore, he was also tired when he wrote it.

His *Diccionario de Escritores* is another extremely useful work. I believe that I already said that Cordoba did not receive this man with the generosity that I, have no doubt, believe he deserved.

The clergy

Two names suffice to describe ecclesiastic Cordoba during the last century. Fray Ceferino González was swiftly forgotten. The other, so-called the Masterly, was Manuel Gonzálvez Francés.

He was, without a doubt, the finest public speaker in the city, including the forensic and the politicians. He is listed as a religious speaker in the catalogues, but he was not one. He employed his declamatory talent before the crowds, for debates and conflicts, not for a professorship without contradiction. Proof of this can be found in his writing and his forays into journalism. His temperament as a leader was eclipsed by the religious pulpit. As eloquence is an art that dies as it is born, copies of his speeches are of no use. There is no way that one can evaluate the different types of orators that Cordoba produced during the 19th century.

A didactic group

An indication regarding the men who belonged to the Institute is lacking. One who stands out, Rivera Romero, was a Latinist who began his work on Cordoba only marginally and only published the Code of Laws. He started to become a collector.

Díaz Carmona, another great translator of Latin poets (Juvenal), was very modest and had little influence in the city.

In truth, the tradition that Ramírez Casas Deza had bequeathed the Instituto was such that it remained unbroken for many years. Gutiérrez, from Granada, appears to have attempted it, as did Manuel Sandoval who was a bit of a poet.

The schoolmasters

I would like to point out two Cordoban schoolmasters who lived very modest lives. One, Antonio Montero Nieto, an excellent educational writer for children and unpretentious annotator of the Gospels; and another, Miguel López Copé, possessed of such humanity as a teacher that he was far ahead of his time, more like a teacher of today.

Of course, the technical side of Education was represented by Pedro Alcántara García, a Cordoban who was known beyond the city as a scholar and a teacher.

Other types of erudition

These do not altogether fit in this simple literary history. I know that I have not mentioned physicians, attorneys, experts, those who represent that which is called scientific intellect, in particular Social History in its various aspects. How has the life of the worker changed? Why have industries that were the pride of Cordoba disappeared? (I am speaking of the silversmiths.) What have architects done?

In short, all this would distance me from the required confines of this book. It is subject matter for future writers. Briefly, as an inheritance and as a creation of today, it would be impossible to collate the moral and intellectual inventory of present-day Cordoba. This would have become controversial even though I intended to restrict myself to the historical aspect.

Female Cordoban writers

Adding this topic to this brief outline of literary history is of interest. Historians have given us quite a few names from the Arab era but very few have remained from the Hispanic period onwards. Of course, it should not even enter one's mind that none reached the high sciences.

The causes of this literary absence are common to an entire civilization where they were deliberately absent. Until the 19th century, in no city, not even in the entire literary History of Spain, do any names with an authentic literary lineage stand out. It is not the purpose of this study to name them.

In the case of Cordoba, the work in which we might find female Cordoban writers is Serrano Sanz' *Biblioteca de Escritores Españoles*, where Leonor López de Castro (1361-1412) is named for her famous *Memorias* and her tragic, romantically hard life. She was the daughter of famous Martín López de Córdoba, the most outstanding representative of Spanish self-respect.

Leonor is buried in the Rosario chapel of San Pablo, that she had built. Serrano Sanz presumes, as other writers have, that she was a sister of Alvaro de Córdoba, the Cordoban saint who founded Santo Domingo convent in the mountains.

The *Biblioteca* briefly mentions Isabel Losa for whom Cordoban writers have searched but in fact, have found no information. She appears to have been a poet, judging by *Versos laudatorios en las justas sagradas del Insigne y memorable poeta Miguel del Cid*, Seville, 1647.

There is mention of traces of an 18th century poet, a Countess of Hornachulas, in the *Biblioteca,* but this does not appear to be anything very profound.[117]

References to María Isidra Guzmán de la Cerda (buried in Santa Marinha) are also very unreliable. She is not a Cordoban, as we know, and her fame must have been greatly exaggerated as it seems proven that her translations of the Greek classics from the French were brilliant.

There remains the popular History of Cordoba that could easily be entitled *Entre dos repúblicas* (1873-1931). This is a task for the present generation which has witnessed the birth and the development of all the Republican movements, beginning with federalism, its initial activities and strife. It knows of the group of people who promoted the different ideals. It has witnessed the genesis of Socialism, of Syndicalism and of unrest in the countryside. There already is a great wealth of information for such a task. In summary, this is a new genre of History in which the entire community is the new subject.

---

[117] Ms. British Museum.

REYNANDO LA MAGESTAD CATOLICA DE S.ᴰ
CARLOS III.

Antonio Caballero y Góngora
Viceroy of Colombia 1782-1789 and Bishop of Cordoba[xxvii]
(Buried in the Mesquita/Cathedral)

HISTORY OF CIVILIZATION
B. ARTS, ACADEMIA, AND ARCHITECTURE IN CORDOBA

CHAPTER XXXII
The noble Art of Printing

It appears that printing in Cordoba did not begin until 1556 when the first book on record is a French Jesuit's, André des Freux, translation. The most ancient, printed book is *Juan Bautista Escudero*.

At first, Cordoba printing was a poor, itinerant affair that was absorbed by printers in Seville. The foundation of the Company of Jesus and its schools in 1553 had some influence on the art of printing.

During the short period of time in which this art was pursued during the 16th century and throughout the entire 17th century, there are very few printers and equally few books are published.

The most important printer during the 17th century was Gonzalo de Cea, a member of the Cea family who founded a printing dynasty in Cordoba.

The number of printers rose during the 18th century, namely Juan de Medina, among others. The Colegio de la Asunción printer, which was particularly active during the 18th century, and the printer of the Augustiniana also stood out among those who cultivated this art.

The art of printing was relatively fortunate in sustaining its activity in Cordoba during the 19th century.

* * *

Ramiro de Arellano affirms that there were no proper printers in Cordoba before Gabriel Ramos Bejarno established himself as a result of Ambrosio de Morales' desire to have his work printed in Cordoba in 1585.

The oldest continuing printer in Cordoba is that belonging to the *Diario de Córdoba*, which has borne this name since 1864 but actually dates to 1739 when it was created by Diego García Rodríguez after taking over another printing establishment. Exhaustive research has attributed its most ancient origin to Esteban de Cabrera in 1713.

There also was a printer at the end of the 17th century in the Alhóndiga side streets. Its directors in 1700 were Diego Valverde and Acisclo Cortés.

Another interesting printer was the Colegio de la Asunción - Instituto printer, which appears to have been only active between 1730 and 1767. The one which disappeared during the riots at the beginning of the 19th century, appears to have been of little or no importance as it operated in the remains of the older establishment. Apparently, it was only used for small jobs from from 1767 onwards, when the Jesuits were expelled, as few or no books or brochures were printed by the said Colegio.

Of the most interesting books it printed, *Vida de San Eulogio* by Lopez Baena and *Historia de Córdoba* by Reverend Ruano come to mind.

The first book

It is extremely difficult, almost impossible, to state, as some insist on doing, exactly which was the first book printed book in the city. All that is known is that in 1503 the City Council acquired a Latin-Spanish copy of the *Siete Partidas*.

One can discover extremely useful information regarding our literary history from amongst the three thousand books and brochures that it is estimated were published in Cordoba since the creation of the first printing establishments.

There is no classification of printed material by subject. It is, however, absolutely clear that books dealing with religious matters predominate. There are many addressing History, relatively few Poetry and extremely few dedicated to the study and development of subjects which the old classification of human knowledge termed Books of Science.[118]

The characteristic of our local printed output can be seen in the proliferation of romantic novels. Almost all are very bad and there are so many that it has been very difficult to catalogue them. It is, however, interesting to see how the Romance is a genuinely Cordoban production, not just by the number of books but also by the unsurpassed excellence of those who promoted them. The study of novels produces extremely interesting data regarding the Literary History and the psychology of this city.

History of the printed press and journalists

The ancestor of the newspaper is the news report, of which there are curious examples in our press, such as the notable one by Paéz de Valenzuela in 1624, in which he reports on Felipe IV's entrance in El Carpio and the festivities in his honour.

The oldest one that I know of and of which some copies still exist, is the *Compendio Semanal de Noticías de Córdoba*, a weekly paper published in 1790 and whose first issues were challenged by a short-lived paper entitled *Phylopatro*.

---

[118] *José María Valdenebro* wrote the *Historia de la Imprenta en Córdoba* (1900). We must however bear in mind that he naturally does not list all the books by Cordoban authors because many were either unknown, unpublished or published outside Cordoba.

Gutiérrez del Caño, in his *Catálogo de impresores españoles*, cites twenty-seven printers in Cordoba between 1556 and 1798, that is, from Juan B. Escudero to Luís Ramos. This list completes Valdenebro's data and provides a history of Printing in Cordoba and of the men who engaged in this profession.

The *Correo de Córdoba* was first published in 1801.

The *El Correo político y militar de Córdoba* was published during the French invasion, that is between 1810 and 1812. The Instituto holds an almost complete collection of this paper.

The *Colonia Patricia* published some very nice issues in 1843.

The *El Liceo* also was an interesting magazine that deserves being mentioned. Likewise, *El Ramillete* that Burell created.

Without a doubt, the greatest Cordoban journalist of the entire 19th century, albeit somewhat forgotten, was Carlos Rubio (1832-1871) or Pablo Gambara, the pseudonym he chose for himself.

Passionate about democratic ideals, he was one of the most characteristic victims of political ingratitude when he was scorned by the triumphant revolution with which he had collaborated. There are numerous writings of his. Of special interest there is *Historia filosófica de la Revolución* of 1868 and the historic play in which he praised liberty and was staged as *Rienzi y Teoría del Progresso* in 1859.

The magazine *Córdoba* in the 1860s also needs to be mentioned, as are many other political magazines influenced by the heat of the 1868 Revolution.

During the last years of the 19th century, the newspaper *La Unión* was perhaps the sole shining attempt at modern journalism in Córdoba.

Before it, the *La Crónica* had a distinctly Cordoban flavour, followed by the *La Lealtad*, the finest political newspaper. Lastly, the *Diario de Córdoba*, dating from 1848, benefited from the opportunities arising from many years of publication. It reflects the life of the city with articles signed by countless ardent Cordobans and by masters of the pen. The collection of its issues is extremely interesting.

Lastly, because of its unusual viewpoint, there is *Córdoba* (1915), a defunct magazine.[119]

Other newspapers and magazines have been published and continue today. I shall only mention one, the *Boletín de la Real Academia de Córdoba*, solely for its technical nature.

There were good journalists in Cordoba during the 19th century. In my opinion, the most brilliant in the entire town was the Valdelomar group. The Madrid press also benefited from the gifts of Cordoban journalists. The most significant of these were Julio Burell (not from the Cordoban capital but it is here that he began his profession) known, according to the popular saying, for the genius of his pen. José Sánchez Guerra (1859-1935) whose career as a statesman he concluded with all decorum, began in the field of political journalism

---

[119] I refer the reader to my comments on this subject at the beginning of this Chapter.

There are other Cordoban journalists today; their names and accounts over time shall be left to another author.

Although the Carlos Rubio was essentially a journalist, he has skills and another standing as an author in his own right. To the work I already mentioned, I must add the *Prólogo to La Mujer* by C. Torralba (1870).

Francisco Silvela presented an interesting study regarding Carlos Rubio at a conference in the Ateneo Madrid, 1886, entitled *Origins..., nature of the Press.*

Schools

When studying the History of Cordoban Culture, we must not fail to mention the Colegio de la Asunción, today attached to the Instituto Góngora, for the influence it always had. It is almost certain that its foundation dates to 1560, although Pope Gregory XIII's Papal Bull formally creating the Colegio is only dated 13 August 1577.

This institution was founded by Pedro López de Alba "to succour poor individuals who wish to follow an ecclesiastic career".

The Jesuits, although they had a Colegio of their own, always showed a fondness for the Colegio. When they were expelled in 1767 the Colegio de la Asunción came under the patronage of the Crown, the curiculum was changed and the Colegio occasionally was referred to as the Colegio de Humanidades until Institutos were founded in 1847.

As already mentioned, this Colegio's printers published important works until it was destroyed in 1814.

Colegio de Santa Catalina and the Jesuits

The entry of the Jesuits in Cordoba, so greatly helped by the famous dean, Juan Fernández de Córdoba, led to the foundation, among other institutions, of the Colegio de Santa Catalina – the Compañía. One of the most important in Andalusia from 1553 to 1767, it was attended by students and teachers of great literary and scientific merit. To a certain extent the institute became a self-styled literary centre thanks to its distinctive literary fetes.

Following the expulsion of the Jesuits, its vast library was transferred to the Bishop's Palace with the obligation of making it available to the public.

In Cordoba, this Colegio was truly emblematic of the Jesuit manner of teaching as described in the history of teaching, a theory whose effectiveness, so highly praised by some and so reviled by other scholars of teaching, will not be discussed now. The names of several Jesuits have already been mentioned. To those from the 16th century one should add the orientalist Diego Martínez and Ferdinand Pérez, co-founder of the University of Évora.

There are many names, although those that have remained commonly known are Roa and Ruano, who have streets in Cordoba named after them, because of all the Jesuit writers, these are the ones who truly felt most Cordoban. Francisco de Toledo is probably the best of all, but I have seen how he did not think of Cordoba.

One can say that the idea of founding this Colegio was established as early as 1553, although its legal charter is dated 24 February 1554, when it was signed.

Antonio de Córdoba was the first Rector of the Colegio. He was very young, only twenty-six years old and the son of the Marquis of Priego who greatly helped the Compañia. Nonetheless, the institution's great benefactor was Deán Juan Fernández de Córdoba.

The Colegio opened its doors 23 June 1555. Some details of its history can be found in Astram's book. The greatest literary figure it produced was Father Roa, described nevertheless by this modern Jesuit historian as "sickly sweet and affected", unjustly so, in my opinion.

The history, *Memorias de la Compañia* (1543-1741), studied by Astraín in 1900, can be found in a British Institute manuscript.

Other *Colegios*

There was another Colegio in the building that today is San Roque church. Run by the Carmelites, it lasted and shone for some time during the 17th and 18th centuries until it, too, was closed in 1820 with the secularization.

The Augustine religious community, rivals of the Jesuits, was perhaps generally considered the most cultured in Cordoba. It owned one of the good printers in the city and had a pedagogic sense greater than other communities. It was especially interested in Art.

San Pelagio Seminary

The San Pelagio seminary was founded by Bishop Antonio Pazos in 1583, under the provisions of the Council of Trent. The subjects taught there were expanded by order of Cardinal Salazar.

Almost always well attended, from its beginnings in a very modest building, it grew over time. The last building work, including the façade, was done during the 18th century, between 1772 and 1781.

From its founding, students attended classes at the Jesuit Colegio de Santa Catalina until Cardinal Salazar created the chairs of Theology and Art. A bishop whose biography, like that of many others such as Mardones, remains to be written.

It is interesting to note that Sanz del Río was one of its most famous students. Perhaps the most illustrious individuals who began their studies there but did not enter the church were Rey Heredia and Amador de los Rios. Quintana also studied there.

Like a gust from the Renaissance, all forms of disseminating culture were employed in Cordoba during the second half of the 16th century. This explains its 17th century, not that I believe that it was a great century nor that I am being parochial. The great names of Christian Cordoba appear up to the mid-17th century and almost end with Góngora. Their literary credentials were nurtured in the second half of the previous century, precisely during the days of this flourishing of teaching.

That is where we find the tradition of episcopal education, a tradition that ultimately was not the Seminary but rather the new teachings of the Jesuit Order which were launched with such vigor in the Colegio de Santa Catalina and the private Colegio La Asunción, a charitable institution. This charitable element was accentuated in the short-lived Colegio-Refugio de la Paz.

At the beginning, everything was absorbed by the Jesuit Colegio. Patron of the La Asunción (the Assumption), the seminarians attend classes there, it organizes festivals and solemn events, it is the cultural centre of its day. There were even thoughts of turning it into a university.

The founding of the Colegio La Asunción was due in part to the Jesuits who certainly always held the school in high regard. Pedro López de Alba contributed his wealth to its foundation.

The creative spirit, however, belonged to the pious Juan de Avila, whose story has not been written. Even today, all that is known regarding his chapel, considered one of the most beautiful examples of the Cordoban baroque, is that its foundations were laid in 1708. Its sculptures are generally attributed to Duque Cornejo, although the validity of this attribution is questionable.

The 18th century and education

After the foundation of all these establishment, there are no independent cultural movements until the second half of the 18th century.

The *Sociedad de Amigos del País* was founded in Cordoba in 1779, more as a charitable than a cultural institution. It did not possess the typical form of its original patron, at least at the beginning. It is possible that the primary impetus came from Padre Pérez Pavía, a priest and book collector and sometime writer.

The Sociedad published a historical summary of what it had done between 1779 and 1815. In 1823, we see it attacking silkworm breeders and its concern with the well-being of the people. It is also called *Sociedad Patriótica*, but this must not be confused with the *Tertulia Patriótica* of the beginning of the 19th century.

It has already been said that the new era and the new sense of culture during the 18th century is represented here by Bishop Caballero Góngora (1788-1796) who, better than anybody else, protected teaching, especially that of the Fine Arts.

The 18th century stands out for the cultural fervour that marks the second half of the century; it is what is called the era of 'enlightened despotism'. There is a revival, a desire for knowledge and for caring for the people according to the formula that has become famous: Everything for the people and nothing by the people.

It is a period of reforms that in Cordoba coincides with Francisco Fernández de Córdoba's foundation of the Escuelas Pias on the site of the old Colegio de Santa Catalina. The two institutions for women were the Colegio de la Piedad and Colegio Santa Victoria, dating from the end of the 16th century and from 1791, respectively.

The Sociedades Económicas de Amigos del País represent a pedagogic and social reform. Their most productive actions were during the 18th century. They were active in Cordoba as from 1779. They soon gave way to the Cordoban Academia. The Económica was sporadically active and appears ended today. Campomanes, the first Liberal breath in Cordoba, can be considered as the most illustrious and representative of these Sociedades.

Another lay cultural institution is the Academia de Ciencias, Bellas Letras y Nobles Artes, founded in 1811 by the poet and writer, Canon Manuel María de Arjona, as already noted.

The 19th century

There are several different eras in the history of the Academia; generally speaking, it has always been an intellectual home, solely Cordoban, passionate in its love of the city. There are interesting documents in its *Memorias* and it has edited several very interesting publications.

There also was a Free University, founded in 1870, where Angel Torres y Gómez, among others, distinguished himself. He was a very interesting figure in Cordoban jurisprudence. There also was an *Ateneo* that was often created and renewed and last functioned between 1880 and 1890. Our Ateneos have never had a sense of enduring.

Over time, the State created the *Escuelas Normales* and the *Escuela de Veterinaria*.

The Instituto, the Escuela and the Normal were the typical cultural note in Cordoba for seventy year and that which illustrates Cordoba during the 19th century. There was nothing else, except for the *Seminario* - occasionally the latter and its men intermingled in the life of the city - and a rudimentary teaching of arts and trades limited to Drawing.

There remain the efforts of the Academia that, until 1920, did not revive its great initial period and those of individual members. Individuals - and mistrustful, I must say.

The intellectual almost always believes that he is his colleague's rival and not his cooperator. To crush a news item, disprove a date, hide one's sources, criticize poems, all are his greatest of pleasures and sole victory. That, and when possible, fleeing Cordoba. A centrist always, Madrid was or could represent a triumph, to return with acclaimed success. All of this marked the spirit of Cordoban culture. It has no focus, it simply leaves a city that had been dead to thought for many years.

These are the bullfighting years – I am not going to criticize them. Cordoba, as regards the frivolous Spain of the Regency and the minority, was no more than this or that bullfighter. When Cordoba began to also resound with the name of Romero de Torres – those who may dislike his style must recognize this truth – we began to reclaim our own soul. This retrieval, helped by the new times and Spain's introspection in recent years, corresponds to the great generation of 1915 to 1935. Those also were the days when Mateo Inurria fully triumphed.

Spain, today, looks at Cordoba with different eyes. Especially since nobody has written the book of Cordoba. Ortega y Gasset would have done a superb job, as he promised himself that he would, were he to do so.

Cordoba's prestige during the 20th century is undoubtedly greater than it has been since the 16th century, when it was smothered in Andalusia by Seville on the one hand and, like all of Spain, by the insufferable gloom from Madrid on the other.

CHAPTER XXXIII
Dramatic Art

The history of the Theatre in Cordoba is equally interesting as it had to struggle a lot. It evokes the death of Lope de Rueda, in 1565, who is buried in the Cathedral, although where is not exactly known. His sojourn in Cordoba is also very interesting. The documents referring to him in the *Archivo de Protocolos* (Last Will and Testament Archives) have been most useful. Our archives contain considerable information regarding comedians, the theatre and authors of comedies.

Comedies were fiercely persecuted at various times, especially by Padre Francisco Posadas (1644-1713) who, in 1694, managed to get the City Council to agree that there would never be any more comedies and, furthermore, that the theatre should be torn down. This agreement was confirmed by the Council of Castile in 1695.[120]

Later, Fray Diego de Cádiz raged against them in his sermons and frequent visits to our city (1778-1786-1792).

At the Bishop's insistence in 1784, the king, Carlos III, also agreed to the suppression of comedies, decreeing that from then onwards, no comedian shall be permitted to enter the diocese of Cordoba.

Fray Diego, the tenacious persecutor, says so in one of his January 1778 letters: "Since I brought up the question of comedies, they have ended once and for all."[121] That is how matters stood until the French invasion when the ban was lifted.

The list of Cordobans who wrote for the theatre, from Fernán Pérez de Oliva's adaptations of Greek and Latin classics in the 16th century to today, is considerably longer than one would expect:

Roque de Figueroa (16th century and beginning of the 17th), Diego de Aguayo, author of *El Gran Capitán de España*, perhaps the brothers Diego and José Figueroa y Córdoba, Góngora himself with *Las firmezas de Isabela*, and Francisco Delicado, author of *La lozana andaluza*, a dialogue.

However, as far as we know, until the 19th century Cordobans did not produce any play or comedy worth being included in an anthology.

The city again agreed to absolutely prohibit the use and practice of comedies, declaring that they are not allowed, not now or ever again.

That was the end of comedies in Cordoba during three quarters of a century. The theatre was closed and when it fell into ruin, was demolished in 1734. There only were presentations of classical works by students as actors in the Jesuit Colegio.

There is no news of the return of actors until soon after 1769, two generations after they were driven away from Cordoba by Padre Posadas, when they again had to face the tough assault of a great speaker, Fray Diego de Cádiz.

There also was a type of rural theatre in some locations in the Cordoba Sierra. Toboso y Alfano, an Asunción student, speaks of them in 1768. Professor J. M. Camacho has recently published some of these works.

Cotarelo speaks of the Figueroa y Córdoba brothers and praises *La dama capitán*, *La hija del mesonero* and *Mentir y mudarse a un tiempo*, which appear to have been popular in their day (second half of the 17th century).

Except for the outstanding figure of the Duke of Rivas whose great passion gives rise to romantic theatre in Spain with *Don Alvaro o la fuerza del sino*, the

---

[120] *Vide:* Emilio Cotarelo's interesting work: *Controversias de la licitud del Teatro en Espanã* (Madrid, 1904).
[121] J. Torres Asencio, *Vida de Fray Diego de Cádiz* (1894).

remaining Cordoban contributions to dramatic literature cannot be considered of the best quality.

There is Dionisio Solis (1774-1834), better known for his adaptations of classical Spanish theatre, namely *García del Castañar, El rico hombre de Alcalá,* among others, than for his original work.

When mentioning Solis, I must also point out that he is the only Cordoban poet, in addition to the Duque de Rivas, produced by the 18th century. He writes romances that Góngora would not hesitate to claim as his own. Hartzenbusch praises his great culture and his tenacity as a self-taught individual. His improved translations of Italian poets show him to be an artist. He is another forgotten Cordoban who deserves to be studied.

Music

Music in Cordoba deserves a few lines of its own, although Averroes' saying is commonplace: "When a wise man dies, his books are sold in Cordoba; but if he is a musician, his books end up in Seville."

The Arabs cultivated music with fondness and a great many compositions believed to be typically Andalusian, owe their origin to them. They had their experts and essayists, such as Faradjí, who wrote the *Grán colección de tonos,* and Farabí, author of *Elementos de la Música.*

The most noted modern musician from Cordoba, however, is Ferdinand de las Infantas, born in 1534, in the middle of the great era, who has no reason to envy the great Hispanic composers. He travels a great deal, especially in Italy. He participates with great success in the renovation of the Gregorian chant and later, when he is older, becomes a minor theologian, although he preaches little.[122]

The music chapel of our Cathedral acquired some fame and one can name many of its teachers and organists. During the second half of the 19th century, Cordoban music enjoyed a period of splendour and promised great things. Eduardo Lucena, extremely inspired and very private, should also not be forgotten. This supremely aesthetic trend later appeared to become limited.

During the last years of the 19th century and the beginning of the 20th, Cipriano Martínez Rucker was more technical and more artistic, although when he isolated himself in Cordoba, he exhausted his temperament as a great composer and maestro.

---

[122] Rafael Mitjana, his biographer – *Don Ferdinand de las Infantas, teólogo y músico* (Madrid, 1918) – says that as a composer, *de las Infantas* should be listed as one of the finest in our country. A fine work, executed with all the technical rigor one would expect today, is *La Capilla de música de la Catedral de Córdoba en el siglo XVI,* by Mitjana, illustrious critic and researcher.

We owe Ferdinand de las Infantas' biography and that of others related to him, to J. Latorre. Julián Rivera's works regarding Arab music are also of revindicating and even sentimental interest to Cordoba.

Lucena lived only from his inspiration, he was intuitive. Rucker, who had formal training, did not get involved in the great conferences as he could have.

Popular song and dance

The names recalled here do not illustrate the musical panorama nor the past, which produced many excellent organists and composers of religious music, which only Mitjana has begun to research. A research that appears to be almost unknown in the Cordoba Cathedral.

There is another facet, the genuinely popular. Now that the guitar has taken on a higher esthetic category than previously enjoyed, the great guitarists should be rescued from oblivion.

With them also, folk music, which has produced no outstanding representatives in Cordoba, compared with other musical provinces in Spain. In this respect, furthermore, the city appears almost erased from what we could call the Hispanic musical map. Nevertheless, unique and very beautiful musical nuances emerge in the provinces.

In addition to the visual physical landscape, with its three different features: mountains, rivers and countryside, there is an auditory landscape which also belongs to culture and to emotions. Today it is sought not only for its intrinsic beauty, but as a psychological and historical study, as accurate as any document, with which to fully understand the soul of a city.

It exists in Cordoba and then spreads to the land in the South, in the same way that it huddles amongst the canyons in the North, such as in the Pedroches Valley, across the somewhat irregular administrative boundary. Cordoba boasts at least three provinces in one, better expressed as three great natural boroughs, whose spirit flows into the city.

These features remain unstudied by those who could have done so. An example of this, although somewhat beyond the limits of this book, is the Cordoban *saeta*. Does it not possess a serene singularity, is it not an authentic lament that differentiates it from all the others in Andalusia? What about the songs from the mountains? Are they something that arrived with the Reconquista? At times the mountain appears to be revived or one hears the sounds of La Rioja on the border with Navarra. Or is it that the songs were preserved here and are not coming, but going (or went) Northwards?

Are there no elements of border ballads in the countryside, which like the river flows towards Seville, or in the hilly and rugged South that is more focused on Granada? That is what I would call them, as I think of the Romances that gathered in those regions.

As another example, I believe that I heard the 15th century *El enfardelar judíos*, published several times, the last time by Rivera, in a popular song in Iznájar. Those who know and do not just feel may find some value in these suggestions.

Biographies

This subject is also of interest. There are listings in the *Guía Bibliográfica* of many ancient and some almost current biographies. Have these been further developed? It is difficult and, to an extent, dangerous to generalize. For a biography to be a living document, one must know the the subject's historic time as much as his personal time and rhythm.

The old Cordoban biographies all initially date back to the 17th century and they are centred on the Morales and on Vaca de Alfaro's *Varones ilustres*. This 68-page manuscript, so frequently mentioned by earlier essayists but barely described, is simply a July 1770 copy by Vázquez Venegas whose mark in the research is more extensive than it appears, of a 257 folios quarto book in Vaca de Alfaro's handwriting: "the original of which is kept among the manuscripts in my office." Díaz de Ayora's copy of Venegas' copy is kept in the Colombina.

It appears, therefore, that Vaca de Alfaro was the individual who ploughed the widest furrow across Cordoban biographies. His work is very uneven. Few dates and occasionally this or that poem.

His only somewhat lengthier studies are of Juan de Mena, Gonzalo de Ayora, Juan de Castilla y Aguayo, Luis de Góngora and Enrique Vaca de Alfaro the elder.

These are the fifty-five biographies by Vaca de Alfaro:

1. Juan de Mena
2. Gonzalo de Ayora y Córdoba
3. Pedro Tafur
4. Rodrigo de Queto
5. Alonso Guajardo
6. Fray Gregorio de Alfaro, Benedictine
7. Rev. Ferdinand de las Infantas
8. Fray Petro de Soto, Dominican
9. Ferdinand Cívico de Montemayor
10. Gonzalo Gómez de Luque
11. Juan de Castilla y Aguayo
12. Hernán Pérez de Oliva
13. *Licenciado*[xxviii] Pedro de Valle
14. Juan Rufo
15. Dr. Luís de Sanllorente
16. Antonio de Córdoba y Lara

17. Dr. Juan Ginés de Sepúlveda
18. *Licenciado* Juan Bautista Navarrete
19. Sebastián de León
20. Andrés de Angulo
21. Ferdinand de Córdoba
22. Pedro Viedma
23. Luis Cabrera de Córdoba
24. *Licenciado* Pedro Cabrera, Geronimian
25. *Licenciado* Benito Daza de Valdés
26. Dr. Gaspar López Serrano
27. Fray Miguel Muñoz, Carmelite
28. Luis de la Vega
29. Alonso Carrillo Laso de Guzmán
30. *Licenciado* Martín Alonso del Pozo
31. *Licenciado* Juan Páez de Valenzuela
32. *Licenciado* Antonio de Paredes
33. Andrés López de Robles
34. Alonso Carrillo Lasso
35. Andrés Pérez de Ribas
36. Fray Martín de Córdoba, Augustinian
37. Fray Alonso de Córdoba, Augustinian
38. Luis Carrillo Sotomayor
39. Luis de Góngora y Argote
40. *Licenciado* Henrique Vaca, the elder
41. Dr. Gonzalo del Alamo
42. Dr. Pedro Díaz de Rivas
43. Francisco Fernández de Córdoba
44. Francisco de Leiva y Aguilar
45. Pedro de Cárdenas y Angulo
46. Andrés Ponce de Léon
47. Pedro Ruiz Montero
48. Dr. Enrique Vaca
49. *Licenciado* Pedro González Recio
50. Francisco Carrillo de Córdoba
51. Fray Juan de Rivas Carrillo
52. Pedro de Blanca
53. Fray Luís de la Santísima Trinidad
54. *Licenciado* Luís de la Vega
55. Dr. Andrés de Pitillas

CHAPTER XXXIV
Architecture in Cordoba – First Group

The artistic prestige of Cordoba has always, and quite rightly, been attributed to the uniqueness of the Mesquita. Nonetheless, all the peoples who passed through this city have left some trace of their passage and we need to point this out in this brief description.

Cordoban architecture is best understood if it is divided into two large groups:

1. Architecture prior to the conquest of Cordoba by Castile, i.e., pre-Roman, Roman, Visigoth and Arab.
2. Strictly speaking Christian architecture.

Prehistoric remains

Regarding what is currently described as prehistoric peoples, nothing more is known about their houses or industry[123] within the Cordoba municipal boundaries, other than that which is mentioned at the beginning of this book.

Roman

There exist remainders of the wall that encircled the city, beginning in front of the La Salud Cemetery and the corner of the Old Alcazar, as far as beyond the Puerta de Almodóver city gate, a bit in the Tejares neighbourhood and the Calle San Ferdinand. Without a doubt and despite the controversy regarding certain ruins, the wall was originally built by the Romans, retouched during the Arabic reconstruction and with later Christian additions.

There are remains of the authentic Arabic wall from the Marrubial barracks to the wall of the Misericordia, mostly in ruins.[124]

As regards the bridge, it is both customary and traditional to say that it is Roman. It was undoubtedly built by the Romans, but it has since undergone many later alterations as time and use have required. The remaining foundations are Roman but there are evident traces of all the later periods. The last repairs

---

[123] Regarding the Iberians, already a protohistoric people, and others that appeared before the Romans, the chapter on Sculpture briefly describes some artworks that can be attributed to them.

[124] Cordoba has been totally devastated and, as far as Art is concerned, has been entirely abandoned and unloved by Man as it suffers the ravages of time. There is no Spanish city with a greater artistic heritage, where the most civilized roots of the Peninsula were centred and where the least number of traces are preserved, considering the proportion concerned. It was somewhat unusual for children in our schools to be taught to love Art.

to the bridge deprived it of all its character.[125]

The sections of the walls I just pointed out and part of the bridge are the only architectural remainders from the days of the Romans whose authenticity is indisputable.

Cordoban archaeologists and historians have spoken of the great Roman buildings in Cordoba and how they were distributed around the town; aside from some beautiful capitals and pieces of columns that attest to the grandeur of the past, nothing is left but a memory.

Visigoth architecture

It has always been believed that there are Visigoth architectural remains and fragments in Cordoba, magnificent examples of which are the column capitals in the earliest section of the Mesquita. Regarding architecture, none until Gómez Moreno brought up the question of the survival of a great part of the Visigoth façade next to one of the doors on the eastern side of the Mesquita. This subject has impassioned many and has only been sustained by this archaeologist's authority.

Be that as it may, one must sincerely say that the opinion is weighty and must not be disdained nor discarded as a matter of course.

I believe that the same essayist attributes the architectural remains next to the Seville gate to the Visigoths. There is no unanimous opinion in this respect, and it appears that local essayists consider that they are the remains of a 14th century watch tower.

The discovery of some burial sites in Salud cemetery itself, have led some to conclude that this was the Visigoth necropolis.[126]

Arab Architecture. The Mesquita

The Arab Mesquita has been described innumerable times. We are still waiting, however, for a concise study of the entire construction: the mosque and its addition, the Christian Cathedral.[127]

---

[125] The arguments regarding the bridge have been summarized and judged in the fine work by Blázquez y Delgado-Aguilera - See *El Puente romano de Córdoba, Boletín Academia de la Historia*, 1914. There have been, however, a few small studies since then. In truth, there is nothing Roman about the bridge today. Very little of the Arabic and almost all is Cristian art and work. The locals still call it the Julius Caesar Bridge. Nevertheless, the study of works contemporary with Caesar, the description and dates of his campaigns, lead one to believe that there was no such bridge in his days and that it must have been built later by Emperor Augustus.

[126] *Nuevas antigüedades visigodas*. Academia de la Historia 1909. Enrique Romero de Torres.

[127] The concise work, a bit old, that best summarizes all that refers to the Arab part is *La Mesquita Aljama*, by M. Sentenach. There also is a brief history *La Mesquita-Catedral de Córdoba*, by Romero Barros (Academia de San Ferdinand, 1884). To this we add the third volume of Ramirez de Arellano's *Historia de Córdoba*.

The Mesquita was built by the Arabs for two fundamental reasons: religious need and political convenience. Abderramán I, creator of the independence of Arab Spain, founded it in 785 AD, although he did not live to see it completed. It was inaugurated by his son Hixem I in 793AD, that is, in the 177th year of the Hegira.

The poets sang this event. Since then, Arab and Christian travellers and poets and people of all races have praised its grandeur; this is why they said: "The gold on your ceilings shines like a lightning bolt that crosses the clouds…"

Arab history says, and the Christians later accepted it, that the Mesquita was built over the ruins of a Christian Basilica.

The Mesquita is not the work of a single man; better still, it is the work of an entire race. As Cordoba grew, all the caliphs increased its grandeur.

There are four clear architectural periods in the Mesquita:

First. The initial work (785-793) by Abderramán I, when by adding the covered area and patio, the Mesquita becomes totally square-shaped, with its main door on the northern side, the entrance to the patio. Within, eleven grand arches led the way to the eleven naves of the covered area (the middle nave was the widest).

This is the oldest construction, for which they used Roman and Visigoth columns and capitals, creating a lovely effect that was like a museum.

Second. Abderramán II extends the Mesquita southwards towards the river, increasing the number of arches to twenty, almost doubling the area for prayers (833 to 848), the *el dhamir.*

Third. Al-Haquem II, during the most magnificent period of the Caliphate, extends it again, also southwards. He does not remove the outer wall enclosing Abderramán II's Mesquita but opens it with eleven arches and extending the naves, adding thirteen columns to each row. The Mesquita assumed the shape of an extremely prolonged rectangle (964 to 965).

Abderramán III also left his mark on the Mesquita, reinforcing the northern wall that was having difficulties retaining the building, a reinforcement that is obvious in the construction.

The extremely famous *mihrab*[xxix] was built during the days of Al-Haquem, an extension directed by the architect Motharrif-Abderramán. Curious graphics with the names of the Arab artists who worked on this building ten centuries ago are preserved in the columns.[128]

---

[128] These two sections of the Mesquita are the most genuinely Arab; in the second, Abderraman's extension, we saw how the Arab artists created their own style, whilst in Al-Haquem's building work, the magnificence of this unique creation demonstrates caliphal art in all its splendour.

In those days, Cordoba and Constantinople were the only shining lights in the world, the two sole centres of civilization. For political reasons, Cordoba had received embassies from the Byzantine emperors since the beginning of the 9th century.

Constantine VI sent a magnificent embassy to Abderramán III and from then onwards, they enjoyed a closer relationship. In Cordoba, Abderramán II received artists and scientists from Constantinople. The admirable decoration of the Mihrab, produced by Greco-Byzantine artists, testifies to this relationship and is the only documented example of genuine Byzantine Art in Spain.

Fourth. The expansion that occurs under Almanzor, Hishem II's hágib. The building could only now be extended eastwards, although this would destroy the symmetry of the building and leave the main door off-centre. Great arches were opened in the Eastern wall and eight naves were added (987).

Almanzor's expansion does not strengthen the walls. The marks of his extension are also clearly visible. The old doors of the first Mesquita, on the western wall, are now inside the building and although somewhat worn, some are clearly evident.

Expanding the Mesquita increased the amount of space left in the last nave (northern wall), but this did not quite line up with the nave that it was extending. To resolve the problem, two arches were built to create the effect of a pier. However, because this was done in a smaller space, it resulted in the swollen pointed arch that has drawn so much attention. According to the experts, this was not the result of an arbitrary or purely aesthetic creation, but of a building necessity.

The later reconstructions are much less important, even so they all added something: the Almohades added the Perdón façade.[129]

Almanzor's contribution was more trivial, with indications of decadence and simplification, haste and less attention to details.

The entire building formed a rectangle measuring 179 metres x 129 metres, encompassing an area of more than 23,000 square metres.[130]

The wall that surrounds the building, whose conception clearly shows an Assyrian-Persian influence, is braced with towers and buttresses. The southern

---

[129] There have been innumerable discussions regarding the Villaviciosa chapel: some call it Almohade (Berber) which others believe it was built by the Arabs (10th century) and decorated in the Mudejar style by Enrique II; others state that it was built entirely during his reign. *Vide:* Amador de los Ríos *La capilla de Villaviciosa en la catedral de Córdoba,* R. *España,* and volume III of the *Historia de Arellano,* examples of widely diverse opinions.

[130] Arab authors have often described it; Velázquez states that Al-makari's reports are pure fantasy; in exchange, he considers that Abben-Adzari's, who must have seen it just before the Christian conquest, are very accurate.

wall is the strongest, as it has to bear the entire forward weight of the building. It is believed that the door that led to Abderramán's *maqsura*^{xxx} was in this wall. It was also the wall that has suffered the most from the Christian alterations.

The entire wall is surrounded with battlements, of which only a few in the shape of a fleur-de-lys in the area that corresponds to the atrium are believed to be modern. Not all the battlements are the same.

The interior consisted of 19 naves from north to south, and 35 naves from east to west.

The exact number of columns has never been established. Today, it is believed that there are 856 free columns. There is no doubt that in its day, there were more than 1,000 columns. The shafts vary a great deal, and their capitals are admirably rich; in some, we can detect traces of polychrome. In the old days it was believed that there were no foundations for the columns. Although simple, all the columns in the original Mesquita had foundations and they are visible today.

The original ceiling in the Mesquita was a coffered ceiling covered in sculptured arabesques (great beams connecting thick boards). It appears that the floor, despite fantastic descriptions, was covered in small red tiles, probably like the ones that served as the source of the colour the builders wanted for the arches. Later, it has been proven that the Mesquita had an earthen floor during the time of the Arabs and that tiled floors were only introduced in the 16th century.

Coat of arms on Santa Catalina gate in the Cathedral.
4th edition of Historia de Córdoba, 1971

Another coat of arms on the west gate to the cathedral, facing northwest towards Calle de la Encarnación, shows the tower as it must have been at the time of the first Christian alteration and before the addition of the third element and with the little "bonnet" which was carried away by a storm and made the present modification necessary.

The minaret, or tower, built by Abderramán III, was 16 metres tall and had 14 mullioned windows.[131] its original shape is shown on the shield on the Puerta de Santa Catalina in the cathedral.

That was the marvelous Mesquita, the one with the twenty-one doors and ten thousand lamps, which according to certain hyperbolic authors, illuminated it on great days. Oil was first used in the lamps and later, wax.

The Arabs consider that the classic candelabra is the one that hung from the cupola of the vestibule of the mihrab, and which contained 1,054 glass lamps in various colours.

After the Mesquita and the city walls, there really are no more traces of Arab architecture in Cordoba, except for some baths on Calle Céspedes and others on Calle Rubio, both of which were earlier called Calle del Baño. These have almost totally disappeared.

As regards remains of Arab constructions and the countless palaces that they owned, today we are beginning to know something of the grandeur and many times incredible Medina-ah Azahara, where there are ongoing excavations.[132]

On one of his trips to Cordoba, Mohidin, a poet from Murcia at the end of the 12th century, wrote some touching verses on Medina-Azahara, whose ruins he said had become a mansion for vermin.

We must not forget the beautiful, though greatly changed, Santa Clara minaret, and the recent discovery of the minaret in San Juan church.

According to Velázquez Bosco, there were three stages in the life of Medina-Azahara: Abderraman's construction, between 936 and 961, Al-Haquem II's work from 961 to 976, and lastly, until the fall of the caliphate in 1031.

---

[131] After the conquest, the Christians changed it, adding a spire. Destroyed by an earthquake in 1585, the City Council ordered that it should be rebuilt in 1589 and work began in 1593, directed by Hernán Ruiz the younger, that is the third Ruíz in that dynasty. He was followed by Juan Ochoa and concluded by Juan Hidalgo in 1664. It has remained unchanged to this date, except for some retouches during the 18th century.

A summary of this can be found in the article *Sello de Córdoba en el siglo XIV*, by Ramírez de Are lano. (Excursiones, 1892).

[132] "Apuntes para la historia monumental de Córdoba durante la dominación musulmana", R. Amador de los Ríos, *Revista España,* 1885.

Medina Azahara y Alamiriya, Ricardo Velázquez Bosco. Madrid, 1912.

Los Alcázares musulmanes de Córdoba. R. Ramírez de Arellano, Vol. XIII. (Sociedade Españcla de excursiones.)

Excursión por la España árabe, L. Mª Cabello, (Vol. VIII, idem).

Más sobre Medina-Azahara, N. Sentenach, (Vol. XIII, idem).

R. Amador de los Ríos. *Inscripciones árabes de Córdoba.*

As a joint summary, *La civilización árabe y sus monumentos en España*, Gómez Moreno. (Octavo curso internacional comercial), Barcelona, 1914.

Medina-Azahara was sacked by the Africans in 1009, by the people of Cordoba in 1010, and after some feeble attempts to restore it, pillaged again in 1025, which rapidly led to its decline and subsequent disappearance.[133]

The Mozarabic. Is there anything left?

The several histories of Cordoba, especially the books by San Eulogio and Abbott Sansón and Bishop Recemundo's Calendar, speak of San Vicente church, of the Basilica, of Fausto, Januario and Marcial, San Cipriano and Santa María churches believed to be inside the city, and other churches in the slums and outlying districts.

The ferocious 9th century persecutions demolished the monasteries outside the city and mutilated the churches. As we gather from the document entitled *España sagrada*, Volume V, chapter V, Santa Maria Church still existed during the last days of Mozarabic Spain.

When speaking of Cordoba, Pedro Madrazo sees important Mozarabic traces in the layout and ornamentation of present-day parishes churches.

Lampérez says that his conclusion regarding the layout appears correct, which is the same today, but not as regards aspects of constructions and ornamentation which are well-known as being in the Romantic style of the transition.

The Visigothic

Another matter is the case of San Vicente church, the original Visigoth cathedral, apparently built during the 6th century.

The Christians claimed it as their own until 748 AD when they were forced to cede half of it to the Arab invaders. Although separated, both the victors and the defeated worshiped under the same roof. There was nothing new to such an unusual custom. Alma-Karl attributed it to the advice of Caliph Omar who, after conquering Syria, did the same in Damascus and in Emesa.

In 748, however, that is seventy-three years after its joint possession by Arabs and Christians, the latter were dislodged by Abderramán I who purchased their half and built the Mesquita on the site.

It appears that the original Mesquita was already built in 786. Several Arab authors say that it was not in the Emir's plan to create a new building but to take advantage of the Christian one which itself was quite sumptuous.

Some say that the Arabs did nothing more than dismantle the five naves in the larger basilica and rebuild them with a new orientation, thereby using almost all the materials and even leaving some untouched.

---

[133] In Velázquez's Memoria, 1923, there is a kind of summary, later expanded with great care by the local Committee, especially Hernández and Castejón, that has continued the excavations and research of the site.

The principal façade of the basilica remained as a side wall of the Mesquita, and it remains so to this day. This opinion is defended by Gómez Moreno who in fact first advanced it.

CHAPTER XXXV
Architecture in Cordoba
Second group – Christian architecture

Arab Art set an indelible stamp on Cordoba and every building reflects this influence and gives character to the city.

This is the architecture that has been built from the 13th century to this day. All the styles that have marked Spain, within the general history of Art, are represented. First, however, a general word of warning: it is almost impossible to find a building with a pure style. All have endured renovations, every era has left a clear indication of its artistic feeling, and although originally they may be attributed to a specific period, it is difficult to classify them exactly.

The Cathedral - the Christian part of the Mesquita.

At the beginning it appears that some of the building was respected. Later, the needs of the worship, very often the whims, least often the artistic sense of the conqueror, began a barely interrupted series of profanations.

During the second half of the 13th century, Bishop Mesa converted the space in the middle of the central nave into the main chapel, the one that was later named the Villaviciosa Chapel, and decorated it with paintings.

During the second half of the 13th century, Bishop Mesa converted the space in the middle of the central nave, the *luminario*, into the main chapel, later named Villaviciosa Chapel, and decorated it with paintings.

In 1371, Enrique II founded, or simply decorated, the San Ferdinand chapel, creating a masterpiece of 14th century Arab art, comparable to parts of the Alcazar in Seville or the Alhambra in Granada. In 1377, the same king had the Puerta del Perdón façade decorated in the same manner.

In 1489, the spacious nave that formed the first Christian transept was created under Bishop Iñigo Manriques. Three Arab arches wide, it went from the Villaviciosa chapel to the Western wall. Vicente Lampérez believes that the reconstruction of this nave is considerably older than Bishop Iñigo's, perhaps as early as the 14th century. He says that the ceiling of this nave is an exotic example of artistic carpentry in Spain. He suggests totally unusual, probably English, influences.

The era of great artistic profanation arrives soon afterwards. Since the 13th century, Spain had peopled itself with gothic cathedrals. Leon, Toledo and Burgos, as typical examples, had built their marvellous churches. Gothic Art, however, was already declining, overwhelmed as it was by the Renaissance, and they were only building in the gothic style. Cordoba Church Council, perhaps resentful of the competition and of Seville's obsession with its cathedral, also dating to the end of the Gothic era, desired a cathedral that was not Arab. Thus, following a proposal from Bishop Alonso Manrique, construction on a new main chapel was agreed to 22 July 1521 and work began in 1523.

The city, the Council and the Mayor, all the populace, were firmly opposed to the new work. Together they declared that no one should dare touch the building, nor work on anything in it, because it could not be redone with the care and perfection with which it was built. They protested in vain, and the building work continued.

Once the construction work which occupied all the 16th century was completed, it was the Church Council's task to decorate and furnish the main chapel, which it did during the 17th century and part of the 18th.

The rich marble and bronze main altar was built from 1614 to 1628 by Alonso Matías, Juan Aranda and Luís González. The tabernacle was completed in 1653, the stalls date from 1753 and the pulpits from 1766. Some beautiful carvings and sculptures of great ornamental beauty adorn the vault in the chancel and although more beautiful than those in the transept and choir; none are ornate enough to arouse any great admiration.

The chapels

However, as one sees after a simple inspection of the Mesquita, the transept was not the only Christian addition as additional chapels began to be built from the beginning. The *Conquistadores* funded the first one, San Clemente chapel. Afterwards, there was not a noble family, not a wealthy prebendary, not a restoration-inclined bishop who did not decide to fund yet another chapel and soon the Mesquita was almost always populated with inartistic Christian chapels. [134]

---

[134] These are described in some detail, although some rectifications are required, in *Descripción de la Iglesia Catedral de Córdoba* by Luis María Ramírez-Casas Deza, 1886.

Before the stalls by Duque Cornejo, the present ones, there were other seatings. What where they like? There is no specific data. Some suggest that Lucas Navarro used some wood from the old seats to fashion the lectern in 1593. The stalls in La Concepción chapel were ordered by Bishop Alonso Medina y Salizanes, in 1682, and those in Santa Teresa or that of Cardinal Salazar, concluded in 1703.

The vaults that cover the original Arabic ceilings today date to the 18th century, but it was well into the 19th century before the value of the Mesquita became apparent and people began to respect it and also do a bit of restoration. Bishop Trevilla began it in 1826 and it was continued by Albuquerque and Fray Ceferino González. The State later took charge of the restoration of the Mesquita after it was declared a national monument.

In the minds of many, the Cathedral has suffered several unfortunate dates: the first Christian work in 1260, in 1489 and most especially, in 1523. This was followed by disastrous 1713 when the original coffered ceilings in the Mesquita were covered over with lathes of wood and plaster. Today, the care and the restoration of the Mesquita have continued during the 20th century under the excellent management of architect Velázquez Bosco.

Numerous local and foreign artists worked in the Cathedral chapels and on the building itself. Among these, painters César Arbasia and Pedro Campaña and Orta, a Flemish artist, in the Tabernacle in 1578.

Especially noteworthy, Pedro Campaña, also Flemish (1503-1580), left numerous works of art in the chapels of the nave of the Sagrario (Concepción and San Nicolás chapels). The critics attribute the Coronation of the Virgin altar piece to 1558. His principal works are in Seville. He had a considerable influence on 16th century Andalusian painting.

There have been recent studies of the Cathedral tower. The reconstruction that gave the building its present style was undertaken by several architects. Special note is made of Hernán Ruiz's work on the Giralda in 1593. Hernán Ruiz did not finish it all, however. Another architect, Juan Sequero, worked on it in 1617 and it appears that despite some minor alterations, the tower did not achieve its present state until 1664.

Villaviciosa chapel in the Mesquita-Cathedral[xxxi]

CHAPTER XXXVI
Architecture from the 13th to the 15th centuries
Predominance of ogives

Having, superficially studied the Cathedral, as befits this book, we shall now look at the other monuments, classifying them in order to make them easier to understand.

Bear in mind that the art of the ogive – the pointed Gothic arch – predominates from the 13th to the 15th centuries. The Renaissance begins in the 16th century and in Spain it consists of three styles: the plateresque; the Herrerian, classical or in the manner of the Escorial; and the baroque or churrigueresque. They span the 16th and 17th centuries. In the 18th century, there is a kind of Renaissance called neoclassicism. We recall that the 19th century has no characteristic style of its own. All styles are imitated, and the only novelty is the use of a new material, iron, which modifies constructions.

The Cordoba churches

The original Cordoba churches are all very noteworthy. Tradition had it that all had previously been Mozarabic, that is, built by Christians who lived in Cordoba during the Arab dominion. It is possible that some were built on the same sites, but there is not even a trace of that so unique and attractive past in the present-day churches.

All belong to a period of transition, in which Romanesque Art disappears and gives way to the Gothic during the second half of the 13th century.

Their façades, with slightly pointed arches, are in a simple Romanesque style, an art brought by the conquistadores. Lampérez classifies them as belonging to the Romanesque-Ogival-Mudejar group, which is indicative of the merging trends. Their Mudejar style is archaic and severe, differentiating itself from the more filigreed previous style.

San Pablo Church

Perhaps the first in terms of age and without a doubt, the most interesting church in Cordoba after the Cathedral.

In 1241, Ferdinand III cedes the land for the building of the church. It was likely completed at the end of the 13th century and is located in an area of great architectural traditions, over an Almohad palace which itself was built over a

Roman building that, although it cannot be identified today, is generally believed to have been an amphitheatre.

Inside, it still preserves an enclosure with an Arab ribbed vault. The Romanesque features in its architecture remind one of Poblet monastery and the beginning of the Cistercian school.

Built in 1537, its perfectly preserved ceiling of decorative knots is a beautiful example of Mudejar carpentry. All the architectural styles that formed a period in the general history of Art and in local history have left their mark and traces of their work, from the existing Roman columns to the most modern restorations. This adds value to its importance and makes it unique.[135]

Santa Marina Church

Founded in the 13th century, it later suffered some truly awful restoration. The bell tower dates from the 16th century. It has a very beautiful central apse from the original period, and it likely has a 13th century coffered ceiling in the central nave that has been covered over. Outside, the doors retain the slightly pointed Romanesque arches; this is particularly evident on the Puerta del Evangelio.

San Lorenzo Church

It is possible that the first half of the tower is all that remains as an authentic example of Mozarabic construction. The façades of the present church date from the 13th century, the transition of the Romanesque to the Gothic, and it is adorned with a most beautiful ogival rose window. The transept was built in 1517.

Although greatly neglected, it is one of the finest churches in Cordoba. "Completed in the year 1555", says the inscription on the rosette.

There are three doors on the outside. The one that opens below the portico is very beautiful and has since been restored and has recovered all its beauty. During the 1960s, this temple enjoyed a major restoration: its walls were uncovered, its

---

[135] This is why Master Lampérez says that it is "the most archaic of the Reconquista, the most complete and the one that best enables one to determine the nature of Cordoban architecture of those days". *Historia de la arquitectura cristiana en la Edad Media española,* 1918.

San Pablo is built upon an Almohad palace, which in turn was erected over a large Roman building. Of this palace, there remains an enclosure with an Arab knotted wood ribbed vault and various capitals that were put to good use in the church.

Juan de Ochoa, a great architect, built the church cloister, which no longer exists. There is also mention of a lay monk, Fray Antonio de Herrera, who was active during the 18th century. Rosario chapel, one of his additions (1401), is interesting, as is the altar, reminiscent of the Carthusian Monastery in Granada, and the most opulent example of baroque in Cordoba. In 1601, Ochoa also built the first theatre on Calle de las Comedias in Cordoba.

vaults were cleaned, revealing stunning paintings, and its primitive gothic state was restored. In 1963, on the occasion of the Centenary of Abend Hazem, the church was associated with the mosque in the Abul Moguira quarter.

Other churches

- *San Pedro* – Retains nothing prior to the Conquista. There still remain the apses and two 13th century façades, as well as some ogival gates from the 15th century in the main chapel.[136]
- *Santiago* – Dating from the 13th century, the principle and original façade in the old Calle del Claustro is a beautiful façade with a rosette. The church has been very badly treated and deserves to be restored.
- *La Magdalena* – Of the same period as the previous churches, the details of which are particularly visible from outside only because, like almost all churches in Cordoba, it underwent considerable reconstruction during the 17th century.
- *San Miguel* – Built at the end of the 13th century, only a portion of the original building remains outside. The façade is very similar, if not the same, as Santa Maria's, and there is a well-preserved lovely rosette that we will speak of later.
- *San Francisco* – Only the apse remains of the original 13th century building.
- *San Nicolás de la Villa* - Only the main façade facing San Nicolás square remains. The gothic church has a square apse on the outside, a typical feature of our churches. Its magnificent chapel is plateresque. It is said to date to 1554 and is attributed to Hernán Ruíz. Other authors are not so sure. It is unique in that it boasts the queen of Cordoban towers. Certainly, there are remains of its original coffered ceiling, as in Santiago and in almost all original churches that were built soon after the Conquista.
- In this original group we must include the *Capilla del Hospital*, which has been at the root of interesting discussions. This chapel is all that remains of the San Bartolomé hermitage that was merged with the Hospital. The horseshoe arch and the remains of columns and capitals, in addition to its lovely, tiled decorations, have created a splendid jewel with several artistic styles, although its beginning dates from the end of the 13th century. It has also been restored.

---

[136] The Cathedral and San Pedro have always been churches of great prestige. San Pedro is traditionally known for its antiquity, the invention of the martyrs (16th century). Like all, it deserves a special study and essay of its own.

When in 1772, Carlos III manages to cut down on the number of asylum seekers in the churches, refuges for delinquents, the only churches that retained this privilege were the Cathedral and San Pedro.

Next, we have the following:

- *Santa Marta* – One of the 15th century churches that have suffered little or nothing. Completed in 1470, its main gate, a gothic arch of the last period although not excessively adorned, is one of the most beautiful arches of its kind in the city.
- That which was *Regina* church, completed at the end of the 15th century, and still has a beautiful, coffered ceiling.
- *Santa Cruz* – established in 1435.
- *San Hipólito* – Begun during the 14th century, it retains its ogival nave from its first period, although its apse has suffered several alterations, such as its fleur-de-lys adorned façade.
- Perhaps the only thing that remains of *San Augustín*, initially built during the 14th century, is the apse.
- A few arched windows are all that remains of the *Bishop's Palace* on Campo de los Mártires
- The *Caridad* Church façade is a simple example of gothic art.
- That which once was the *San Jerónimo monastery*, admirably located on the hills above Cordoba, was also in this style and from this period. It was lucky that when it was about to be lost, it was restored with exceptional care and affection. It boasts a simple façade and a totally intact, very beautiful gothic cloister, the finest in Cordoba.

16th Century

- *San Jerónimo*'s foundation first dates back to 1408. It has gone through different architectural styles, of which the finest, the cloister and the patio, are from the 16th century.
- The description of this monastery's history appears in *Historia de la Orden de San Jerónimo* by Padre José Sigüenza and continues in the work of Padre Santos.[137]
- Pedro Madrazo published the first article written after its secularization in *Semanario Pintoresco*. Padre De Arellano continued this in *Boletín Excurcionistas*, as did Antonio Jaén Morente in his doctoral thesis.[xxxii]
- The *San Jacinto* church façade is built somewhat tardily, in 1572, as ogival art was gradually giving way everywhere to the invasive momentum of the Renaissance. It is the most attractive example of the florid Gothic art in Cordoba and already exhibits the influence of the new art of the period: the plateresque. The new art begins to make its influence felt.

---

[137] Ms. Escorial.

- *La Compañia* is from this period. It belongs to the so-called Greco-Roman style, a dry and sober art. Probably the work of the Jesuit Juan de Bustamante, it is built from 1564 to 1589 and paid for by its Dean, Fernández de Córdoba. Alonso Matías, another Jesuit architect who also worked there, died in 1629.
- It boasts a magnificent staircase and a patio somewhat in the style of the Escorial. The architect of both of these is unknown. The staircase, given the materials used and its drawings, could be by Alonso, although this remains to be resolved. It is one of the monumental Spanish staircases.
- *San Augustín* – 16th century façade decorated in in the plateresque style, covered with paintings.
- Façade of *San Pedro* – Built in 1542 and an example of the Renaissance style, too strong, unattractive, and lacking any possible beauty.
- *Carmen Calzado* (Puerta Nueva). The church dates from 1580. Beautiful, coffered ceiling reminiscent of the one in *Jesús Crucificado* church, built in the same style in 1588 with a single wide nave.

17th century

The sober Greco-Roman style that left its magnum opus in Spain in the Escorial Monastery, appears to have set the pace. There are four religious buildings in Cordoba in which it is represented.

- *San Cayetano* begins the century. Although devoid of any unique architectural feature, the building was completed in 1614, at the same time as the church of the Trinitarians, established in 1607 and known as *Los Padres de Gracia*.
- This is followed by *Fuentesanta*, founded in the 15th century. Other than a small well, very little remains from that period. The present church dates from 1640 and is perhaps inferior ascompared to the former.
- *San Pedro de Alcantara*, concluded in 1699, ends the century with a polychrome effect - a black façade, built by Luís de Rojas and Baltasar de los Reyes.
- The *Corpus* is also built at the beginning of the 17th century

18th century

This is an unfortunate century regarding architecture and, generally speaking, all the arts as the end of the previous century is subjected to the invasion of the churrigueresque style. This century begins first as baroque and then becomes neoclassic. The baroque is the art of ornaments and spirals, which in Cordoba most often appear on the profusely gilt altars that invade all the churches. The baroque is succeeded by neoclassicism, which represents a return to the fine Renaissance Art, albeit a servile copy lacking in inspiration and taste.

- *San Andrés* – How this church must have been remains visible in an ogival apse and a walled-in arch that is visible outside. The church dates from the 18th century, as does the tower, both completed in 1733, and like San Jerónimo, also subject to a barbaric restoration in the 18th century.
- *San Francisco* – The façade dates from 1782.
- *San Rafael* – The façade from 1796, the best façade of the period but with little esthetic impact, is the work of López Carderera.

Exalted baroque

There are, however, two typical examples of the baroque delirium that twisted columns and grouped ornaments in a disorderly manner. One is the façade of *San Pablo*, built of white and blue marble in 1796 and opens onto Calle Ayuntamiento. The other is at *La Merced*, dating from 1745 and served as an inspiration for the *San Pablo* façade.

A neoclassic example

There remains a unique and quite acceptable church, built during this period: *Santa Victoria*, in which a Frenchman named Graveton worked in 1761, and which was concluded in 1788 by Ventura Rodriguez, the famous architect, designer of the cupola and the façade.

It is cold, like all that style, but not lacking in beauty, and perhaps the only church in Cordoba in which the style is perfectly defined and not mixed with any other.

The 1708 *Instituto de la Asunción* chapel is a truly beautiful baroque church hardly mentioned in books.

19th century

This century was, as we have said, appalling for Cordoba. Everything that could be destroyed was destroyed. This was the century of perfectly conceived but badly implemented disentailments, and a time when in Cordoba, as in the rest of the country, looting of art was a systematic and methodogical business. Very little was respected, and the artistic character of the city was irretrievably lost.[138]

---

[138] From an architectural viewpoint, the 19th century was disastrous; nothing worth mentioning was built. Today we must gather and accentuate Cordoba's tradition of art. All cities with a tradition of art are guided by this principle, although adapting it architecturally to the modern way of life. Cordoban houses are built in an anti-artistic manner and that is why we still do not have an urban aesthetic, although some are thinking of this, as we see elsewhere. Seville, for example, has begun to build along the lines of what they, more or less correctly, call *Sevillian Art*, which to a certain extent has influenced the latest buildings in Cordoba, although with few examples.

CHAPTER XXXVII
Civil architecture

Cordoba boasted a wealth of palaces during the Arab period. The Cordoban house of the times was little concerned with the exterior. Almost no traces remain of the way the Arabs lived - a family life, in seclusion, in the strictest intimacy.

After the Reconquista, Cordoban nobles began constructing their palatial homes, each with a special seal. Almost none had an exterior façade. Unconfirmed tradition speaks of royal sanctions.[139]

There are still beautiful remains of some of these homes. Some examples are *Las Campanas*, built by the Hoces y Fernández de Córdoba family, where Sánchez de Feria lived and still has three magnificent 16th century mullioned windows. Also dating from this period on a street named Calle de la Pierna, a house with for some other decorative work contains a window that, although sealed today, still shows traces of beautiful Renaissance artisanship. There are noteworthy remainders in several homes on the Plaza de las Bulas.

The façade of the Páez home on the square of the same name, although in a very poor state of preservation due to the poor quality of the materials with which it was built, still looks very nice as a whole. Built in the 16th century, in 1540, it has a splendid frieze and well-defined Renaissance-plateresque lines. The broad outline of the house reminds one of the Puerta del Puente.

On Calle Ambrosio Morales, where the first City Hall was located, there are two gorgeous 10th century mullioned windows which bear the Cordoba coat-of-arms, overlooking the Calle de la Feria.

Dating from the 16th century, there is a truly lovely remainder of a house on Plaza de San Andrés, in front of the church. There are the remains of a façade dated 1520 on Calle de Santiago, at the corner with the Plaza.

The *Casa de los Villalones*, without a doubt the finest remaining façade in Cordoba in a pure Renaissance style, also dates from this period (1560).

The *Casa del Bailío* from the 16th century, has examples of plateresque workmanship.

---

[139] Pedro el Cruel is said to have ordered rebellious nobles to build their houses without an outward facing façade, a temporary measure that may have had some impact on the city. It is more likely that this was simply the carryover of an Arab and even Roman, tradition.

The *Marqués de la Fuensanta del Valle*'s house, thus called from the 19th century onwards, built in 1551 in mid-16th century, is a curious mixture of styles, and more than any other building in the city, sports unusually padded doorjambs. The façades of the City Hall buildings were built between 1594 and 1631. The Municipality moved to its present installations in 1587.

Construction in Cordoba experiences something of a rebirth during the 17th century. In 1683, Corregidor Ronquillo Briceño orders the building of the Plaza de la Corredera according to Antonio Ramos' plans, assisted by Francisco Beltrán and Antonio García.

The purpose of this simple, schematic book is not to exhaust the subject, but to point out vestiges of style or places that might jog the memory or inspire future architects, such as the patio in the *Casa de los Ríos*, the most beautiful patios in the *Casa de D. Gómez*, the so-called *Casa de las Pavas*, and so on.

As a reminder of long-lost constructions, those which are spoken of as if a dream, we have for example, the *Puerta de Baeza, Torre de los Donceles*, and so on. One recalls the *Casa de los Bañuelos* that could not be saved, despite the campaign in its favour. Other buildings, lacking defenders or champions, collapsed and were lost forever.

The house

The history of the Cordoban house, as that of its patios and gardens, is another chapter.

Regarding the patio, there are examples from the 14th to the 19th century. The 20th century hates the patio, and nobody builds in the Cordoban style. Between the economy, hardships and squalor as well as sleazy architects lacking in style, the traditional was lost. The hall porter's booth killed the entrance hallway, a neutral and welcoming area. Shops did away with the ground floor, thus giving birth to the odious multi-apartment house with hardly any personality, where the tenant is less of a man, and certainly less of a *Señor*.

Further details regarding the Hernan Ruiz family of architects

This is very interesting from the viewpoint of the history of Cordoban architecture. Having three architects with the same name (father, son and grandson), all active during the 16th century, encourages confusion.

Hernán Ruíz Senior, the Old Man as all of us called him as we copied each other, though born in Burgos, is Cordoban to the core, like Alejo Fernández, as de La Torre discovered and proved in his intelligent work.

It appears that the strongest of the three is the second Ruiz, Hernán Junior, who first worked in the plateresque style, which is why he is confused with works by Berruguete. There is his altarpiece in San Nicolás chapel in the cathedral, in 1567, and the San Nicolás baptismal chapel. The façade in the Páez house has artistic motifs that come to mind in this chapel. Some dates are given: 1525 for the façade (1540 is preferred); 1554 for the chapel.

This is the Hernán who works the most, especially alternating with Ochoa, building houses and windmills, among them Lope García's mill. This is followed by an evolution in Hernán Junior's work as he turns towards the Herrera style, in which he builds the Puerta del Puente in 1571. Later, his work shines in Seville, namely the Giralda bell tower. He is attracted by Seville and there he remains.

His son, the third Hernán, has his father's work on the Giralda in mind when in 1593, he rebuilds the cathedral tower.

Just what was Hernán the Youngest's personality? A master of the techniques of his trade, he has been denied a personality of his own. Experts said that he followed the styles too closely. Be that as it may, nobody can deny that he was a first-rate artist who should be singled out and one who stood above all other architects of the Christian Cordoba era.

Other architects

Who built the great Cordoban stately homes, all which date from the 16th century, such as that of the Méndez de Sottomayor in 1551, later wrongly called of the Marquis of Fuentesanta del Valle, and in 1560, the Orive's house with its birth certificate on its façade, and the Duque de Medina Sidonia's (Calle José Rey), also from this period?

So far, although there are no greater architects other than Ochoa, the Ruizes, and later, Ordóñez, this does not mean that there no other architects during the 16th century.

Juan de Ochoa, whom we already spoke of when talking about San Pablo church, works well. In 1596, Santa Ana, one of the cathedral's best-preserved chapels, is by him.

Jerónimo de Ordóñez, is another name during this period, whose 1580 work on the Los Ríos Hospital façade remains.

The architectural tradition continues with those we have already mentioned regarding the Cathedral, such as Alonso Matías. The work on the Company of Jesus church as well as the major altarpiece in the cathedral, between 1564 and 1589, are attributed to him. It is said, and so it shall remain unless other research comes to light that contradicts it, that he began working on the altarpiece in 1614 but that it was Juan Aranda Salazar who would finish it.

There still is another important work during the 18th century, the Bishop's Palace that was concluded in 1769 by Espinosa, who was born in 1724.

At the very end of the century, there is Santa Victoria church by Ventura Rodríguez, and the work of other lesser-known architects such as the Triumph of Saint Rafael, the façade of San Pelagio Church, and so forth.

Military architecture

There are very few remaining examples of the city's ancient defences, except for the Calahorra Fort, the Malmuerta tower, and bits of the wall surrounding the city that we have mentioned earlier.

Cordoba's city walls have also been better studied. The existence of the Arab Alcazer's double or triple enclosure has been confirmed. The strongest and most forward of these appear to be the tower on the western side of Belén hermitage and the remaining northern and eastern walls of the Bishop's Palace. What has been established without a doubt is that the portion which today is called the Campo de los Mártires was inside the Alcazar.

The original Roman wall is not believed to have gone beyond today's Calle de Santa Ana, although it may have been extended later.

There are three sections of wall: A) from la Victoria to the Campo de los Mártires, where there are authentic caliphal remnants. The Roman wall is believed to be somewhere around here, along the same paths; B) the Marrubial walls, authentically Arab but earthen and of very little importance; and C) the third and last section formed by the walls that go from the Puerta de Sevilla to the bridge, along the entire Alcazar.

There are different opinions regarding the wall. There are those who believe they are Mudejar and those who say they are Arab. It appears that they are Arab, although the entire southern wall suffered a great many alterations during the 14th century that are clearly visible. Changes were also made during the 16th century. The great polygonal tower in the Alcazar wall, next to the river, is of the same period as the Malmuerta tower, early 15th, both built under the orders of Corregidor Pedro Sánchez.

The watchtowers present another problem. Today, the only remaining one is the Torre de la Malmuerta and local archaeologists believe that the arches on the Puerta de Sevilla, thought to be Visigoth in origin, are the remains of another 14th century watchtower.

This section of Cordoba, from the Puerta de Sevilla to the Alcazar prison, must be totally restored to recreate one of the most beautiful settings in Cordoba, one overshadowed by the Inquisition and during a century, by the prison.

The construction of the Alcazar, today so dilapidated, began between 1327 and 1328 and incorporated houses belonging to Gil Gómez de Sosa. One of the first Mayors, if not the first, was Pay Arias de Castro, married to Urraca Téllez in 1351. The only interesting and moving moment of its history occurred during the reign of Isabel la Católica. In its interior, there are precious architectural remains of ogival art. The Inquisition established its headquarters in the Alcazar in 1482 and would remain there until 1821.

The only remaining artefact of military art is Calahorra Fort, which increasingly likely was built under Enrique II, albeit on the site of ancient buildings.

The walls of Cordoba have almost all disappeared, but it is not difficult to find their remains and above all, locate them. According to local lore, more than 50 rods of walls and the adjacent houses collapsed in 1597, from the Puerta del Puente to the Ribera, after which they were replaced by was called the walls of the old Rastro.

CALAHORRA FORT

Calahorra Fort
Photograph Sam Guimaraens 2017

Special comment

The Calahorra Fort is of Arab origin, although it is believed to be older, and built in the same place as a Roman fortification. The Christians carried out repairs, especially Enrique II and the Reyes Católicos, changing the direction of the road a bit, which had probably been straight. The entrance may have been through the fortification which may have had other military additions, long since disappeared.

When Enrique II passed through Cordoba in 1369, he ordered the bridge repaired and the Calahorra Fort strengthened and improved.

The fort was again renovated during the 15th century. As a mere verbal curiosity, I recall that, according to the book *Aves de caza*, Pedro el Cruel stated that Calahorra was his nickname for his favourite noble.

The name of the Fort

Many have researched the etymology of the word Calahorra. Someone even once attempted to connect *Calat* (castle) with *Al-Horr*, the name of the emir who established Cordoba as the Arab capital, so to say *Calahorra* meant Al-Horr's Castle. In this case, what do we do with all the other locations with the same name in Spain? Did Horr visit all of them? This etymology is useless.

What recent studies say is that Calahorra comes from *calat* (castle) and *horr* (free, exempt). In other words, an isolated, free or exempt castle or tower. Supporting this is the modern word, *jorro*, also meaning free, which come from *horr*.

Regarding the word Calahorra, in *Homenaje a Codera*, Eguiláz wrote that the ancient name Calahorra is the diction composed of two Iberian words: *cala* (castle) and *horra* (red), undoubtedly a primitive name for the fortress, referring to Granada, which the Arab conquerors translated as *calá-al hamra* (alhambra). The expression Calahorra is also found as the name given to the castle or fortification which controls Cordoba's bridge. Although the latter etymology makes some sense, it has been corrected by the previous one.

The place name

This is not a futile study. Toponymy can lead to some very interesting concepts and today's advanced philological studies shine light on new worlds. Today, nobody says that Andalusia comes from Vandals, not even that it was named after Al-Andalus, attributing its present name to the Arab one.

Some have turned to previous designations, whereby *lus* (extreme or final), is said to refer to its extreme location, the last frontier according to the ancient knowledge of geography, at the end of the known world where the *Elysian Fields* could be found. *An* or *en* would mean 'the'. According to current essayists, its name comes from a geographic situation, meaning the extreme, the far distant.

Speaking of names, another small note, not as weighty as *Don Gomar*, but regarding *Don Gome*, which was quite fashionable a few years ago in Cordoba as a substitute for the now classic *Don Gómez*. This was the name of a street since the 16th century, and everyone was happy with that. However, one day a writer, with good faith and philology, argued that if the name López was originally Lope, Gómez must come from Gome, thereby creating a tradition. This would be a mildly acceptable, though distasteful theory, if Gómez were Latin, but it is not.

Since the 13th century, the Castilian Chronicles wrote the name as Don Gómez. For example, the most famous Count to bear this name since the days of Ximénez de Rada, is Don Gómez de Candespina. Interested parties have signed Don Gómez on diplomas. All nobles are called Gómez. Lastly, experts state that:

> *Don Gome is unacceptable because the z at the end of the name is from the origin. Gome does not exist. In the same way that there is Lope and López (son of Lope). The ancient forms of Gómez are Gáumiz, Gomecius, and so forth., always with a z at the end. The etymology of Gómez is unknown, but that has no bearing on what has been said. Lope, on the other hand, is Lupus (Llop in Catalan).[xxxiii]*

Other experts the author consulted said, rather interestingly, that perhaps originally it could have been Gomar, changed but always with a z at the end. As regards its origin, there even are those who presume that it is Berber. No one believes in the shortened Don Gome. I, an authentic traditionalist, called and will continue calling him Don Gómez, with as clear a z at the end as possible.

Other comments

The Malmuerta, an octagonal tower with a massive lower half, was attached to the city wall and according to its inscription, built between 1406 and 1408. The Puerta de Almodóvar, at the entrance of the Jewish quarter, was restored at the beginning of the last century, in 1802.

Originallly, there were 13 gates or *puertas*, to the walled enclosure of the city: Nueva, Andújar, Martos, Baeza, Excusada, Colodro, Rincón, Fonsario, Gallegos, Almodóvar, Seville, del Puente and Plascencia.

The Puerta del Puente had very little of the military, as the Calahorra served for that. Built by Hernán Ruiz in 1573[140], it was subjected to a restoration that totally changed its appearance as it always was a gate with a single façade. Today

---

[140] This artistic façade, which surely was only half-finished, is the work of the third member of the Hernán Ruíz family. An interesting summary of its history was written by R. Romero Barros in his *Estudios sobre arquitectura española* (Boletín Academia de San Ferdinand, 1888).

it has two façades, is now free standing and an arch of triumph in the Roman manner.

In 1868, a year when Cordoban architecture was totally vandalized, we were deprived of several gates of interest, among them the Puerta de Andújar and the beautiful Puerta de Baez, represented in a somewhat idealized engraving in *España y sus monumentos*, in the volume on Cordoba.

The Christian Alcazar is built on land that belonged to the Arab Alcazar and all that remains of the building is dedicated to a public prison. Its towers, dating from the 14th century, in which there are traces of past constructions, were built by King Alfonso XI in 1328. It housed the Inquisition until 1821.

Mudejar Art

Finally, comments regarding Cordoban Mudejar art have been left to now. It has become very fashionable to speak of Mudejarism and of the Mudejar; we frequently give these names to matters that are difficult to classify.

Mudejar is no more, no less, than Christian Art blending with Arab art, almost always executed by Arab artists working in the service of Christianity.

It appears that with it and as it developed, we would have created a national art, had it not been cut short by the Renaissance. Its principal characteristic is the use of tiles and blind arcades reminiscent of the Arab.

The Mudejar is not identical in character in all Spanish districts, and one speaks of a Romanesque and an Ogival Mudejar art. The Cordoban Mudejar is an art that is created, not in imitation of another, but as an Arab memory used for Christians purposes. There are dates and names of many Arabs who continued to work for Christians after the Conquista.

There are extremely beautiful examples of Mudejar art in Cordoba, the finest of all being on the Gospel side of the façade of San Miguel Church that imitates Arab Art at the time of the Caliphate, a doorway in La Magdalena church, the 14th century chapel in San Bartolomé church hospital, and the *Casa del Indiano*, albeit from the 15th century, not entirely Mudejar.

One also needs to mention several chapels in Santa Marina and Santiago churches, the extraordinary baptismal chapel in San Miguel church and another in San Pablo church, recently renovated. Remember Lampérez' magnificent studies of Cordoban churches and that which he called Romanesque-Ogival-Mudejar.

The so-called Casa de los Caballeros de Santiago, located on a square across from the Escuela de Artes e Industrias, probably dating to the mid-15th century, where the most typical character is preserved, as well as the Casa de Augustín Sam in general:

We, who turn our faces to the Holy Land in the East when we pray, never open a door to the Synagogue on the eastern side. In this wall we build a hecal, or small tabernacle shrine, where we keep the toras, or parchment scrolls of the Pentateuch.

The Synagogue never had a door that opened directly onto the Calle de los Judíos. The entrance must have been, as it is today, through the atrium or patio. Suffice to recall the similar layout of some synagogues in Morocco. There must have been a gateway to the school on the Western wall, across from the tabernacle.

It is possible, almost certain, that all that remains today is the actual Synagogue, part of another, larger building, remnants such as those which can be found in ancient houses. Padre Fidel Fita believes that there was only one synagogue in Cordoba. This, despite his learned opinion, is extremely difficult to prove.

The other modern study by Santos Gener is a precursor of the current restoration, which as regards the entire building has remained incomplete. It is, without a doubt, a perfect and very well carried out work. The Synagogue has been restored today, although repairs to the remainder of the building are not yet complete.

One must presume that this was not the only synagogue in Cordoba. Very possibly, remnants of a large one that was being built in the 13th century, shortly after the Christian conquest, are to be found in the traditionally named Casa de los Bulas on the Plaza de Maimonides. The Papacy ordered the work stopped as it offended the Christians.

There is another house in Santiago neighbourhood that contains remnants of a strange building that could perhaps be attributed to Judaism, given the layout of the building, not because of anything specifically or privately artistic, something which, as we know, the Jewish people did not possess, not even in its great historic days. I have not attempted to write a complete and organic guide to Cordoba. Just a very summary indication of what appears to be most important.

The beautiful and ancient Cordoban homes are slowly disappearing, and the modern buildings are built without any thought of renewing their style. The latest major building in Cordoba – the Civil Government - has not been blessed by Fortune.

This could be and should be told to children, the future artists and, undoubtedly, future leaders of their city. This modest *Guide* is only here to help them *see*. *Seeing* is the secret of Art, and the examples that have survived devastation, a great many of which still abound in the city, shall guide them better than anyone along this road of an aesthetic renovation that we all yearn for.

A summary, for reading, can be found in *La Arquitectura en España* by Puich y Cadafalch, Curso Internacional, Barcelona, 1914, recently extended and improved.

CHAPTER XXXVIII
The Art of Painting in Cordoba

This brief chapter will address the principle artistic expressions that the Art of Painting has displayed in our city. Painting as an independent Art is a modern art, although Man has experienced the wonders of colour since the dawn of time.

There are no paintings from the Arab and Roman periods in Cordoba. It is doubtful whether the Arabs cultivated this art. Although much has been said and written about a *surah* in the Koran that prohibited drawing animate beings for fear of idolatry, there are some examples of art that would indicate that they ignored this rule, if it ever existed.

The most ancient painter in Cordoba of whom we know, is Alonso Martínez, a 13th century artist whose work was discovered a few years ago on a wall in the cathedral's Villaviciosa chapel. The paintings are of saints and were signed and dated 1286, an unusual occurrence.

Following in age to the above, there are other wall paintings behind the high altar, in the apse of San Lorenzo church. They are in an acceptable condition and appear to correspond to the 14th century and represent Saint Peter and other apostles. Other extremely faint and difficult to make out paintings in San Nicolás church, also behind the high altar, are believed to be of the above period. To this list, we add work from the 15th century, also wall paintings, in extremely interesting San Miguel church.

After these anonymous artistic manifestations, we begin to find artwork with known names and signs of marked technical progress: Bartolomé Ruíz, Pedro de Córdoba and Bartolomé Bermejo, great artists whose works are signed and dated 1450, 1475 and 1490, respectively.

Bermejo, the most admirable painter of *tablas* or panels of his time, painted the famous *Piedad* in Barcelona Cathedral. I will say more about this great artist later. Pedro de Córdoba is the (signed) author of the great panel, *La Anunciación*, in the Cathedral. There is more of his work in museums and private collections. Perhaps also, *San Nicolás de Bari*, in the Museo de Bellas Artes of Cordoba.[141]

---

[141] *Los primitivos cordobeses Pedro de Córdoba y Bartolomé Bermejo.* E. Romero de Torres. (B. Excursionistas, 1908).

These 14th and 15th century works, generally known as primitives, are of great interest today in the study of the evolution of the several schools of pictorial Art.

To these painters, we must add, in chronological order and artistic value, Pedro Romana, author of the 1504 altarpiece in San Andrés chapel in Espejo, Cordoba, and who may be the artist of *Virgen de escuela alemana*, in our museum.[142] Also, Alejo Fernández, a Cordoban who first flourished in Cordoba, and worked on the first altarpiece for San Jerónimo church in 1525. [143] In 1532, Lorenzo Fernández painted the San Gregorio altarpiece in the Cathedral.

Pablo de Céspedes

After these painters, in chronological order and that of the evolution of painting, is the aclaimed Pablo de Céspedes (1538-1608). Céspedes, who has been mentioned several times in this book, is an artist (painter and sculptor), poet, architect, antiquarian, humanist and sage. He studied in Alcalá and in Rome, thereby acquiring an extensive classical education.

Creative and easily tempted by the seductive pull of beauty, he presents a grand figure. His drawings are admirable, his compositions are elegant and grandiose, and he dominates colour. With him, painting in Cordoba leaps forward and we see the establishment of what one could call our school of painters whose works are found in the Cathedral and churches of Cordoba.[144]

The inventory of the goods that Céspedes left when he died is curious. He had an untidy lifestyle and he lived like a poor man. He left very little of value other than his books. Céspedes is an example of how the Cordoban middle class lived in the 17th century.

Alcalá is the University founded by Cisneros, and in those days, Rome was the centre of light and knowledge.[145] From the 16th century, although not of

---

[142] So believes Ramírez de Arellano in B. de la Academia of San Ferdinand, 1915, in the brief prologue to the publication of *Ordenanzas de Pintores* (held in the Municipal Archives) for 1493 and 1543. This is an invaluable document for the study of the technique of those days, just how this trade organized itself and what were the procedures.

[143] Alejo Fernández painted *La Virgen de la Rosa* and *La Virgen de los Conquistadores*. In Cordoba, I believe wrongly, he is attributed the *Poliptico de la flagelación* (Museum).

[144] Art was predominantly religious, because among other reasons, the Church was rich and was its only, or almost only, market. Around every cathedral, such as in Cordoba, there is always a great nucleus of artists involved in daily renovations and foundations.

[145] Céspedes represents the Renaissance; that is to say, the new modality, the new way of living at the time, the best life, the best learning, progress, the modern life of his time. Italy was, in those days, and afterwards for a very long time, the single attraction for artists. It had already produced the great schools of pictorial art and giants such as Leonardo da Vinci, Rafael and Michelangelo. Céspedes studied in Italy where he learnt how to handle colour. Pacheco, a good painter and even greater writer,

Céspedes' school, we have Francisco del Rosal, a notable artist who has left works from 1553. He has not yet been studied.

Disciples of Céspedes

Antonio Mohedano (1563-1625) is Céspedes' first disciple,[146] and the one who was most strongly influenced by Italianism. It is possible that his work has been mistaken with that of Luís de Vargas, the famous Sevillian who was so greatly inspired by Italy. According to Céan, he left his finest work in Lucena.

Next, Cordoban Juan Luís Zambrano (1598-1639) is without a doubt Céspedes' best disciple and one of Andalusia's noted artists. He employed colour with great force and vigour, as is evident in his *David con la cabeza de Goliath* (that

---

said that "Andalusia owed him the good light of the tones". He had enormous influence and created a school in Cordoba.For example, there is *La cena* in our cathedral and *Las bodas de Canaán* in the Provincial Museum. He wrote books on painting, of which only fragments remain. He is famous for his poem *La Pintura*, in which his description of the horse is a classic:

> Que parezca en el aire y movimiento
> la generosa raza, do ha venido
> salga con altivez y atrevimiento,
> vivo en la vista, en la cerviz erguido;
> estribe firme el brazo en duro asiento,
> con el pie resonante y atrevido,
> animoso, insolente, libre, ufano,
> sin temer al horror de estruendo vano.
> Brioso el alto cuello y enarcado,
> con la cabeza descarnada y viva;
> llenas las cuencas, ancho y dilatado
> el bello espacio de la frente altiva;
> breve el vientre rollizo, no pesado,
> ni caído de lados, y que aviva
> los ojos eminentes, las orejas
> altas sin derramarlas y parejas.
>
> ....
> Arroja por el cuello levantado
> El cerdoso cabello al distro lado.

[146] All of Céspedes' disciples are, or wanted to be, poets. Mohedano is really the only poet in the group:

> En vano es resistir el mal que siento
> si echada por el suelo mi esperanza
> sujeta a mi azón con tal pujanza
> que ni aun libre le deja el sentimiento ...
>
> ....
> Estoy a padecer el mal tan hecho
> Que en el bien estará, si viene, extraño.

He must have also been a portrait artist, as Pedro de Espinosa, in a beautiful sonnet, speaking to him of a portrait that he painted of his beloved, says:

> Cuando el original me diese enojos
> quejaréme al retrato.

some today wish to attribute to Antonio del Castillo) in Cordoba Museum, and his *Martirio de San Esteban* in the cathedral.[147]

Juan de Peñalosa y Sandoval (1581-1636), born in Baena. Like his master, he followed the style of tse Renaissance men. In addition to painter, he was a poet, architect, Canon and an erudite man.[148]

Another Cordoban disciple, Antonio de Contreras (1589-1654) was famous for his portraits. He moved early to Bujalance where he founded a kind of local school. Palomino, his countryman, said that many Cordoban gentlemen went to Bujalance to be painted by him.

Regarding Leonardo Henríquez, another follower, little more is known than his name and the remainder of some of his works in Fuentesanta sanctuary.

As regards Hermano Adrián, who died in 1630, we know that he painted for Carmen church, today San Cayetano church, and that some samples of his precise work are in the Museum.

Related to this group of Céspedes', are Fray Cristóbal de Vera (1577-1621), Cordoban, member of the Order of San Jerónimo and painter of fellow members, Juan Francisco de Quesada (1632-1677) who painted a *Santa Helena* in the Sagrario, and Antonio and Cristóbal Vela.

Antonio Vela, Cordoban (1614-1676), son of Cristóbal Vela, also a painter, was, born in Jaen and a follower of Sebastián Martínez (1602-1677). He studied at Céspedes' school in Cordoba and became an eminent painter with much influence in his homeland. There are examples of his work in Corpus church, Cordoba.

This completes the group of disciples of Céspedes whose work covers the reigns of Felipe II and Felipe III. This being well into the 17th century, we must not forget to mention César Arbacia whom Céspedes brought from Italy. He died in Spain in 1614, leaving several paintings in Andalusia and in Cordoba where he painted the walls of the Sagrario.

We need to add Baltasar del Aguila, an unknown artist who was discovered by Ramirez de Arellano. There is some beautiful work of his in the Concepción chapel of the old cathedral.

Antonio del Castillo y Saavedra

This illustrious artist and his group of disciples make up the second period of Cordoba Art.

---

[147] R. Romero de Barros began the critical biography of this painter. *Juan Luís Zambrano*, ir Boletín de la Academia de San Ferdinand, 1892.

[148] He leaves his best work in Astorga. He was a prolific painter and painted *Santa Bárbara* in the Cathedral. There are samples of his work in the Museum. As regards his poetry, with the best will n the world, one cannot find a grain of inspiration. In the restored San Jerónimo monastery, there was or is, *La Cena*, that was brought there from the dissolved Los Mártires convent.

Antonio del Castillo (1603-1667), born five years before Paolo de Céspedes' death, belonged to a family of painters, son of Augustín and nephew of Juan, one of Murillo's teachers.

The Spanish painter who is credited with having the greatest influence on Castillo is Francisco de Zurbarán, with whom he studied in Seville.

Castillo is more Spanish, less Italian and more sober than Céspedes in his composition and use of colour. He excelled at drawing and became a magnificent draftsman, so skilled that he could dare give Alonso Cano lessons in drawing. He had a very interesting life which he spent between Cordoba and Seville. In Seville, he is said to have declared that he was outshone by Murillo.[149]

Castillo had such a delicate feeling for Nature that he initiated and sometimes accentuated, a love of landscapes that announced the coming of genre paintings. In addition to religious paintings, he also painted a great many portraits. It is believed that he painted himself in *Negación de San Pedro*, a painting that hangs in the Museo de Bellas Artes in Cordoba.

He is the author of a great number of admirable drawings that can be found in collections in many places: the Museo de Bellas Artes in Cordoba, Instituto de Jovellanos in Gijón and the Academia de San Ferdinand.

Hanging in the Provincial Museum, in addition to *Cristo en la Cruz*, there are *San Ferdinand* and other paintings from the dissolved San Pablo convent. No one has yet catalogued his numerous paintings.

Like almost all Cordobans, Castillo is literate but his verses, although correct, lack poetic inspiration. He appears to have portrayed himself in his last poem, when he says: *Es de mi ingenio bronco el instrumento.*

E. Romero de Torres has rewritten much of the information about Antonio de Castillo. After publishing his baptismal certificate,[xxxiv] he reestablished the painter's true date of birth (1616) and that of his death (1668).[150]

The best of Castillo and where he really triumphs as a great painter, is where he masters colour, softens it and gives it elegance, as in the beautiful sky in *La historia de José* which hangs in the Prado Museum.

He seems like a different painter.

There are many paintings by Castillo all over the city, and if we are to believe some notes in the inventory of the Colegio de Plateros, the famous *Virgen de los Plateros*, originally attributed to Valdés, is by Castillo.

---

[149] So far, nobody has made the proper study that this great painter, barely known outside his country, deserves. As regards what he said about being outshone and other things, these appear to be myths. That which is no myth is the humour with which he signed, *Non pixit Alfarus*, instead of his name, because he was bothered by Juan de Alfaro's exaggerated prestige.

[150] Magdalena parish archives

This is a delicate matter because that painting was restored, albeit with great care, by Romero Barros and if in there are bits of the painting – the chasuble, for example – that appear to be by Valdés, there are other fragments that appear, although it may seem strange, closer to Castillo.

A better study of Ambrosio del Castillo's work should provide some surprising information and add to this artist's fame.

Disciples of Castillo

Pedro Antonio (1614-1675) imitated his master very well although perhaps he was more of a colourist. He left a good name but not many works and his *Santa Rosa* in San Pablo may serve as an example.

Manuel Arias y Contreras, born in 1644, spent his childhood with Castillo. José de Sarabia (1608-1669), a Sevillian, is classed as a member of the Castillo Cordoban school as it is there that he studied and did a lot of work. A great colourist, he distinguished himself painting *Concepciones*. His Italianate feeling distances him a bit from Castillo.

Juan Alfaro y Gómez (1640-1680), Castillo's principal disciple soon became his rival. Until then, Cordoban painters had established their principal ties with Seville, the artistic centre at the time, perhaps the first in Spain. From this point onwards, with the creation of the Madrid school, they became closer to the Court. Alfaro goes to Madrid where he studies with Velázquez, and imitates him a lot, especially in his portraits. For many years, Alfaro was attributed the honour of having painted Calderón de la Barca. His main skill which characterizes his work is small oil portraits. His authorship of the Calderón de la Barca painting is refuted today.

Alfaro belongs to a family of artists, his brother is Doctor Enrique Vaca de Alfaro, and he is a nephew of Bernardo Cabrera, the antiquarian. Furthermore, he is something of a man of letters and a poet.

In 1667 he produced his collection of portraits of Bishops of Cordoba, in the Bishop's Palace today. His portrait of Bishop Salizanes, in the cathedral's Concepcion chapel, is one of his best works.[151]

---

[151] The 1918 Madrid Exhibition of Portraits of Women contained the portrait of the Cordoban Isabel Díaz de Morales y Muñoz de Godoy, attributed to Carreño. This is, without a shadow of a doubt, Alfaro's finest work, and if it is his, as I truly believe, suffices to prove his worth as a great painter. He also painted a series of portraits in Cordoba in the Díaz de Morales home in 1676 and 1677. "The portrait of Salizanes exhibits a stunning, well drawn and coloured, head, as well as some baroque and saffron-coloured hands." Luís Siret, *Diccionario de Pintores*.

Another fine portrait by Alfaro is that of the Jesuit Padre Moya. (Library of the Instituto de San Isidro, Madrid).

Apart from their poetic proclivities, it is interesting to draw attention to the historicist and didactic bent of almost all Cordoban painters that makes them feel a need to write.

Alfaro has the mind of a learned man. He collected Céspedes' writings and corrected them by hand. Later, Palomino became most famous as an essayist and historian of the Art of Painting. Fortunately, this very typical Cordoban love of critique and of learning has been handed down to us to this day.

Other 17th century painters

This class of painters, grouped in these two schools, can be said to encompass the entire 17th century, encouraged as they were by the city's artistic output and the artistic renaissance that, to a certain extent, is supported by the bishops and by the works in the Cathedral.

In addition to them, however, there are other greater or less talented painters who are not trained in these schools but whom we need to discuss.

These include Luís Rufo Carrillo, son of the poet Juan Rufo, of whose work nothing remains, and who is better known as the author of the Quinientas *apotegmas*.

Fray Juan del Santisimo Sacramento (Juan de Guzmán 1611-1680), a heroic adventurer with a tempestuous and interesting life. His painting of *Santa Marina*, in the church of the same name, signed in 1678, is an example of his worth as a painter, as are other paintings of his in the Museo de Bellas Artes, where he imitates Van Dyke. He also cultivated the art of the portrait. A characteristic feature is his having translated and expanded Pietro de Ascolti's book *Perspectiva práctiva*, to his advantage.

Antonio García Reynoso (1623-1677), born in Cabra, reflects the Cordoban school where he produced many paintings and, influenced by the poor taste of the baroque, seems to have only achieved success with landscapes. Clearly, he is a good draftsman. He made a great many drawings for the silversmiths.

Antonio Escalante (1603-1670) who also goes to Madrid and studies under Rizzie and became known as a good painter. The Prado Museum has a very acceptable *Sagrada Familia* of his.

Painting in the 18th century

This bring us to the 18th century, to the third group of Cordoban painters among whom we can say there is no school nor even a local tradition. A greater contact with foreign works of art and the enormous decadence of the Art of Painting in Spain after the colossal efforts of the 17th century, exhausted production.

Acisclo Antonio Palomino de Castro y Velasco

An excellent artist (1653-1725) who, despite the decadence of his time, composed and drew, but was unable to master colour. His paintings had a baroque decorative feeling that made them very famous. He was prolific and there are works of his in most of Spain. In Cordoba, these can be found in the Cathedral, San Francisco Church and Santiago Church.

Palomino's fame, however, is that of a didactic writer for his work *Museo pictórico y escala óptica* in which he included the *Biografías de pintores ilustres*.[152] This is the first important history of Spanish Art and by 1744, was already translated into English.

From this period, we must mention Antonio Fernández de Castro (1679-1739), known as Prebendary Castro. In the opinion of some, he was greater than Palomino, with some works in the museum, and *San Ferdinand ofreciendo la conquista* in the cathedral.

Juan de la Cruz Molina, another canon of the church, painted at the beginning of the century, in 1729.

Fray Jerónimo Espinoza, who died in 1791, was a lay member of San Pablo monastery who distinguished himself with his admirable copies of Castillo, with whom he is occasionally confused. He left some acceptable portraits.

Alvarez Torrado also dates from that period and is the last painter of the 18th century.

José Pérez Ruano, author of the murals on the outside walls of San Pedro church, died in 1810. José Cobo Guzmán was also a painter of note between 1666 and 1746. His *San Pedro Nolasco* hangs in the Museo de Bellas Artes.

The 19th century

The Art of Painting in Cordoba reached such a nadir that one can truly say that nobody knew how to paint. Paintings from this period do not appear to be the work of artists.

Academicism in Cordoba at the beginning of the 19th century is represented by brothers Antonio and Diego Monroy, especially the latter.

---

[152] In Palomino we see the peak of Cordoban didactic writing, and the name of this painter is very much used by painting scholars, such as Pons, Ceán Bermúdez, Count of Viñaza, and so forth. That is all that has any literary value; the rest is intolerable.

However, when the traveller arrives at places far from Cordoba, such as the famous Cartuja del Paular, and finds work by this artist in the domes of the Sagrario chapels, even though he does not admire the painter he is touched by this breath of the Cordoban. His paintings have a touch of the Cordoban that one cannot deny.

Regarding the work in Madrid City Hall, there is *Excursionista 1911*, Conde de Polentinos. Painted at the time of Mayor Ronquillo Briceño, who probably knew Palomino in Cordoba.

Diego de Monroy (1799-1856), a follower of Maella, is less of a painter than his father, who painted the *Retablo de la calle de Lineros*; it is no longer in Cordoba. Diego de Monroy left several paintings of no merit in Cordoba. I have seen the odd portraits, some of which could be said to be acceptable.

José Saló y Junquet (1810-1877) appears to be more of a miniaturist and restorer. He paints a great many miniature portraits, as well as the *La Trinidad* medallion in a cathedral chapel. He created a notable and impressive collection of paintings, drawings and sculptures.

The creation of the *Escuela de Bellas Artes* in 1866 is a major step forward in the history of Cordoban painting. One of the foremost artists was Rafael Romero Barros, who died in 1895, a renowned painter and illustrious master. This school was preceded by the *Escuela de Bellas Artes* that was founded at the end of the 18th century by Bishop Antonio Caballero y Góngora, in imitation of the Academias that were so fashionable at the time.

The Escuela de Bellas Artes, which as it evolved became the *Escuela de Industrias,* has contributed to the rebirth of Art. It produced extremely distinguished graduates, most notably, Mateo Inurria and Julio Romero de Torres.

There is also mention of the miniaturists at the end of the 18th century when this genre of painting reached its peak.

Mention must be made of Isidro Espejo (born in 1788) and, as an example, the three medallions in Cruz de Santiago parish church.

This should be the end of this brief summary of Cordoban painting, if adding a small appendix dedicated to Juan de Valdés Leal were not required. Not so long ago, until modern critics deprived us of him,[153] Valdés was the jewel in the crown of the Cordoban school. Today, research has unearthed documents that show that he was from Seville.

Valdés Leal

Valdés represented one of the peaks of painting and his spirit and his adaptation to our city are so deeply Cordoban that only in its spirit could he conceive the marvellous paintings of *Los muertos* of the Hospital de la Caridad, Seville. From that viewpoint, he continues to be Cordoban.

A great part of his magnificent work is to be found in Cordoba, in museums, private homes and churches. *La Virgen de los Plateros* and the incredible *Retablo de la iglesia del Carmen*, are the finest examples of painting that one can find in Cordoba.

Valdés was an excellent draftsman who influenced the silversmiths of his day, guiding them and providing drawings, several of which still exist. An example

---

[153] *La patria de Valdés Leal*, Enrique Romero de Torres, 1912.

of this is his unique pedestal for the *Virgen de los Plateros*, which, more than a pictorial work, could serve as a model for the art of the silversmith.

There are quite a few paintings by other, non-Cordoban, artists in the city. In addition to works by César Arbacia, whom I mentioned earlier, perhaps those by Vicente Carducho in San Eulogio cathedral are finer.[154]

Valdés, born in 1622, six years after Castillo, was of the same period and he survives him, as Castillo died young. Valdés died in 1690, twenty-two years later. There is very little truth to the stories of their rivalry. Valdés spent much of his time in Seville. Castillo almost never left Cordoba, and this was to his disadvantage as it hampered the development of his great ability. Antonio del Castillo's influence on Valdés Leal is particularly evident in the latter's earliest paintings.

---

[154] See Narciso Sentenach's most interesting book, *La Pintura en Madrid*, a book that truly is the most modern history of Spanish painting during the 17th and 18th centuries, and the *Diccionario de artistas cordobeses* by Rafael Ramírez de Arellano (Inéditos, Vol. 105).

In summary, to complete the modern, see *la Pintura moderna española* by M. Rodríguez Codolá, Barcelona, 1914. Today, one absolutely must add *Historia de la Pintura española* by Augusto Meyer, 1928.

IMMACULATE CONCEPTION by
Juan Antonio de Frías y Escalante (1603-1670)

CHAPTER XXXIX
Cordoban iconography before the 19th century

Authentic iconography, that which is made with a desire to ensure that a person's image lasts over time, in other words the portrait, has not been collected as a complement to local history. Iconography, in addition to its biographic value, is also sometimes of artistic value and there are examples of this. The only example of this as a series is the *Colección de retratos de obispos de Córdoba,* which as a pictorial work has a very uneven quality. It is possible that although one or another are acceptable, none are the product of gifted painters.

The best, as is generally accepted, are attributed to Céspedes. Thus, the portraits of the brothers Juan, Diego and Francisco Simancas hang in the space that used to be called the Chapel of the Bishops in the Cathedral.

Céspedes' self-portrait is believed to be found in the *Annunciation* altarpiece in Santa Marta convent. Others doubt this.

By Castillo, the painting that hangs in the Museum signed *Non pixit,* is believed to be his self-portrait.

There is a very well drawn self-portrait of the physician Daza Valdés among his work.

The Colegio de la Asunción rectory has an acceptable portrait of Bishop Caballero y Góngora.

The portrait of Captain Antonio Fernández, founder of the Colegio Santa María de Gracia Asunción Rectory, cannot be attributed to Castillo and is attributed by some to Espinosa. Nor can Castillo have painted the portrait of López de Alba, founder of the Colegio.

There is a portrait of *Padre Juan de Rivas,* a competent writer, in San Pablo church. On the other hand, there are numerous portraits of *Padre Posadas.* The oldest oil portrait in Cordoba is on the Encarnación altar in the Cathedral, although Arellano speaks of another, referring to some paintings in the Cathedral, the *Campo de la Venda* by Fernández de Córdoba, but this cannot be proven.

A good painting of the Cathedral by Salizanes, is in the Concepción chapel. Also acceptable, *Fray Juan del Sacramento*'s painting in Santa Marina parish church.

This appears to be a list of those saved from oblivion, but a search would provide many more as one only mentions portraits by famous artists, leaving out artists who might have made engravings, and even 13th century miniatures, which as we know, attained a certain artistic peak.

Regarding the portraits, it is fair to say that Romero de Torres doubts whether it is correct to attribute the portraits of the Simancas and the self-portrait in Santa Marta convent to Céspedes.

He also does not believe that Castillo's portrait in *El bautizo de San Francisco* in the Museo de Bellas Artes, is truly a self-portrait. Instead, he believes that it probably is a portrait of Gómez de Figueroa, constant protector of Castillo's and donor of the painting. The self-portrait that one sees most often repeated in the artist's paintings is that of a much younger man with a different appearance. It was Romero Barros who spotted this figure and pointed it out as a likely self-portrait of the artist.

There are other portraits that we can mention, that Romero de Torres identified, namely Medina Requejo (Chacón, 1738) and Pedro Salazar, Bishop of Cordoba and nephew of Cardinal Salazar, surrounded by students and signed by Cobo y Gusmán (in the Bishop's Palace). Also, the portrait of Pérez Pavía, painted by Espinosa.

ADDENDUM
Summary of painting in Cordoba.
From Bermejo to Julio Romero de Torres

The Cordoban school of painting, whose existence has been denied, nonetheless acquires a great standing with the person of Bermejo.

His actual name appears to be Bartolomé de Cárdenas (c.1440-c.1495).[xxxv] He came from Cordoba, painted in Aragon and Barcelona (1490, *La Piedad*).

Bermejo's work possesses the features that are typical of the Cordoba school: the great draftmanship, the sense of the dramatic and the elegance, and he stands head and shoulders above all Spanish painters of his time.

His work, *Santo Domingo de Silos* is an extraordinary example, painted between 1475 and 1479. The *San Miguel,* from Tous (Valencia), now in England, is another great painting of his. We do not believe, despite authorized attributions, that there is any altarpiece in Cordoba that can be attributed to Bermejo. By Pedro de Córdoba, yes. I have already pointed to the great altarpiece in the Cathedral and to his painting of the *Natividad*, in which he declares that he is the son of Juan de Córdoba.

Alejo Fernández, who we know died in 1543 in Seville, is another great painter and the most celebrated artist in Andalusia. We presume that his *Cristo atado a la columna*, the altarpiece of the San Jerónimo convent, has remained in Cordoba.

The *Virgen de la Rosa*, in Santa Ana, by Triana, regardless of what the most demanding critics say, is one of the most beautiful images of the Virgin in Spanish painting, The same can be said of his *Virgen de los conquistadores* who shelters many figures under her cape, portraits of individuals of the period, another excellent work of art, not forgetting those that he left in Seville, the centre of his activity. He depicts women with an Andalusian grace, which is quite rightly noted and withstands comparisons with the best Italian masters.

Cordoba did not paint women with such grace until Julio Romero de Torres in the 20th century. Between these two artists, there is a sense of that which is worth painting that has not been pointed out.

The other great pictographic moment in Cordoba, led by Céspedes, in other words, the second half of the 17th century, has been very well studied. Castillo is very Cordoban and of whom a joint study by E. Romero de Torres is announced. The latter has re-established Castillo's correct genealogy and his lifetime (1616-1668). He was baptized in Sagrario parish, and he filled the first half of the 17th century with his work. The second half of the 17th century and well into the 18th, is filled by Palomino who, more than a painter, is an essayist.

We arrive at the end of the great names of Cordoban painting. The 19th century gave us a painter who attained a certain fame, Tomás Muñoz Lucena. A good painter and colourist.

With a reputation greater than all others, Julio Romero de Torres (1880-1930) is *the* Cordoban painter par excellence. No one has surpassed his identification with the soul of his city, nor did anyone immerse himself so completely in it. Much has been written, and frequently well, regarding Romero de Torres, however, there is as yet no catalogue of his work, which is very disperse and difficult to locate. Nor has there been an in-depth, extensive study of one who played such an important part in the triumphal period of painting in Cordoba.

Of all his work, attention is drawn to *Poema de Córdoba*, for its soul imbued with all the nuances of the great spirit of the city that so splendidly inspired him. His draftmanship, his use of colour, the beautiful and chaste nudes, the excellence of his art, not forgetting his marvellous portraits of women, and best of all, those works which he painted without the primary intention of producing a portrait and in which ordinary people were his model.

CHAPTER XL
Sculpture in Cordoba

Our nation appears to be less rich in sculpture than in paintings. Researchers have attempted to attribute this to race and to religious education. Because of a hatred of paganism, images were anathema to early Christians. Later, as the medieval Christian spurns and mortifies the body, naked sculptures are forbidden in churches. There are times, however, when this is unrivalled. The best studies today prove that in terms of quality, sculpture does not compare unfavourably with painting.

Nueva Carteya Lion Iberian sculpture [xxxvi]

Cordoba had – we said – fewer sculptors than painters. Here we see two traditions that complement each other: the Christian, and the Muslim one that tenaciously excluded images from its Mesquita, although it is not correct to say that they scorned the artistic representation of the body, as there are numerous examples of this, especially in industrial circumstances. There may be other reasons that explain why the city contributed fewer sculptors. There probably is a single one: an economic one. Today, however, after Juan de Mesa and the Rivas, the city boasts a prestigious, first-class school of sculpture.

Pre-Roman civilizations

Cordoba's provincial Museum of Archaeology has some, albeit few, prized examples of primitive Art from before the Roman occupation. The following are clearly Iberian:

1. A small sandstone male head that, despite its being in an extremely poor condition, reminds one of the sculptures from the Cerro de los Santos.
2. A marble slab with a bas relief sculpture of a hunting scene.[155]

Roman sculpture

The Roman people loved sculptures. Rome extended its power over all the countries surrounding the Mediterranean and in all it left artistic traces of its passage; the number of Roman statues found is enormous. Rome learnt the Art of the Statue from Greece, that it could never equal. Greek statues primarily personify elegance and beauty, Roman statues, strength and majesty. People today are more discerning and more admiring of Roman sculpture.

The Archaeological Museum of Cordoba has greatly prized examples of this art. The principal ones are Minerva and Head of Caligula.

There are two Roman statues in Romero de Torres' private museum that stand out for the remarkable way that cloth is carved. The Escuela de Artes y Oficios has the fragment of a puteal[xxxvii] that reproduces a subject found on the western side of the Parthenon: the battle between Neptune and Minerva.[156]

---

[155] There have been contradictory comments regarding this bas relief, but the belief that it is Iberian prevails because, in addition to the style, it reminds one of the "Wild Boar Hunt" bronze found in Merida, whose Iberian provenance is undisputed. The carts in the Cordoba Cacería are the same as those on the Merida bronze and correspond to the restored Iberian carts on the ex votos found in the Iberian sanctuary of Despeñaperros and in excavations in Peal de Becerra (Jaen) and Galera (Granada).

A Carthaginean statuette was very recently found: it represents a go ddess with an animal's head. It is of an Eastern style and feeling. One can accept as correct that this work of art is witness to the presence of the Carthagineans in Cordoba, a fact that was already presumed from findings in Andalusia and in this province, at Fuente Tójar and Almedinilla.

For further information on this period, *Vide:* a very useful manual entitled *Cronología de las antigüedades ibéricas anterromanas*, by J.R. Mélida, 1916.

The department of Prehistory and Iberian Art, at the Archaelogical Museum, has grown during the last few years. It has interesting examples attributed to the 3rd and 4th centuries B.C.E, mostly originating in this province. The Iberian lion from Nueva Carteya stands out. There are very few artifacts found in the city (small idols, stellae, and so forth.). The Institute also has a beautiful recently d scovered Iberian artifact.

[156] Reproduced and analyzed in *Materiales de arqueología española* by Gómez Moreno y Pijoán (Junta Ampliación estudios), March, 1912. *Civilización romana y sus monumentos en la Península,* J. R. Mélida, (Curso internacional de expansión comercial), Barcelona, 1914.

Visigoth sculpture

There are very few examples of Christian sculpture prior to the Arab period: the Visigoth altar in the Mesquita, some marble latticework, bases of columns, friezes and capitals in the Museum and the precious artistic nook formed by the capitals of this period in the early section of the Mesquita. Very little sculpture properly speaking.

Employed as the pylon for a fountain, there was a tomb on Calle Cardenal González with a beautiful central relief carving; the figures are half a metre tall. This Christian sarcophagus is one of the finest examples of early Christian art, probably from the 3rd century, although some would like it to be Visigoth. It is now located in the Mártires hermitage.

Arab sculpture

Surprisingly, one of the rare examples of Arab sculpture found in Spain, except perhaps for the Fountain of the Lions in the Alhambra, is in our museum in Cordoba.

This is a bronze stag, a horse, rather, from Medina-Azahara. Dating from the 10th century, this represents a somewhat exotic scene compared to other models. It is not a Cordoban work but of Fatimid art with an Egyptian influence.

The Arab capitals in Cordoba are excellent, especially those from the great period, and they still exist in abundance despite the depredations to which they have been subject over time. In Cordoba there were other magnificent archaeological collections in the past, all of which have disappeared, such as the famous Villaceballos lapidary that until recently was in Cordoba.

The Archaeological Museum contains a first-class, extremely important collection.[157]

The National Archaeological Museum contains the white marble basin that Almanzor had made for Medina-Azahara, featuring a sculptured section, yet another example of how contrary to common and widespread belief, the representative arts were cultivated by the Spanish Muslims both during and after the Cordoba Caliphate.[158]

Other Arab capitals with figures are also found in the Museum. The marble basin that was recently found in the Almunia in Alamiriya, is another beautiful example.

---

[157] Saladin, *Manuel d'art musulman,* 1906. Can be considered simply as a whole work. There are others, indicated in the Bibliography.

Almost all the Arab-Cordoban capitals are catalogued and their inscriptions have been translated and are cited in multiple references .

[158] R. Amador de los Ríos. Notas arqueológicas hispanomahometanas.

Medieval Christian sculpture

This now deals with examples of sculpture after the Conquest of Cordoba. The oldest of these appears to be the *Virgen de Linares* which is kept in the sanctuary of the same name and, if true, leads one to believe that this is a 13th century work.

It is, however, very possible that the oldest image of all is the *Virgen de las Huertas*, currently part of the cathedral treasure.

The statue to San Bartolomé in the Archaeological Museum, by an anonymous sculptor, is from the 14th century. The group of figures representing the Annunciation, attributed to a Juan de Cordoba,[159] is from the 15th century.

As of the 13th century, its evolution, is marked with representative examples not only in stone and marble, but also includes works that led to the great art of silver working.

Cordoban sculpture, like its paintings, deserves a book of its own.

The 17th century

It is at this time that we see a kind of sculptural renaissance, mainly triggered by the conclusion of the building work on the Crucero which, like the new churches and chapels which are being founded, needs to be decorated.

Luiz González, born in Cabra, worked on the main altarpiece in the cathedral in 1626 and stands out among Andalusian artists for his skill in polishing marble and jasper. Pedro Freile de Guevara worked on the stone statues on the altarpiece in 1616.

Pedro de Paz, another Cordoban, worked in the cathedral at the same time, especially on the wood and marble San Rafael, in the tower.

Bernabé Gómez del Rio, also a Cordoban, lived in the middle of this century and was the author of the image of *San Rafael del Puente* that was put in place in 1651.

In the same way that Cordoba bore the influence of painters from Seville, the sculptors from Granada were more connected to us. This is motivated by the school founded by Alonso Cano who, at the time, was Spain's sculptor of note. There is a Christ and a Santa Teresa by him in the cathedral.

Cano's two best disciples, Pedro de Mena and José de Mora, worked in Cordoba. Mena sculpted the statues in the Concepción chapel and that of San Pedro Alcántara, in the church of the same name; Mora, sculpted the statues in the Cardinal Salazar chapel.

---

[159] These works have a force and an impact that are quickly lost; they appear to belong to a strong school that awaits evolving. In truth, the examples that came later are inferior, such as the Christ attributed to Mencía de Oliva (1552), that nobody has seen, and even the cathedral's "San Pablo", said to be by Céspedes, surely a false attribution.
These are the works produced by the 16th century.

18th century

This renaissance is accentuated during this century, and its associated art, that of the silversmith, becomes extremely important. An enormous number of sculptures are produced during this period, as are the notorious tasteless baroque gilt altarpieces that invade Spain. Unfortunately, this is a time of bad taste.

At this time, a noted Sevillian artisan, Pedro Duque Cornejo (1677-1751), a follower of Pedro Roldán, arrives in Cordoba in 1748. His sculptured choir stalls in the cathedral are his finest work.[160] The *Asunción* in the Instituto is attributed to him. Duque Cornejo's passage through Cordoba was important to the art of woodcarving which, if not quite awe-inspiring, is regularly cited as a perennial artistic example of that art. Occasionally, led by the churrigueresque influence of the period, he went overboard with a proliferation of imaginative embellishments and fantasies.

José Antonio Ruíz Rey, from Puente Genil (1695-1767), assisted Cornejo in sketching the designs for the choir stalls.

Master Frei Juan Vázquez (1689-1757), a Cordoban monk at the San Pablo convent, left some average sculptures, one of which of *San Felipe de los Dolores*. Frei Gabriel de Ordónez wrote his biography in 1774.

Juan Jiménez, a modest artist who in 1772, together with the stonemason Alonso Pérez, created the statue of San Rafael in the Compañia.

Miguel de Verdiguier, a French sculptor, who together with architect Baltasar Graveton represent the French academic influence, carved the pulpits in the cathedral, created the monument to San Rafael in San Hipólito square, and in 1781, concluded *El Triunfo*. His influence was actually negative as he lacked a sense of balance, and his works cannot be considered as models. Perhaps the only good thing he did was to have introduced sculpting to José Alvarez Cubero, the best sculptor in the province of Cordoba about whom we will especially speak later.

Juan Navarro León is another Cordoban, of no great skill, who sculpted the *Cristo de los Dolores* in 1794.

Alonso Gómez de Sandoval (1713-1801) is the only Cordoban sculptor who showed some artistic spirit during this period, with intuition rather than study. The *Virgen de la Luz* in Santa Marina and the *Beata Ana* in the Iglesia del Hospicio

---

[160] See *La sillería de coro de la Catedral de Córdoba*, by M.A. Ortí (Arte español, 1919). A beautiful, documented work.

In the *Relación de cosas notables del templo material de la Santa Iglesia de Córdoba* (Academia de Historia, Vol. XXV, Chapter XVI), written by a chaplain in his twenties who entered the Church as a choir boy in 1711, there is a careful description of the old ogival choir stalls that existed before those carved by Duque Cornejo.

are examples of his work of which he produced quite a bit. His best work, a total triumph, is *Los cuatro Evangelistas* which belongs to the Gracia Fathers.

Lorenzo Cano (1750-1817) created, among others, *La Virgen de los Dolores* and *Santiago*, in the church of the same name, considered his finest work. His son José, who died in 1835, left nothing worth mentioning.

José Alvarez Cubero (1768-1827), born in Priego, son of a marble supplier, is the finest Cordoban sculptor. He and Salzillo were the only Spanish sculptors during the 18th century. He studied a great deal, went to Paris and Rome where he competed with the famous sculptor Cánova and, in 1845, was honoured by Napoleon. He is a first-rate classical sculptor, as proven by his *Venus* and his *Diana*.

Alvarez Cubero was attracted by historic sculptures, and he produced the great group *Los Numantinos*, his famous *Ensueños de la antigüedad* for the Quirinal in Rome, the statues of Carlos IV and Maria Luisa in the Museum of Modern Art in Madrid, and many more.[161]

He had no influence in Cordoba. He soon left and until very recently our museum did not even have a poor copy of this sculptor's statues, one of the best that Spain has ever produced. He was a genius who, as the Duke of Frias said, knew how to shine for a time in the famous city of Romulus.

José Tomás (1795-1848), who died in the mid-19th century, is the last Cordoban sculptor, whose work *La Cena*, sculpted on an inner column in the Caballero de Gracia church in Madrid, is worth praising.[162]

Inurria

There is an addendum to this note regarding Mateo Inurria who, during the 19th century and beginning of the 20th, was the one who broke the almost century-old sculptural silence in Cordoba.

Inurria, with his refined and later cultured art, produced magnificent work. Unlike Romero, his contemporary, he is owed a study by the Cordoba School of Art. He was born in 1867 and died in 1924.

---

[161] As you can see from this summary, sculpture flourished little in Cordoba, neither in terms of great works nor Cordoban artists, as except for Alvarez Cubero, there is rarely a name that might be worth being remembered by posterity.

The great Cordoban names, *Mesa* and *Rivas*, worked in Seville. During half a century, there were practically no sculptors in Cordoba during the 19th century.

As regards sculpture, little attention has been paid to the aesthetic of our city and until recently, only religious works dedicated to San Rafael existed, with very little to recommend in terms of works of art. The statues that were so plentiful in the Cordoba streets, as in all Spanish towns, almost totally disappeared in 1841.

For a study of sculpture, *Vide: La escultura en España* by Folch y Torres, 1914.

[162] *See* Serrano Fatigati, *La Escultura en Madrid,* Excurcionistas, 1911.

A new chapter for Art.

The Cordoban school of sculpture has grown notably over the past few years, thanks to research work in Seville especially, completed in Cordoba. Nobody knew who Juan de Mesa and Felipe de Rivas were.

The oh so powerful name of Juan Martínez Montañés, the sculptor from Alcalá la Real, whose centre of production is in Seville, and who is so identified with this city he swathed, that all great and brilliant works were attributed to him. Studious critics however, discovered other notable names as great as his and which turned out to be Cordoban.

Why is it that Cordoba, in an almost traditional manner, forced such great artists as Bermejo, Mesa and Rivas to shine elsewhere?

This is what critics have asked but not yet obtained an answer. There are perhaps several subtle causes for this, among them, the economic aspect and Cordoba's shifting away from the great routes of the Hispanic world.

When Cordoba was the great central city, she was sufficient. Later, these artists had to find a field for their achievements. What is great, that which we do have to point out, is the Cordoban artistic fertility that has never been extinguished.

Juan de Mesa, born in 1583, is followed by Felipe de Rivas, born in 1609. Both left magnificent work in Seville. The *Jesús del Gran Poder* is by Mesa as is the unbeatable *Cristo de Vergara*. Rivas is a great master of altarpieces, the finest that Seville produced in the 17th century, such as his *Santa Paula* altarpiece.

Monumental fountains

Among the sculptural works we must not forget to mention the monumental fountains that, in different places and at different times have decorated our city. The most monumental is the 16th century Potro fountain, sculpted in 1577.

This is followed by the Campo de San Antón fountain in 1746, similar to the one in the Patio de los Naranjos.

The last one, created with an artistic nature, must be Corregidor Vera Zúñiga's so-called 1721 *Piedra escrita* .San Andrés fountain, dating from 1664, is from the Plaza del Salvador.

CHAPTER XLI
Art and religious themes

From the 13th to the 19th centuries, Cordoba has a very interesting history of religious worship that influences its literature, its customs and its art. The history is of a previous life, it is shown in its fundamental guidelines.

The oldest known object of veneration is the cult of Saint Sebastian. This produced the extremely popular San Sebastian hermitage until the national worship of this saint was completely lost in 1845, only to live on as a popular municipal festival with a religious nature.

The 14th century and much of the 15th century were marked by the people's devotion to the *Virgen das Huertas*, later renamed *Virgen de la Victoria* only to completely lose its identity when religious orders were abolished between 1810 and 1836 and the convent of the same name, in present-day Victoria parish, was destroyed. The Cordobans were extremely devoted to the cult of this Virgin during the entire 16th century.

The early days of the 15th century also witnessed the birth of the cult of Fuensanta in 1420 and a sanctuary that was added to at different times, as well as relatively extensive religious literature.

Also, the object of worship during the early days of the 17th century, was the cult of *San Nicolás de Tolentino*. Born spontaneously in a neighbourhood house in 1602, this cult lasted off and on until the 19th century. It bequeathed nothing of note in artistic terms.

The cult of *San Bartolomé* dates to the days of the Reconquista and is very old in Cordoba where numerous chapels were dedicated to this saint. To this day several neighbourhoods are still named after him.

Devotion to *Jesús Nazareno* began in 1579, thrived during the 16th century and continued during the 17th century with the unusual name of *Cristóbal de Santa Catalina* until the 19th century when it lost its popular appeal.

At the beginning of the 16th century, Juan de Avila's influence in Cordoba with his founding of the Colegio de la Asunción and his outstanding sermons that contributed to the founding of hospitals such as the one dedicated to *San Bartolomé*.

A new religious boom provided the basis for the popular devotion to the relics of the martyrs beginning in 1575, greatly encouraged by Padre Andrés de Roelas who declared that Archangel Saint Rafael had appeared to him five times in May 1578, as saviour of plague-ridden Cordoba.[xxxviii]

This encouraged the cult of San Rafael which has inspired many literary and artistic works which lack any aesthetic skill.

Thus, the great literary festival of 1651 which is, as I have said earlier, is an example for our local literary history. The best literary work relating to San Rafael was by the Duque de Rivas.

From the 16th century onwards, this saint provided the greatest source of inspiration. In Astorga Cathedral, there is a *San Rafael* signed by Vela. Valdés, followed by Palomino, and painted by all artists.

It is curious to see how all the artists, painters and sculptors portrayed him with a sense of Roman victory. This classical feeling is also interesting as regards a history of local art, and indicates a classical influence that was never lost, not even during the flowering of Arab art.

The *Virgen de las Angustias*, adopted by a religious Brotherhood created for the devout in the 16th century (specifically 1570, I believe), is unique in that it produced the finest religious work in Cordoba. Authoritatively believed to be a work by Juan de Mena, particularly the Christ, some insist that two other artists are also involved.

Near the end of the 16th century, in 1580, Cordoba was said to be visited by *San Juan de la Cruz* and *Santa Teresa*. This would give rise to religious foundations and cults, followed over time by religious festivals, but except for certain occasions during the 17th century, would have little impact on the mass of the people.

Fray Luis de Granada's stay represents another religious orientation. He resides in the Santo Domingo convent. It is there, in the hills, that he writes some of his great books; his influence extends to preaching and local literature, which to a certain extent reflects the erudite nature of his learned path.

It is with him that we see the boom in the cult of San *Alvaro de Córdoba*, which I see is still confused in serious works with the Mozarab Alvaro Cordobés. San Alvaro de Córdoba dates from the beginning of the 15th century, a devotion that has continued, adapting to the times, until today. There is a reason that cults such as that of the *Virgen de Linares*, which dates to the days of the Reconquista, endure. Located in rural sanctuaries, they are sustained by the religious devotion of the people and an enduring love for the countryside.

The festivals flourish in Spring, under a splendid sun. Instinctively, unconsciously, the religious motive is accompanied by an ancient cult of the sun, not the mythical sun, but the perennial attraction of the Sierra and light.

This had some influence on the city's legendary and religious literature. On its Art, little. The ancient painting of the Virgen de Linares, however, has been the object of several archaeological studies.

The great influence on the Cordoban environment expands at the end of the 17th century with Padre Posada's sermons (1644-1713). They revert into literature and certainly contributed to the banning of the Theatre. I already expressed my opinion of his talents as a writer. As a preacher, he became extraordinarily famous. Mind you, judging from his writings, which should reflect his thoughts and prestige, it appears that although he was excessively popular, he was always unknown outside the city.

Much stronger than he, at the end of the 18th century, is Fray Diego de Cádiz. From his passage, there remained the very 18th century cult of *La Pastora*, whose artistic representations were of no artistic merit.

Some believe that this might be appreciated through its music.

Religious fervour and its observance, although aspiring to the divine, cannot be detached from the human. Thus, the changes in cults, their passionate beginnings, radiant booming, and then oblivion.

As an example, the beginning of the 18th century is marked by the extraordinary worship of the *Cristo de la Merced*. As a work of art, it is truly at the bottom of the list, but this frequently has no effect on popular beliefs and enthusiasm.

It appears that the cult of the *Virgen de los Dolores* begins in 1699, at the end of the 17th century. The images and the appeal of the cult in the city, date from this time. As regards sculptures, these are of the to be clothed kind, in that only the heads and hands are visible, which consequently reduces their artistic value compared to other types of statues.

A very old religious current in Andalusia, one that influenced Art through superb creations, was the people's devotion to the *Concepción*, a cult that has its own chapter in the story of Cordoba, with debates, arguments, controversies and fights. Some art was produced by Palomino, and there were some artistic works in silver. His work is decidedly better than the latter.

This worship carried the day when on 19 September 1650, both the Secular Council and the Church Council swore to protect and defend the mystery of the Immaculate Conception in perpetuity.

San Rafael, sculptural icon

The influence of San Rafael on art is especially apparent in the working of precious metals. I do not believe that silversmiths ever produced anything superior to Damián de Castro's 1765 *San Rafael*, which is kept in the cathedral's treasure vault.

Other sculptural works materialize in the *Triunfos*, or monuments, honouring San Rafael, which for hundreds of years, have been the only statues in the city. Beginning in 1651, these monuments to San Rafael appear on the bridge and elsewhere in the city. In 1736, there is such a statue on the Plaza de la Compañía. In 1743, a statue on the prison esplanade, today's railway station. Later, in 1747, the one that still exists at the so-called Puerta Nueva. In 1763, one on Aguayos square, next to San Pedro. In 1772, one on San Hipólito square, today the Plaza del Potro. Lastly, in 1781, the best, the monumental statue next to the Seminary, closes this series. As you see, these statues reach a highpoint in the 18th century.

Of all the pictorial conceptions of San Rafael, as I said earlier, the best are by Valdés Leal, even though they are not first-class works. Valdés' powerful realism did not allow for those abstractions.

Also, one can say that the History of the Church in Cordoba ended in the 18th century when Gómez Bravo stopped writing. Local history received Padro Ruano's appreciable tribute from the clergy. Later, except for worthy contributions, there has been no work such as that required by its own history and own defence - worship, cults, men, churches, images, institutions, sculptures and statues, teachings, and an almost unedited field despite interesting viewpoints in suggestive essays such as *Indicación del conjunto histórico de la Iglesia de Córdoba*.

Statue of Our Lady of Sorrows in Los Dolores church
4th edition of Historia de Córdoba, 1971

CHAPTER XLII
Ancient Cordoban stone inscriptions

The study of ancient inscriptions (epigraphy) is in itself remarkably interesting and one that deserves clarification of its guidelines. The most numerous are Hispano-Latin and Arab, followed by the Hispano-Christian of which very few remain. Of the Hebrew, there are even fewer, only those in the Synagogue.

From the so-called Hispano-Christian period, that is, the one prior to the Conquista and that includes the Visigoth and the Mozarabic, there are very few. There are a few examples in the Museum and in Romero de Torres' private collection.

There still has been no proper survey of the purely Christian inscriptions, those from the period that followed the expulsion of the Arabs from Cordoba. This, even though there are many of great local interest on tombs and house façades, either as mottos or for identification, such as Casa del Duque de Medina, Calle Rey Heredia, Casa de Orive, among others.

Also included are religious inscriptions on monuments to San Rafael and funerary ones on tombs. The best collection of the latter is in the Cathedral (Góngora, Céspedes; bishops, such as Austria, Mardones, and so forth.). Also, of interest are those found in many churches such as San Pablo, Santa Marin, Padres de Gracia, as they refer to persons who made their mark on local life.

The Arab inscriptions were not properly studied until Rodrigo Amador de los Rios did so in the last third of the 19th century.

This work was later followed by corrections. The research that best satisfies our interest is Levi-Provençal's recently published work, with an abundance of images and corrections and clear observations for the student.

Indicative of Cordoban interest and research into 18th century epigraphy can be found in *El Erario corduberse* by Pedro Leonardo de Villa-Zeballos. Villa-Zeballos wrote part of the 188 folios and Díaz Ayora completed the work. Thus, we discover that Villa-Zeballos lived until 13 June 1774 and that he was buried in San Pedro de Alcántara church.

Padre Pedro Ruano appears to have contributed to the study of the Exchecuer, which he describes as created in 1740 and set up and established in the first patio of the principle houses in the city and in the home of Don Rafael, his father,

Knight of Santiago, on Calle de las Pabas, a side street bearing his name, in the parish of the Santa Iglesia Catedral."

His study contains a long list of silver family medals and imperial coins or medals and a description of the Museum as explanatory of ancient stone inscriptions. There are also numerous (bad) pen and pencil sketches of coins and stone inscriptions.

Emil Hübner

This *Corpus*, or body of information regarding the Hispano-Latin inscriptions is well-known to everyone, namely Hübner's first book, *Inscripciones hispanolatinas* and the *Suplemento*, and the one entitled *Inscripciones cristianas*.

Hübner's work continues to be fundamental, although critics today talk of mistakes and corrections. That is natural, but despite all that, until someone publishes a new Cordoban Corpus it still is the only book on the subject. Hübner's book is extremely interesting, although perhaps the fact that it is written in modern, easily understood Latin, has prevented it from drawing the attention of the Cordoban aficionado. I know that the experts know it well.

It is also interesting because it reveals all the Cordoban antiquarians. He includes all the epigraphists, from both Cordoba city and province, with all their comments, not forgetting the fantastic Pozoblanco from the mountains (16th century) nor López de Cárdenas (18th century) from Montoro.

With Hübner as the guide, the list of epigraphists is also of extreme interest.

In truth, Hübner's stay in Cordoba is important. He was there in October 1860 where he met with Ramírez Casas Deza and gleaned a great deal from the Vázquez Venegas collection.

The value of Vázquez's miscellanea varies considerably as there are useless, almost ingenious, volumes; a stack of papers. Today there are only fourteen volumes that are kept at the Comisión de Monumentos, but there remains something that might be explored.

In volume VIII, Hübner does not conceal his studies of Vázquez as he states that when he examined it, the said collection contained 24 volumes. When speaking of the monuments, he says:

Cuius schedæ tam epigraphicæ quam historicæ et miscellanæ vigente quator voluminibus comprehensæ (sunt 13 vol. Fol. 11, vol. IV). Servantur in Bibliothecæ provinciali quæ Corduba est.

In addition to this information, which is neither secret nor published for the first time, there is much of interest such as mention of the lapidary belonging to Pedro Leonardo de Villa-Zeballos, of whom Pérez Bayer spoke. I believe that in Hübner's time, it belonged to Rafael Villa-Zeballos.

Hübner had the following to say regarding the founder: *Vir non indoctus et rerum antiquarium amantisimus,* continuing with his description:

Et enim in domo sua, quæ etiam nunc extat, quanque olim solebant et Museo, nuncupare titulos collegerat, tam cordubensis quam universæ provincia Bætica plus sexaginta. Quorum hodie si miharios exceperis de quibur dicetur suo loco, incuria et aviditate posteriorum ejus perierunt undevigente. Supersunt quadraginta plus minus.

The author complained of negligence and greed and the negligence worsened when in 1885 the lapidary was lost. After an absurdly low amount was offered for it, most of the lapidary ended up in a private collection in the Finca de la Concepción, Malaga, thus depriving Cordoba of a valuable artefact of a richness that was very much its own. One cannot be surprised that today there is so little left of antique Cordoban inscriptions in our museums, both private and public.

Hübner published his study of 140 Cordoban headstones in *Inscripciones hispanicolatin*as (nos. 2,191 to 2,321) and extended his research with his description of 14 Roman miliaria.[xxxix]

His *Suplemento* contains additional, less important, information, but it is here that we note the names of Romero Barros and Rivera Romero as collaborators in these studies.

There is also some value to the data, as he uses engravings, regarding Cordoban epigraphy that he knew and personally studied concerning the Hispano-Latin inscriptions.

* * *

This research did not cease with Hübner, who we can say drew attention to these studies. Everything regarding Cordoban epigraphy can be seen continued in the *Boletín de la Academia de la Historia.* There already was a better way to conduct this study and it is interesting that Padre Fidel Fita and other Cordoban and out-of-town experts followed the path of our epigraphists.

We still need a Cordoba Corpus that can use and itemize existing inscriptions, such as a beautiful one in the Seville Municipal Museum, and add new studies or newly-discovered ones.

The most interesting find, a Greek inscription, occurred some time ago.[163]

I believe that neither will add much to the general History of Cordoba. We must not, however, ignore these historic landmarks that are an easy road, like so many others, leading to local studies.[164]

---

[163] See Boletín de la Academia de Córdoba.

[164] Similar to this is the case of Cordoban heraldry: a great many coats-of-arms have been photographed, I believe by Sarazá. There still are large collections in Cordoban homes but, generally speak-

Documentary wealth

As in many respects, as this is just a guidebook, I shall now address sources for documents. In Cordoba, these are found in several places:

- A) Archivo de Protocolos
- B) Archivo Catedral and Biblioteca
- C) Biblioteca Espiscopal
- D) Archivo Municipal and
- E) Biblioteca Provincial.

The city has a great researcher at the Archivo de Protocolos, José de la Torre, who obtained more than 12,000 slips of paper from the 16th and 17th centuries notary files. He has published some of his work on these and they are kept in the appropriate place. However, little has been made public regarding his so far, unpublished work.

The *Archivo de Protocolos* (Official Deeds) is in the Casas Consistoriales, a totally inadequate place. At least 10,000 such documents are stored there, the oldest dating back to 1442.

There are thousands of dowry agreements, wills and testaments, deeds of purchases and sales, contracts, and so forth., that reflect the life of almost everyone who has lived in Cordoba since the middle of the 15th century.

This great researcher who, as he says, has only examined a third of the archives (15th century, almost all the 16th century and half of the 17th century), annotated some 20,000 documents that might be, and certainly are, of interest, although in different degrees.

He points out the name and number of approximately two hundred painters although, from the onset, they are not all of artistic merit. There are some noteworthy artists such as Pedro Fernández and his son-in-law Alejo Fernández, both Cordoban, of course, Pedro de Córdoba, Pedro Romana (who called himself thus because he had lived in Rome), Agustín and Antonio Castillo, Valdés Leal and Cristóbal de Vela.

There are names of sculptors, stone masons and architects.

What appear most are names of leather workers and silversmiths, Cordoba's two great industries from the 16th to the 18th centuries. There are 300 leather workers and an equal number of silversmiths.

When it comes to the history of the Theatre, beginning with the great Lope de Rueda, the Archivo has notes of almost all the authors of comedies and farces that passed through Cordoba in the 16th and 17th centuries.

---

ing, they have not been identified. The only known study of these is in Alfonde's *Nobiliarios de Morales*, Ms. Academia de la Historia, Biblioteca Nacional and Municipal Archives. I only mention this as indicating roads and paths to follow.

This flow of research, however, remains almost totally unpublished, but not because of the author's greed. Quite the contrary. It is, today, a magnificent work, only small parts of which have been incorporated in the ordinary files. I know perfectly well that it is not that data that is going to change the bases of any literary, artistic and economic history. However, the material needs architects, and it is very possible that it will give rise, as always, to new points of view, especially regarding the history of the leather workers, some of which has only been studied in part, not as a whole, and could be completed. Something similar has occurred regarding the history of the Cordoban silversmiths, magnificently begun by Ramírez de Arellano, and better known than that of the leather workers as regards its genesis and development.

We are, therefore, faced with research and a study that could provide the necessary matrix for the great amount of knowledge that we already have of Cordoban life.

When this worked stone becomes organic and comes to life, Cordoba will have done a great service for its local history. Local histories provide the basis and the origin for all national histories.

The Cathedral Archives have been relatively little explored. In modern times, perhaps the most ample exploration is by Carlos Lea, regarding the Inquisition. The attention of scholars has been drawn to the curious codex of the *Indiculus*.

There is some local research by Latorre, Orti and E. Romero de Torres, but little of that is known so far.

The most extensive oldest research was, without a doubt, during the 18th century, organized by Vázquez Venegas. His colleague, Domínguez. Bravo, Bishop of Cordoba, also used it and did some work on his account. I believe that because of the truly little use that has been made of it, this Archivo harbours some surprises of local interest.

Additional information

The Cathedral Archives are divided into two sections: one, attached to the *Biblioteca del Cabildo*, contains pontifical and royal documents, mostly prior to the 16th century; the other section contains documents from that century onwards.

The most interesting of these are the books recording the Meetings of the Chapter, correspondence between with the Chapter's agents at Court and in Rome and the personal information and dossiers of individuals for the filling of positions.

The Biblioteca del Cabildo began to be created almost at the beginning of the Christian conquest, founded in the 14th century following Dean Pedro de Ayllón's donation of manuscripts.

Later, it received the collections from Bishops Deza and Angulo, as well as books from Ruiz de Morales, one of the first inquisitors.

It appears that Ambrosio de Morales, in compliance with an order from Felipe II, sent a great many Arabic manuscripts to the Escorial, thereby reducing the wealth of the Cordoban collections.

This library, like all others, has suffered from negligence and thefts. The masterly Gonçalo Francés, who jealously explored them, declared that there were many books left to study.

The manuscript collections are, as I said, of interest. Canon Bravo almost limited himself to examining the records of the Chapter meetings, but he still left a very worthy unfinished book.

Rodolfo Gil declared that the several papers and legal arguments contained in one hundred and ninety-four exceptionally large volumes, buried in the Biblioteca Capitular Eclesiástica and acquired by the Chapter from Reverend Gregorio Pavia's Last Will and Testament, have not yet been studied.

The episcopal Bibliotheca is less valuable but is nevertheless most important. It is so long since I last consulted it, that I cannot at present determine its value. There are, however, notes, manuscripts, books, and so forth, for the 17th and 18th centuries, some which have been coming to our attention for inclusion in our local history.

The *Archivo Municipal*, however, is extraordinarily rich. It has constantly been consulted since the days of López Runo and by all the young archivists who followed him (La Torre, Ortí, Rey Díaz) and who have contributed something. Nevertheless, it still contains complete sections, such as the *Archivo de los Jurados*, that although I have only briefly consulted, believe to be extremely important. Always, of course, from the viewpoint of a focus on a specific history.

The Archivo Municipal is estimated to contain some 36,000 documents grouped in more than 3,000 bundles of papers, and whose value varies considerably. Its archivists have always worked most efficiently.

Of the collections in the *Archivo Consejal*, one that stands out is the Fuero de Córdoba, the charter issued by the Chancellery of Ferdinand III in 1241. Compared to the Archivo de Protocolos, these archives have been very well set up since 1878.

This collection has been greatly explored at different times. The best ancient research, albeit partly lost, is Venegas' during the 18th century. There remains, nevertheless, considerable documentation regarding the guilds (well-studied), municipal ordinances covering all aspects of local life, those identified by their special terminology as *asonadas* (which deal primarily with Cordoban Jewry) concerning Muslims and so forth. Lastly, the special *Archivo del Cabildo de los*

Jurados has escaped any great investigation except for some feeble attempts during the 18th century.

The *Archivos Parroquiales*, or parish archives, are also important, albeit less so than others. They have been more studied and more recently, their most fortunate researcher has been E. Romero de Torres. His dossiers on Antonio del Castillo, Juan de Mesa and Felipe de Rivas, are examples of the quality of his work.

This, basically, is the state of our local history studies and of the sources for their investigation. It is increasingly difficult to consolidate the history of Cordoba. There are many determinant elements that still must be dealt with in order to proceed with a complete historical investigation of Cordoba.

Because of that, I insist, the Cordoba Institute introduced Arab and Hebrew studies. It was our duty to prepare this instrument for future researchers. We did not want to wait for Madrid to act. We do not think it either good or bad that Granada has such studies. These are ours by right and because it is our duty, which is why we acted.

Madrid, who turned a deaf ear to us; who left us without the Hispanic-Islamic Exhibition we asked for in 1921, without the University of Arabic Studies which we requested in 1921 as an introduction to training staff from Morocco, in 1931 also deprived us of the initial creation of a Centre for Andalusian Studies that several worthy Cordobans had funded. We shall go ahead without Madrid and without help. Some day we will get along.

To this information, I must add a reference to the very interesting *Biblioteca del Seminario de San Pelayo*, containing books that are hard to find elsewhere, such as Jacques Paul Migné's *La Patrología*. Then, there is the *Biblioteca Provincial*. Today, it is well organized and has a small number of manuscripts, all from the Marquis of Cabriñana, and other local items of some interest.

The great private libraries have disappeared from the city. The last one, belonging to Feliciano Ramirez de Arellano, was badly sold and scattered at the end of the 19th century.

This is not to say that there is nobody with books that are useful for our history, but one cannot create a personal guide for each expert or aficionado. I do not wish to end without mentioning the Instituto y Colegio de la Asunción, which appears to have held a number of manuscripts of great interest to our city, but which today, for some unknown reason, has been greatly depleted.

CHAPTER XLIII
Other Arts

Silversmiths, Engravers

Cordoba boasts a long artistic tradition in these fields. First, there were the *guadamacileros*[xl] who created the embossed varicoloured leather work for which Cordoba is famous. Of the various trades which flourished in the city, however, the principal trade, and in relatively modern times at that, was silversmithing.

Cordoban silversmiths filled Spain with works of art. Their most important age, their golden age, was the 18th century. The origins of both trades are extremely old and attempting to determine which peoples developed these skills is a useless task.

Tarif and Bedr are the oldest known silversmiths in Cordoba, creators of the magnificent Arab chest found in the Cathedral of Gerona that Al Haquem commissioned for his son.[165]

Afterward no names and barely any works appear. In the 14th century there are many items of Cordoban filigree work. In 1503, at the beginning of the 16th century, the Cordoba guild of silversmiths creates its brotherhood, with San Eligius as its patron saint. In 1488 the Reyes Católicos issued a proclamation for their silversmith subjects, covering the trade and weights of precious metals.

During the last part of the Middle Ages, both silver and goldsmithing experienced a seemingly incredible boom, especially in Italy and in Flanders where, in Bruges goldsmiths and silversmiths made up various companies of a regiment. Particularly after its establishment in 1443, the Feast of Corpus Christi led to the production of *custodias*[xli] whose influence was so decisive to Cordoba's silversmithing tradition.

The Great Arfe

Enrique de Arfe, a foreign artisan who came to Spain at the end of the 15th century, was the founder of a veritable dynasty of artisans (Antonio, Juan and so forth.) who filled the entire 16th century.

---

[165] Antonio Vives, *"La arqueta arábiga de Gerona"* (*Excursiones*, 1892)

Enrique, who crafted the custodias of Leon and Toledo as well as the last custodia in Cordoba, reached heights of inspiration.

Arfe's influence is very strong throughout Spain and with him the modern school of Cordoban silversmithing is definitely established. The Cordoba custodia was made around 1513 to 1518. The processional cross of the cathedral of Cordoba is undoubtedly also a work of his.

Immediately following him, there is the Cordoban Juan Ruiz, *el Vandalino* (the Vandal), a disciple of Arfe's, who also had his own personal style. The first custodia in Spain that was not pointed is ascribed to him – that of Jaen, finished in 1535. According to Juan de Arfe, Ruiz was the first to turn silver on a lathe and demonstrated throughout Andalucía how to tool well. In other words, he introduced a beneficial change in technique to his trade. He also made the *lunette*[xlii] and the *pyx*[xliii] for the Baza custodia.

**Custodia de Arfe religious monstrance
Santa Teresa chapel, Mesquita-Cathedral**

Studies of these artisans are still being undertaken and amplified, although a book on silversmithing is still unavailable. Several names have appeared, namely in 1523 when twenty-four people signed a statement presented to the City Council,[166] proud examples of the craftsmen who lived at the time of Arfe. "We are rich and have paid our dues" they say, defending themselves from the Council who, they maintain, wished to subject them to somea degree of humiliation which the craftsmen considered intolerable.

The history of local art changes every day, as new names and entries are added, and major surprises may be in store.[167]

The founder of the Cathedral of Cordoba's treasure and the so-called Bishop of Mardones' cross is known – he is another Cordoban. Just as there was a Cordoban school of painters which peaks with names such as Alejo Fernández and Bartoló Bermejo and hundreds of secondary painters, one can say that there is a specific and personal school of silversmiths in this small segment of art history.

The major works (crosses, chalices, pyxes) in the cathedral treasury today date from the beginning of the 16th century.

It is highly likely that older works have disappeared. According to Juan de Arfe, to make the custodia his grandfather Enrique melted much gold and silver which he received from the Church Council.

The Arfe custodia was epoch-making and traced a path and a style. Vandalino, Arfe's immediate disciple, made the ones in Jaen, Badajoz and San Pablo convent in Seville.

Among the many examples of the silversmiths' art which exist in the artistic area of our province, one is in Fuenteovejuna (16th century), attributed to the beginnings of the school and one in Santaella (17th century). They form a small part of the official, still unpublished, *Catalogación* Ramirez de Arellano began.

Included in this beautiful group of custodias is an 18th century work, Damián de Castro's magnificent shrine in San Nicolás church.

Silversmiths

Numerous 16th century Cordoban silversmiths are worthy of being mentioned. Let us cite Rodrigo de León who with Sebastián de Córdoba crafted the image of the Virgin of Villaviciosa, as well as two beautifully enamelled *portapaces*, or sacred images.[xliv] Leon and Córdoba crafted the images in silver,

---

[166] Manuel Merino published them in *Revista Arqueológica*.
[167] Some say that there is now documentary proof that the *Custodia de Arfe* was in fact not by Arfe, that the great reform of 1616 produced a new one and that the original custodia was also not by Enrique de Arfe. Researchers will reveal its author.

leaving the head of the Virgin and the Christ Child in wood. These so-called Duque de Segorbe portapaces are known to have been contracted in 1581. Sebastián de Córdoba dies in 1587. The list of his belongings is very curious, compared to Pablo de Céspedes' for instance, and shows how the middle class in Cordoba - a rich silversmith and a poor canon - lived during the 16th and 17th centuries. Also interesting is the inventory of Ambrosio Morales' goods who, although not wealthy when he died, was far from destitute.

Rodrigo de Leon in his 1603 Will and Testament, describes himself as a Cordoba Cathedral hammer silversmith. Francisco Merino, from Jaen but a follower of Vandalino, dared compete with Juan de Arfe and, in Cordoba, worked for San Jerónimo convent and elsewhere.

The famous embossed brazier from the cathedral by an unknown artisan, is from this century. During this period the *burin*, hallmark of the Cordoba silversmiths, is an engraving tool with a lion and the syllable *Cor*.

Francisco de Alfaro made the cathedral's four silver candelabras in 1578.

Lucas Valdés, without doubt related to the famous painter, is another famous silversmith who had real taste. He crafted the lantern of the chapel of the Martyrs (San Pedro), in 1602.

Martín Sánchez de la Cruz forges the large, 325-pound, lamp in the cathedral transept.

During this century Cordoban art reaches great heights. Valdés Leal and Antonio del Castillo produce models for the silversmiths. There is an increased use of precious stones in Cordoba, as in the rest of the country, to peak in the 18th century. Generally speaking, silversmiths in the 17th century indulged in more artifices than in the previous century, as in Seville for example, where a tendency towards the excessive use of precious stones focuses more on the value of the stones than on the quality of the work of art itself.

18th Century

Although the art of silversmithing was declining in almost all of Spain, remarkable baroque works in silver were being produced in Cordoba during the 18th century by such famous individuals as Damián de Castro and Cristobal Sánchez Soto. Theirs is a singular, unmistakable and immediately recognizable style.

Juan Sánchez Izquierdo and Juan de Torres are the authors of the beaten silver of the Ayuntamiento altar.

Tomás de Pedrajas creates the Del Paular custodia in the 18th century. He worked in the El Paular Cartusian monastery at the same time as Antonio Palomino, the painter.

Barnabé García de los Reyes, appears in 1731, early in the century, as an artist renovating the custodia de Arfe.

Damián de Castro

Damián de Castro (1716-1790) is the great architect of this school of art. His master work, the Sigüenza custodia, once thought lost, was found by Narciso Sentenach and forms the core of the Cadiz custodia.

He skillfully embosses and chisels, as can be seen in the 1757 all silver *Conception* of the Cathedral, as well as several sacred cups in 1776, and the urn of the Holy Week monument. Castro does not have Arfe's artistic vision, but he does possess the steady hand of a brilliant artist. His *San Rafael*, crafted in 1765 and part of the cathedral treasure, is the most beautiful image of Saint Rafael either painted, sculpted or silver-wrought, produced in the city.

Cristóbal Sánchez Soto, like Castro a member of a family of silversmiths, left the silver reliquery chest of the *Mártires* (San Pedro) in 1790, as an example of his work. He is an outstanding artist with a hint of the sculptor.

Antonio Santa Cruz, author of the silver mitre of Saint Eligius, in 1768; and lastly, Juan Segovia y la Hoz, who in 1745 writes his work *Universidad de la platería y compendio de todas las ciencias, which* no one has seen.

Isidro Espejo y Saavedra (1788-1876) seems to have been the last silversmith to have upheld the prestige of the art in Cordoba, although without success.

Closing Notes

For reasons not germane to this book, silversmithing in Cordoba suffered almost one hundred years of great decline. The guild lost prominence and importance with industrial competition seemingly striking the final blow. Recently, hints at a resurgence have been noted and the sector seems willing to reclaim its past glory, although it has declined once again, but not for lack of artists.

Ramírez de Arellano, in particular, has availed himself of new document to study this Art sector: *Estúdios de historia de la orfebrería cordobesa* and *Diccionario de artistas cordobeses.*[168]

Also interesting is *Bosquejo histórico de la orfebrería española*, by Narciso Sentenach.[169]

Regarding the Spanish custodias, see Anselmo Gascón de Gotor's summary, El *Corpus Christi y las custodias procesionales de España,*[170] as well as *Las artes musulmanas de España en la Exposición de Munich* by Ernesto Kuhnel.[171]

---

[168] Unpublished documents, volume 107.
[169] *Bosquejo histórico de la orfebrería española,* by Narciso Sentenach, Madrid 1909.
[170] Gascón de Gotor, El *Corpus Christi y las custodias procesionales de España,* Madrid 1916.
[171] *Las artes musulmanas de España en la Exposición de Munich* by Ernesto Kuhnel, *Museum* 1911.

Damían de Castro has also had commentators. The *Revista Bética*. Seville, produced a not badly written study on him. Pérez Villaamil lectured on *Una joya inédita de la orfebrería Española*. Sentenach gave an academic conference which may not have been printed.

Local scholars, notably Manuel Merino, have collected silversmith burins, and at one time, a carefully organized exhibit of Cordoban silverwork was suggested. A major study could be undertaken considering the number of examples of Spanish silversmithing throughout Spain, some from the 16th century, some from the 17th century and many more from the 18th century. For example, in Cordoba, the *custodia chica* of Santaella, the Fuenteovejuna monstrance, the one from the church of San Nicolás, already mentioned, the one in Teruel and another in Cádiz, and the magnificent chalice from the Cordoba hospital. We cannot forget the scattered and uncatalogued examples in Seville that cry out for a study. There also are several works in Compañia church in Arequipa, Peru, which appear to be and most certainly are of Cordoban origin, and which I admired with some satisfaction.

Just as guadamecí, the embossed and gilt leather, represents the industrial artistic product of Cordoba during the 16th and 17th centuries, silversmithing with its extraordinary dissemination is the great artistic contribution to Cordoba during the second half of the 17th century and all of the 18th century.

This study is most needed in Cordoba, where no inventory of these works of art has been made. There are many such works in churches, monasteries and in individual hands. Furthermore, the cathedral treasure is neither inventoried from an artistic point of view, nor studied, nor even half-decently properly exhibited.[172]

The most heartfelt description of the Arfe custodia, the only work of art which has been studied on numerous occasions, was by Pedro de Madrazo in his book, *Córdoba.*

* * *

The legislation pertaining to the silversmithing trade is very interesting, not only in Cordoba but also in other Spanish production centres, namely Madrid, Valencia and Leon, and to an extent in a style related to Cordoban filigree work, Salamanca. The privileges which Cordoba's guild of silversmiths enjoyed and were studied by R. de Arellano in *Libro de privilegios del arte de la platería,* were not solely theirs but were granted through legislation to all guilds. The works in silver from Madrid, Valencia and Leon have been amply studied. The same can be

---

[172] J. M. Camacho (B.A. Cordobesa) wrote an excellent article on the subject, and it seems that his recommendations are being heeded.

said for Toledo, more a centre of consumption than a school, but nevertheless especially important.

The following is a summary of the fundamental privileges:

- 1483 – Reyes Católicos. Silversmiths are exempt from sales taxes.
- 1556 – Carlos I. Exempts the wives of silversmiths from the injunction against wearing silks, a provision of the legislation regarding clothing, and also allows silversmiths to hold public offices, such as governors, mayors, and so forth.
- 1619 - *Felipe* III – Also exempts them from paying a 1% tax on the price of their goods, to which they were subject.
- 1641 - Felipe IV – Exempts them from having to billet soldiers during the war with Catalonia.
- At the beginning of the 19th century, they were exempted from paying taxes.

Engraving

This branch of industrial art was not very important in Cordoba and although there are others, only one name is especially cited: Juan Bernabé Palomino (1692-1777). A professor at the Academia de San Ferdinand, he was a pupil of his uncle, Antonio Palomino, for whom he engraved the prints for *Museo Pictórico*.

Juan Díez is believed to have been Palomino's pupil and there are signed works by him dated 1760, 1762, 1764 and 1766. There are many mentions of these engravers and others in books with prints from the 17th and 18th centuries.

Then we have Bartolomé and José Vázquez, father and son.

Bartolomé Vásquez (1749-1802), a Cordoba silversmith and engraver, like all others in this chapter, is self-taught. He becomes an outstanding engraver, rivalling Salvador Carmona. Using colour and engraving in various colours, his engravings *La Rosa* and *La Virgen de la Silla* are famous, as are the plates for the edition of *El Quijote* annotated by the poet Manuel José Quitana. His son José (1768-1804) followed his father's tradition.[173]

---

[173] This art, which had a precursor in Lucas Valdés, never was highly successful in Cordoba, and less so in the 19th century; a century which among us, as has been noted, was one of extreme decline, one only interrupted at the dawn of the 20th century.

Information regarding prints can be found in Historia *del grabado* by Domingo Martínez; and *El Grabado en España by José* Caveda. (Discursos ingreso Academia San Ferdinand).

CHAPTER XLIV
Guadamacileros – the embossed leather craftsmen

This has been one of our major industries, whose success is linked to another industry, tanning, which reached great heights in Cordoba. *Guadamaci!*, the art of embossed and painted leather, flourished under the Arabs and continued to thrive under the Christians.

An example of the work of Arab leather craftsmen - guadamacileros - is the *arqueta de Huesca*[xlv] and closer to us, the Hall of Justice ceiling in the Alhambra. During the 14th and 15th centuries the famous cordovan leatherwork was sold throughout Spain and Europe.

In 1502 the Catholic Monarchs codified rules and norms for this guild in their *Ordenanzas* which are kept in the Municipal Archives.[174] In Cordoba, this craft reached its greatest heights during the 16th century but as the century wanes, the sector begins to decline and disappears completely within less than half a century.

The frontispiece of the cathedral altar, with its crimson and silver background, and the frontispiece of the Iglesia del Corpus altar, with its gold background, are two excellent examples. Cordovan armchairs are famous. A beautiful example of the craft can be seen in the La Alegría hermitage, and others, in the Marqués de Viana Collection.

Martín López (1507) was the oldest known leather craftsman, according to the data from the chronicler of Cordoba. Juan Carrillo, the last guadamacilero, is credited with crafting the embossed leather in the Cathedral in 1607. Alfonso Pérez Moreno, in 1678, is also mentioned.

There have been books on the subject since Ambrosio de Morales, whose description of Cordoba decked out in cordovan leatherworks in his *Las antigüedades de las ciudades de España* has been often quoted:

> *They were not only used to cover the walls of churches and homes, but also as rugs, on cushions and bolsters, and frequently as altar frontispieces, on the seats and backs of chairs, and so forth.*

---

[174] Archivo Municipal, volume IV, folio 248, year 1520.

Las Joyas de la exposición histórico-europea, Madrid, 1892, is the best summary of Spanish art. It includes the famous frontispiece from the main altar in Cordoba Cathedral, embroidered in gold and silk, a work from the 15th century.

A short but nice summary is Antonio Sarazá's *Arte industrial guadamacíes*. There was a small exhibit in Cordoba in 1924.

The importance of a related craft in Cordoba, weaving, is seen in Francisco Fernández y González' book, *El Tiraz de Hixem II*.[175]

The origin of cordovan leatherworking goes back to the heydays of the Arabs. Leatherworking depended on the tanning industry which excelled in Cordoba during both the Arab and the Christian eras, when one spoke then of the embossed and gilt leather harness with which Abderramán III harnessed his horse. It is also possible that cordovan leather was originally only used for military garments to enhance their opulence.

There are wonderful examples in museums of leathers worked by Arab craftsmen, such as the Huesca casket and the so-called Cordoba living room in the palace in Naples.

Laws pertaining to leatherworking were passed in 1502, 1529, 1553 and 1579. At the time of the earlier laws their guild was separate from the tanners. Later laws decreed by Felipe II as extensions to existing legislation and in confirmation of that enacted in 1529 by Carlos V, established detailed regulations regarding the manufacture of the skins: they must use sheepskins and the silver must be sterling.

The latest information expands on what has been said up to now regarding the continued presence of the art in Cordoba – although still showing it in a clear state of decline.

Simón de Toro, founder of the Hermita de la Salud, names Alfonso Pérez Moreno, a guadamacilero from Cordoba, as executor in his Will, dated November 19, 1678. It is very possible that there are no more leatherworkers after this date.

The artistic decline began at the end of the 16th century and increased rapidly, to recover during the first part of the 17th century.

The guadamaciles were their best during their 16th and 17th centuries, especially between 1550 and 1650. Although this date is arbitrary, it does give an idea of the main timeline.

Various examples show the differences in style and technique between the 16th and the 17th century when the embossed leather has less relief and designs become ungraceful. Guadamacileros who used silver are from the earlier period. Colour, especially, the subject of intense legislation in the 1553 Ordenanzas, loses its vibrancy and its shine.

---

[175] Museo Español de Antigüedades, volume VI.

An indispensable source, really the only one for the study of guadamaciles is kept in the Archivo Municipal. Some material has been published and the *Actas y edictos del Concejo de Córdoba*, the *Reales cédula y documentos del Gremio* and the *Ordenanzas* still survive.

There are a few written sources which refer to the craft, but the only useful Cordoban sources are recent ones, namely those by Ramírez de Arellano y Sarazá, the well-known *Notas sobre los cueros de Córdoba* by Jean Charles Davillier, 1879, and *Las antigüedades* by Ambrosio de Morales, 1575. [176]

The poem *El Cid* speaks of this industrial art for which Cordoba was so famous, as it equates the original name Guadamex with that of Cordoba – guadamaciles and Cordobans. Verse 85 begins:

> *Con vuestro consejo bastir quiero dos arcas;*
> *Inchámoslas d'arena, ça bien seran pesadas,*
> *Cubiertas de guadalmeçí e bien enclavadas.*
> *Los guadamecíes vermejos, e los clavos bien dorados.*

CHAPTER XLV
Other Crafts

Artistic Woodworking

Other artistic trades flourished in Cordoba. The Arabs and their heirs, the Mudejar, were great carpenters. The ancient, coffered wood ceilings that remain in Cordoba, although crafted by Christian artisans, are proof of the excellence of their work.

Their work can be seen in the Jesús Crucificado church, the former Jesús Maria convent of which only the church remains, El Carmen convent, the Museo Provincial de Pinturas, the former Regina church, that which once was the Military Governor's headquarters and before that San Felipe church, and in private homes such as those of the Páez family.

The ceilings in El Carmen church, which harbours the altarpiece by Juan de Valdés, transform this church into a small museum. Those in Jesús Crucificado church are also magnificent.

---

[176] Their conclusions, and a few personal ones were gathered in Antonio Jaén's unpublished conference, *Los Guadamaciles cordobeses,* at the 1924 *Exposición de Guadamaciles.* Also in a similar venue, the 1927 *Semana Gongorina* and the 1929 *Semana Califal*, two conferences also by Antonio Jaén: *El espíritu de Góngora* and *Política internacional de los Abderramanes.* Some have found their way into this little book.

All these works trace their remote ancestry to the original coffered ceiling of painted and sculpted beams built by the Arabs in the Mesquita.

Lope de Liaño, García Alonso in the 16th century and Alonso Muñoz de los Rios in the 17th century, among others, are prestigious names of Cordoban artisans mentioned by Ramírez de Arellano in *Artistas exhumados*.[177]

The ceilings in the Páez family's house are the work of Francisco Muñoz and Alonso de la Plaza (1530?). The Santiago church ceiling was by Muñoz de los Rios, in 1635, and that of Encarnación church, by Alonso de Aranda at the beginning of the 17th century. There are numerous coffered ceilings to be found in private houses, such as a house in Callejas de Alcántara, one in Calle de la Encarnacíon, and another in Calle de los Judíos, near the Plazuela de las Bulas. The ceilings in the so-called Casa de las Bulas have disappeared. They were taken to Seville where they became a magnificent ceiling which adorned one of the palaces in the Seville Exhibition. Others are hidden from view in several Cordoba churches, notably Santiago and San Nicolás.

Artistic Forging

The art of the forge was also important although never as important as it was in cities[178] such as Cuenca, Toledo, Segovia and others. There is still some nice ironwork as that by Ferdinand de Valencia in the Capilla del Sagrario, in 1554, as well as the wrought-iron Renaissance gates of the Capilla de San Acislo on the eastern side of the cathedral and in the Capilla de la Resurreccíon. The ironwork in the Capilla de Santa Inés is by Pedro Sánchez, in1593. There is more dating from 1569 in this nave of the cathedral.

The smith and the stonemason - important trades in Cordoba - plied their usually anonymous but extremely useful occupations alongside the great architects, painters, sculptors, and so forth.

The pinnacle of artistic ironwork was reached during the gothic period and is one of the marvels in our cathedrals.

Decorative Tiles

Cordoban decorative tiles do not have the splendour of the tiles from Seville – in fact, they seem to have arrived here later than in Seville.

---

[177] *El arte de la lacería* by Antonio Prieto Vives, Madrid, 1901, based on the book by Diego Lopéz de Arenas. *Carpintería de lo blanco y tratado de alarifes*, is a particularly useful work, with explanations of the techniques used by the Mudejar carpenters.

[178] "Y aunque señalándose Córdoba en las labores de adorno en oro, plata y cuero... nunca logró celebridad ni nombre en el trabajar los aceros." Fernández y Gonzáles, *Espadas hispano-arábes*.

The city is full of examples. Some are known only through a reference, such as the tiles in Santa Cruz convent, which practically no one has seen. Of note is a house on Calle Martínez Rucker, which has tiles on its exterior.

Were these tiles made in Cordoba? Probably not – they came either from Seville or later, Talavera. The tile industry was never particularly important in Cordoba although there are nevertheless some interesting examples.

It is recorded that in 1606, the Cordoba City Council contracted Hernando de Valladares from Triana to deliver a large quantity of decorative tiles. The tiles decorating the façades of certain chapels in the Cathedral are more or less from this period.

One example of beautiful, old 16th century tiles remaining in the city is to be found in the Casa de las Bulas in the remnants of old decorations in the entrance patio. The house also has other remnants from various periods as well as possible older constructions. It is one of the most interesting.

The tiles preserved in the old Municipal Chapter Hall are from the beginning of the 18th century, specifically 1732.

Another beautiful example of 18th century decorative tile work belonging to another style (blue and white) can be found in San Bartolomé church in the old Alcazar, the only noteworthy feature in San Bartolomé el Magno convent.

Also noteworthy are the tiles in what once was the Hospice chapel, also known as San Bartolomé church, which are not only the best examples of this art form found in the local churches, but also the oldest (14th century), and the altar frontispieces in the Mesquita chapels.

Mosaics

One industrial art of immense importance especially in ancient times deserves a special mention: *Musivaria* or the art of mosaics.

Mosaics have been found in a considerable number of places in Cordoba, but as a whole, they have not generated any particular interest. Some gorgeous ones appeared recently in the Jesús Crucificado convent, although they have been covered again.

There is a beautiful example from the Roman period that is preserved in a house, once a church, on Plaza de la Compañía. These fragments of mosaics, apparently paving in an ancient Roman home, represent the four seasons, the whole surrounded by an artistic frieze.[179]

---

[179] This has been perfectly explained and beautifully reproduced in *Monumentos arquitectónicos de España* (volume IV), in Rodrigo Amador de los Ríos, Mosaicos *de las cuatro estaciones.*

Related to the ceramic arts, *Vide* also *Mosaicos, aliceres y azulejos árabes mudéjares,* by Rocrigo Amador de los Rios, Museo *Español de Antiguëdades,* Volume VI. Also, Breve *resumen de la evolución*

Examples of the art of mosaics have increased in Cordoba. With each new find, other examples of lesser or greater importance surface. Three cities are buried in the grounds of Cordoba: the Roman, the Arab, and the Christian. The deepest level is the Roman, the several layers of which are seven meters deep in some places, followed by the Arab and then the Christian.

Mosaics are found in the Almedina, in the Villa or Ciudad Alta, in neighbourhoods such as Instituto, Tendillas, Zapatería Vieja and others.

The Hospice mosaic was discovered in 1927. Thought to be from the 2nd century, it represents Victory in a chariot and is very beautiful.

Less ancient is a mosaic in Rafael Cruz Conde's house. It is the best in the city and compares favourably with the most beautiful mosaics in Spain. The place where it was found is located outside the Cordoba city walls.

Ceramics

Ceramics are harder to preserve but there is a magnificent example of a ceramic well covering in Santa Marta convent, considered to be a Mudejar work from the 15th century. Though not as beautiful, there is another such work in the Museo Arqueológico Nacional. Amador de los Ríos studied both.[180] Some, however, believe them to be 13th century Arab work.

The discoveries in Medina Azahara have led Ricardo Velazquez to say that just as the architectural art of Medina is the purest and most original of Cordoba, in ceramics the achievements were frankly revolutionary. It was previously thought that the enameled ceramics dated from the 15th century but thanks to newly discovered shards it is clear that the technique was already known in the 10th century. Ceramic pieces with a metallic sheen, the oldest examples of which were thought to be in the Mosque of Kairuan in Tunisia, were also known in Cordoba before that time.

Textiles: Silk

There were many artistic representations of the art of tapestry in Cordoba, although none were produced in the capital. A major school of tapestry flourished in the palace of the Caliphs where a series of historical tapestries - the *tiraz* – were produced. One of these, that of Hixem II, is preserved.[181]

---

del mosaico by Antonio Aguilar Correa, *Discurso Academia de la Historia*, 1892, and *El mosaico de character romano en España,* by Pelayo Quintero, *Museum,* 1911.

[180] *Brocales de pozo árabes y mudéjares,* in *Museo Español de Antigüedades, Volume III. Industrias hispanoárabes, Lucarnas de cobre,* by Rodrigo Amador de los Rios, *Arch.* 1899.

[181] There is an interesting summary in P. Artiñano's prologue to *Catálogo de la Exposición de tejidos españoles,* Madrid, 1917, in which there were Cordoban works dating back to the 11th century.

The silk industry, whose great flowering occurred under the Arabs, continued in Cordoba under various guises. At the end of the 18th century, according to a 1775 account, silk workers formed an important guild as there were close to three hundred artisans registered as experts in the silk trade.[182]

The linen workers guild was also significant, although as a reminder there is only the name of a street and a rudimentary remainder of the trade.[183] The carding and working of linen was an important industry whose bylaws were rewritten in 1728 and 1776.

The silk trade held its own as an industry up to the end of the 16th century. In Cordoba, silk as a Christian trade also flourished in the 16th century, although it now seems clear that the raw material came from Valencia or Murcia. Records show that in 1650 there were some 1774 looms, small ones, to be sure, and 200 spinning wheels.

Cordoba in Crisis

Cordoba went through a major period of crisis during the second half of the 17th century, during which it was assailed by epidemics and the great plague, which depopulated the city. The number of looms drops rapidly, and only 30 looms and 50 spinning wheels are recorded in 1686.

When citing the epidemics as the cause of the decline of Cordoba in the 17th century, the recollections (compiled in ghoulish detail by T. R. de Arellanos) of local historians who record an exorbitant number of victims come to mind. The number of victims they claim would be enough to populate three cities. According to official population data, there were 6,257 family units or between 30,000 and 35,000 inhabitants in Cordoba at the end of the 16th century. If we assume that there were some were 40,000 inhabitants, as is likely allowing for the unreliability of the official data, one cannot accept the numbers cited by historians and half historians regarding the epidemics.

Seville, Granada and Cordoba were the three principal cities in Andalusia in the 16th century. The first, the largest at this time and the largest urban nucleus in Spain, had 18,000 family units or 90,000 inhabitants. Granada had more than 13,000 units, that is 70,000 inhabitants, and Cordoba, 40,000 inhabitants.

Malaga had 20,000 inhabitants, fewer than Ubeda and Baeza. Ecija had more than 25,000 inhabitants. Cadiz was almost depopulated. Jerez was in the middle, with a population smaller than Cordoba's.

---

[182] Granada, Toledo, Valencia, Cordoba and Murcia fed more than a million men with this work and occupation, with a large part of the proceeds produced by housebound women who nurtured the silkworms, spun the silk, and had been working with it since very early childhood. *Vide:* Ustariz. *Theoría y Práctica de Comercio y de Marina, 1724.*

[183] *Les arts* du tissu, by Gaston Migeon, 1909, a flawed summary that says very little about Spain.

The geographic, economic, and historic reasons which motivated these demographic changes, are extremely interesting. Seville, although losing ground regarding other cities in Spain, maintained its rhythm in Andalusia, Granada lost a great deal, and steadily declining Cordoba, while maintaining its population level, does not recover until the second half of the 19th century.

* * *

Cordoban Numismatics

Because of their industrial arts and archaeological significance, it is important to make a brief mention of the minting of coins in Cordoba.

The oldest coins originating in Cordoba date to the first century BCE and coincide with Julius Caesar's domination of the city. These coins are so beautifully engraved that few Greek coins surpass them in style. The *As*, by this time an imperial coin bearing the image of Emperor Augustus and the inscription *Colonia Patricia* encircled by a crown of oak leaves, is especially noteworthy.

Some maintain that the minting of coins in Cordoba disappeared under Emperor Claudius in the 2nd century. Others state that the mints did not disappear but that a centralizing edict obliged them to depend on the central power and to mint coins under its control and command.

The Visigoths did not change the Roman monetary system. There only were some modificaitons under Leovigildo, and from Leovigildo to Witiza, gold coins continue to be minted in Cordoba. The famous inscription *bis obtinuit* appears on a gold coin from the time of Leovigildo, alluding to when he twice conquered the city of Cordoba, in 572 and 585.

The Visigoths kept the honorific *Colonia Patria* on their coins.

Coin collectors use the term Baetic in which they include coins from Cordoba.

Arab numismatics are extremely curious. At first, they minted coins using Latin characters and no Arab references. There are fully Arab coins from Cordoba under all the Caliphs. In 947 Abderraman moved the *Casa de Moneda*, the *Ceca* or mint, to the newly established Medina-Azahara. They minted copper coins (*felus*), silver coins (*dirrhemes*) and gold coins (*dinares* and *semidinares*).

The Almohades changed the appearance of the coins. Generally square, with only Koranic inscriptions, no date or mint stamp and bear names of princes difficult to identify. In the Christian era, after Ferdinand III took Cordoba in 1236, the Casa de Moneda seems to have disappeared, as no Christian coins were ever minted.

There are those, however, (Chaves, *Congreso Histórico de Sevilla*) who maintain that coins were minted in Cordoba from 1236 to 1248 and that the minting of coins in Seville became firmly established shortly after it was conquered by the Spaniards.[184] A letter dated July, 1297, inserted in the *Memorial Histórico* in which Ferdinand IV speaks of those who are to collect for him the income from the coins which he had minted in Cordoba, leads one to believe that although few in number, there may well have been the remains of the Casa de Moneda in the 13th century.

Constrained by the limits of this book, we close this chapter on the Industrial Arts, on Cordoba's most glorious tradition – and especially refer to the working of silver and leather to: Pablo Alzola, *El arte industrial en España (1892).*

Artes industrials, by H. Giner de los Ríos, is a small volume, to add to the whole. On these topics is a particularly useful and beautiful book, *The Industrial Arts in Spain* by Juan F. Riaño. Also worth consulting is the *Dictionaire de l'ameublement et la decoration* by Henry Havard.

Seals

Because of its age (1360) and because it contains an interesting view of Cordoba in the 14th century, the wax seal found in the Duque de Medinaceli's archives on a document which confirms certain favours granted by King Pedro I is worth noting. [185]

It is not known when Cordoba began to use the present seal, one inferior in beauty and in heraldic authenticity to the seal used by the original City Council - a seal which corresponds more than any other to the written documentation and to the soul of Cordoba.

In the 18th century there was another city seal, one more beautiful and more complete than the present seal which in fact is very similar to the seal of the province.

---

[184] Interesting engravings of Cordoban coin and studies of them are found in the now classic books by Alois Heiss, *Decription générale des monnaies antiques de l"Espagne* and *Description générale des monnaies des rois visigoths d'Espagne,* and Antonio Delgado, *Nuevo método de clasificación de las medallas autónomas de España.*

Tratado de numismática arábigo-española, by Francisco Codera, and *Monedas de las dinastías arábigo-españolas,* by Antonio Vives.

A very simple explanation of numismatics is found in the chapter on this subject in Elementos *de Arqueología* by P. Nadal; which must be complemented by the *Manuale di Numismatica* by Solone Ambrosoli (acceptable engravings), and by the *Indicador manual de la numismática española* by A varo Campaner (without any engravings).

[185] Brought to our attention by Alfonso Herrera: *Sello de Córdoba de mediados del siglo XIV.* (R. Excursiones, 1892)

**Imperial coin bearing the image of Emperor Augustus
and the inscription *Colonia Patricia* encircled
by a crown of oak leaves
Cordoba 19-18 BCE[xlvi]**

EPILOGUE
by Antonio Jaén Morente

I have reached the end of this modest book on the history of the city of Cordoba and her people. I believe, without any false modesty, that this work is not the complete book, not even part of a measured plan, nor the spiritual guide to the city, nor does it go forward as a somewhat sentimental, organic guide. All my efforts to achieve the book as the soul, the complete inventory of our race, have been in vain. There is more there.

Nevertheless, framed by this sincere *non possumus,* I submit it to the worthy critique of future collaborators and active participants in a work that must be a collective endeavour. As the saying goes, between all of us, we know it all…

Let me continue…

On the other hand, each generation has, and must have, a viewpoint of its own regarding History. This is what forces us to continuously revise and explains the speed at which textbooks of this kind become dated. We can never speak too much of our ancestors, but we should always speak of them from different viewpoints. History is rebirth, but as life is a perpetual renewal and a constant transformation, the observer must find a place in this evolving plane of changing methods and content.

Furthermore, to write the history of Cordoba, we need a high point from which landscapes are uncovered and sceneries explained. The pinnacle which our city reached, its unparalleled past located at the crossroads of history, the illustrious paths of life, oblige everyone to make this spiritual climb which, as it touches the motherland, lifts the spirits and encourages a search for the ideal vista of the future.

The geographic concept of Cordoba

Cordoba is a geographic city, created by the dictates of the land and not an artificial concept. There are indications as to why this is and has been so. Thus, once Rome expands it and actually creates it, it lives as a city.

The Roman world was a great association of municipalities. Later, under the Arabs, Cordoba is the leader of a great State, and it does not lose its relative independence when it falls into the hands of the Christians. Although this is diminished, Cordoba remains more personal than later, with very few ties to a central Authority that barely existed as a bastion and incarnation of the State.

The city falls under the general law of the times, the internal movement towards centralization, connected to the monarchy, as every country worldwide was experiencing.

Geographically-speaking, there is a political weakening of the region, of the country and even of the district, geographic units created by a law from which Cordoba cannot escape. This change over time and the increasing distancing of the Arab frontier which moves to the sea, is one of the reasons for its decline as a city.

Assuming that Friedrich Ratzel's concept of a peninsula is correct, there is no peninsula like the Iberian to exemplify this principle. There are three zones in a peninsula: the isthmus, the centre and the peninsulas. The isthmus abides by its mission to usher in the continental contribution, the great foreign cultural links and ideological paths.

The centre is the nucleus of the nation. There is nothing clearer than this explanation, a kind of geographic determination that, as regards Castile, metamorphoses as History.

The peninsulas provide the culture. Hence, Andalusia during the days of the Romans, the Visigoths and the Arabs, and later in literature, art and philosophy, supplys the great names, leads the routes and the cultures, always shining.

The note continues: the peninsula makes romanticism triumph and even today Andalusia exemplifies Spain worldwide, although historically, Cordoba always held that honour.

The case of Madrid confirms the rule. It is an artificial capital whose strength is a synthesis of the general work of Spain, a greater political value that explains other values.

Cordoba lives over a river and in a valley. Referring to the region and the study of the human element, the significance of the rivers varies according to where they flow – upper, middle, lower reaches.

The upper reach of a river, always unimportant, does not boast a great city. It never had one. The middle section of a river has always had a political value; the lower reach produces the economically strong city.

This was the case in the Guadalquivir River valley. There were no outstanding cities in the upper reaches. Cordoba was politically predominant in the valley and to some extent economically, which quickly passed to Seville, especially after the discovery of America.

Cordoba therefore appears as a geographical creation, not an artificial city, but one that had a natural birth in the middle reaches of the river, naturally assuming political leadership in Andalusia. This in turn led to centuries of an often sustained and oppressive intellectual leadership.

All the reasons that have been given at times to explain Cordoba's status as a capital had to base themselves, more or less scientifically or instinctively, on the geographic factor. This is why, upriver or downriver, there has been life in Cordoba since prehistoric times. There was its Iberian city and the later invasions added to this geographic element.

The nature of Cordoba explains many of the events in its history, without invoking geographic determinism but demonstrating the alliance between land and hunger which Carl Ritter advanced as an almost perfect definition of geography. As a synthesis of its region Cordoba expressed this alliance magnificently

It is not that History arises from Geography as the same natural conditions do not act permanently over the passage of time. If the land were to impose itself on human activity, man could also impose himself on the land.

**To prevail over the land, to continue the story,
that is our mission.**

Monument to San Rafael
Patron Saint of Córdoba[xlvii]

ENDNOTES

[i] *Fondo Antonio Jaén Morente, Archivo Municipal de Córdoba.* www. archivo.cordoba.es

[ii] Fondo Antonio Jaén Morente, Archivo Municipal de Córdoba. www. archivo.cordoba.es

[iii] Rafael Castejón Martínez de Arizala, scientist, historian, writer and politician from Cordoba.

[iv] Ramon Otero Pedrayo, geographer, writer, intellectual and politician from Orense, Gallicia.

[v] Ramon Otero Pedrayo, prologue to the posthumous 4th Spanish edition of Antonio Jaén Morente's *Historia de Córdoba*, Ed. Libreria Luque, Cordoba, 1971.

[vi] Downloaded 08/11/2022http://www.racordoba.es/

[vii] Antonio Jaén Morente's 1935 dedication to the *Real Academia de Córdoba* - Royal Academy of Sciences, Fine Arts and Noble Arts of Cordoba - published posthumously in the 4th Spanish edition of his *Historia de Córdoba*, Ed. Libreria Luque, Cordoba, 1971. http://www.racordoba.es

[viii] https://www.romanports.org/images/Italica/1200px-Tartessos.jpg

[ix] Stele found on the grounds of this engineering company specializing in electromechanics, on display in the Cordoba Museum.

[x] As reported in a communique from A. Carbonnell & Trillo-Figueroa. *La Minéria y la Metalurgia entre los musulmanes de España*, 1929.

[xi] https://www.merriam-webster.com/dictionary/delenda%20est%20Carthago

[xii] *Praetor*. Administrative officer who, in the absence of a Consul, administered civil law and commanded provincial armies. *Vide* Encyclopedia Britannica.

[xiii] *Quaestor*. A high magistrate in ancient Rome. The first quaestors were judges in of cases of murder and insurrection or high treason. Later, administrative quaestors were responsible for the administration of the public funds. *Vide* Encyclopedia Britannica.

[xiv] *Mozarabs*. Any of the Spanish Christians living under Muslim rule (8th–11th century), who, while unconverted to Islam, adopted Arabic language and culture.
https://www.britannica.com/topic/Mozarab

[xv] *Medinians*. The people who offered sanctuary to the Islamic prophet Muhammad in the city of Medina following the migration of his followers in what is known as the Hijrah (migration to Medina) in 622. Today generally known as Muslims. https://www.britannica.com/topic/Islamic-world/Muhammads-emigration-to-Yathrib-Medina

[xvi] Abu-Beka, also: Abu-l-Tayyib/ Abu-l-Baqa Salih b. Sharif al-Rundi), poet, writer, and literary critic from al-Andalus who wrote in Arabic. 13th century author of *Rithaa' ul-Andalus* (Elegy for al-Andalus), a poem mourning the Catholic invasion and conquest of al-Andalus.

[xvii] *Cortes*. The medieval assemblies of the various kingdoms. Today, the two houses of the Spanish Parliament.

[xviii] *Judaizers*. Gentiles who adopted Jewish religious practices or sought to influence others to do so. Downloaded 19/10/2022 from https://www.biblestudytools.com/dictionaries/bakers-evangelical-dictionary/judaizers.html.

[xix] Communards. Members and supporters of the short-lived 1871 Paris Commune formed in the wake of the French defeat in the Franco-Prussian War. Downloaded 19/10/2022 from https://er.wikipedia.org/wiki/Communards.

[xx] Joseph Bonaparte, a French statesman, eldest surviving brother of Napoleon who appointed him King of Spain (1808-1813). https://www.britannica.com/biography/Joseph-Bonaparte

[xxi] Prebendary. An Honorary Canon of a church.

[xxii] Source: https://www.pinterest.pt/pin/15692298680932300/

[xxiii] Phillip Pouind Photography https://www.flickr.com/photos/superhoopsa/3051543436/

[xxiv] Archivo Iconograifco, S.A./Cor, https://www.britannica.com/

[xxv] Real Academia de Historia. https://dbe rah.es/biografias/33521/francisco-del-rosal

[xxvi] Downloaded 29/09/2022 from https://i0.wp.com/historia-biografia.com/wp-content/uploads/2018/11/biograf%C3%ADa-de-Luis-de-G%C3%B3ngora.jpg?w=573&ssl=1

[xxvii] Downloaded 27/09/ 2022 from https://upload.wikimedia.org/wikipedia/commons/f/f3/Anto-

nio_Caballero_y_G%C3%B3ngora.jpg

xxviii *Licenciado: G*eneric honorific for a university graduate; also, lawyer.

xxix *Mihrab:* a niche in the quiblah wall of a mosque, facing Mecca, towards which the congregation faces to pray. https://www.britannica.com/topic/mihrab.

xxx *Maqsurah*: in the Mesquita, near the mihrab, enclosure reserved for the Caliph and his entourage to shield him from the public them during prayers. https://dle.rae.es/macsura.

xxxi https://www.ne.jp/asahi/arc/ind/2_meisaku/06_cordoba/xmez_6eng.htm

xxxii Antonio Jaén's 1908 doctoral thesis was unpublished until 2022 when it was transcribed by Manuel Jiménez Jaén and published by the Archivo Municipal de Córdoba.

xxxiii Américo Castro, 11 January 1935. Note received.

xxxiv Sagrario parish archives

xxxv https://www.britannica.com/biography/Bartolome-Bermejo.

xxxvi https://multimedia.andalucia.org/content_images/main_image_55420.jpeg

xxxvii Puteal: enclosure around the opening of a well. https://www.collinsdictionary.com/dictionary

xxxviii Cordopedia, *Padre Roelas*, https://cordobapedia.wikanda.es/wiki/Padre_Roelas.

xxxixlll Miliaria: granite markers placed along Roman roads, marking the distance in Roman miles between two towns.

xl Guadameci: Embossed leather. Guadamecilero: Leather worker who worked with soft sheepskin leather which was tanned, embossed and gilt. https://www.andalucia.org/en/cordoba-cultural-tourism-casa-del-guadameci-omeya

xli Custodias: religious monstranses or ostentoriums.

xlii Lunette: a crescent-shaped clip made of gold or of silver-gilt which is used for holding the <u>Host</u> in an upright position when exposed in the monstrance, securely attached to a small stand or frame. https://www.newadvent.org/cathen/09435a.htm

xliii Pyx: in Christianity, vessel containing the consecrated bread, or host, used in the service of Holy Communion. Commonly, a smalll round silver box with a cover. https://www.britannica.com/topic/pyx

xliv Portapace: a sacred image presented to the pious at mass and forms part of a cathedral's treasure.

xlv Arqueta: small casket, used for relics of saints or to keep consecrated hosts.

xlvi Virtual Coins. https://www.vcoins.com/en/stores/victors_imperial_coins/208/product/augustus_colonia_patricia_from_cordoba/978494/Default.aspx

xlvii https://www.google.com/url?sa=i&url=https%3A%2F%2Fes.wikipedia.org%2Fwiki%2FTriunfo_de_San_Rafael_%2528Puerta_del_Puente%2529&psig=AOvVaw10MT-C2fgFKmD6zCgdLN_q&ust=1684086662879000&source=images&cd=vfe&ved=0CBEQjRxqFwoTCOC8iv3t8v4CFQAAAAAdAAAAABAE